Praise for the Second Edition of *Working Virtually*

"Trina has been thoughtfully examining nontraditional employer/employee relationships for longer than nearly anyone in the industry. What makes this book unique is that presents tangible benefits for both the employer and employee. All relationships must work for both sides or sooner or later they stop working. Trina's book fully recognizes this in a far more workable way than too many other one-size-fits-all plans on the market. Every business and every relationship in a given business is unique and must be treated that way. *Working Virtually* provides guides to manage an ever-changing process, not just a list of policies that may or may not work for my business. As such, it is a go-to outline for making the new workplace work."

—Doyle Albee, President, Metzger Associates

"Virtual is now both the vehicle and the platform for most work. Are you ready? Trina Hoefling masterfully maps the three most powerful paths you'll travel to succeed virtually. She is the perfect guide, simplifier, and coach for every virtual team and overworked manager! Hoefling helps us see that every virtual choice is ultimately about ourselves—our mindsets, our ability to learn and unlearn, and how we embrace change. Get *Working Virtually* now—to get working virtually and to unleash all that is within you and your teams!"

—Bill Jensen, author of Future Strong *and* Disrupt!

"*Working Virtually* does an outstanding job of reminding us that the things that make for meaningful work in face-to-face environments apply more so when working at a distance. Generosity, trust, and collective meaning-making are at the core of very practical approaches to working across distances—geographic or otherwise."

—Jerrold McGrath, President, Intervene Design Incorporated; Leadership Faculty, Banff Centre for Arts and Creativity, Alberta, Canada

"Having worked with Trina both in a classroom and virtually 'across the pond,' I have no hesitation in recommending her and this very helpful book on coming to terms with the new virtual work reality. Organizations, leaders, and individuals—everyone is coming to terms with this new phenomenon and the implications, challenges, and opportunities related. It's an easy read with helpful pointers on what we all need to grapple with in our digitally enabled work/life environments."

—Martin Allison, Chairman, Cimlogic, West Yorkshire, United Kingdom

"The past 20 years have seen a steady increase in the percentage of the workforce that doesn't go into an office every day. Trina Hoefling provides an important addition to any manager's or virtual worker's toolkit, describing in clear, jargon-free language the skills that separate high-performing virtual workforces from their less effective counterparts."

—*Ceil Tilney, Covalent Solutions, San Francisco, California*

"I write this from my favorite table at my favorite cafe. An office? Not so twenty-first centry. And that's exactly what Trina Hoefling is exploring in this engaging new book. Read it while you're sipping a cappuccino, you'll be enlightened."

—*Dave Taylor, Principal, Intuitive Systems, LLC.;
and Ask Dave Taylor blog, Boulder, Colorado*

"A gem of a book! Despite rapid advancements in collaboration technology and dramatic increases in the work-from-home movement, many leaders are left to figure out on their own what it takes to drive high performing teams in this new environment. Trina Hoefling reminds us that the quality of human interaction ultimately makes, or breaks, a team and expertly lays out the tools and techniques for success."

—*John Short, Global HR Business Partner, MilliporeSigma, a business of
Merck KGaA, Darmstadt, Germany*

"Having been involved in this field since 1982—virtually the Stone Age of virtual work—I've seen this field emerge, develop, and morph. This book provides a welcome and needed fresh look at the various flavors of mobile, distributed, and virtual work as it exists today and will grow tomorrow. Managers and organizations that want to work smarter and engage their professionals should follow this guide closely. Those that still resist virtual work and distributed workplaces can bury their heads in the sand and keep sending e-mail with their 1200-baud modems."

—*Gil Gordon, acknowledged expert in the implementation of telecommuting
and telework, author of* TURN IT OFF: How to Unplug from the
Anytime-Anywhere Office Without Disconnecting Your Career

"Successful virtual teamwork does not just happen. Even though members know how to use communication technologies, and have integrated mobile devices into their everyday lives, more is needed. Leadership, shared purpose, clear expectations and trust are all essential but challenging to carry out. *Working Virtually* offers important guidance for virtual team sponsors, leaders, and members. The understandings gained from this book will save time, money, and heartache!"

—*Janet Salmons, Indie Translational Scholar, Vision2Lead; Dissertation Chair & Qualitative Methodologist, Walden University; and Chair, Academy of Management Ethics Education Committee*

"Technology has changed the workplace in many ways. At the same time, creating a high-functioning environment continues to challenge organizational leaders. *Working Virtually* clearly defines the specific issues that call for learning how to work with people in today's work world. Building trust and communicating effectively about the tasks to be accomplished and expectations for performance in the virtual organization top my list of requirements for success in today's companies. Learning how to bring individuals together to best support individual satisfaction has never been easy. Hoefling's depth of experience and wisdom provide ways leaders can engage and increase their personal effectiveness for brilliant performance with their teams."

—*Judith Light, Certified Management Consultant*

"*Working Virtually* addresses organizational team issues and what managers/leaders need to do to be effective in dealing with the changes that the workplace is experiencing—and will continue to do so."

—*Steve Dorn, Pivotal Resources*

"Could not ask for a timelier book. People who work together in the same place at the same time will be a distinct minority before this decade is out. I love this; it's all in one place. It is not only current but also put together so it is constantly curated as new tools are found, new techniques developed. I would say what you have here is not only best practices but also 'next practices.'"

—*Charlie Grantham, Community Design Institute*

WORKING VIRTUALLY

WORKING VIRTUALLY

Transforming the Mobile Workplace

SECOND EDITION

Trina Hoefling

Foreword by Didier Elzinga

STERLING, VIRGINIA

Published by Stylus Publishing, LLC.
22883 Quicksilver Drive
Sterling, Virginia 20166-2102

Library of Congress Cataloging-in-Publication Data

Names: Hoefling, Trina, 1958- author.
Title: Working virtually: leading your organization and team,
and advancing your personal career,
in a mobile world/Trina Hoefling.
Description: Second edition. |
Sterling, Va. : Stylus Publishing, 2017. |
Includes bibliographical references and index.
Identifiers: LCCN 2016035684|
ISBN 9781620362914 (cloth : alk. paper) |
ISBN 9781620362921 (pbk. : alk. paper) |
ISBN 9781620362938 (library networkable e-edition) |
ISBN 9781620362945 (consumer e-edition)
Subjects: LCSH: Virtual reality in management. |
Virtual work teams. |
Teams in the workplace--Computer networks. |
Organizational effectiveness. | Personnel management.
Classification: LCC HD30.2122.H63 2017 |
DDC 658.4/022--dc23
LC record available at https://lccn.loc.gov/2016035684

13-digit ISBN: 978-1-62036-291-4 (cloth)
13-digit ISBN: 978-1-62036-292-1 (paperback)
13-digit ISBN: 978-1-62036-293-8 (library networkable e-edition)
13-digit ISBN: 978-1-62036-294-5 (consumer e-edition)

Printed in the United States of America

All first editions printed on acid-free paper
that meets the American National Standards Institute
Z39-48 Standard.

Bulk Purchases

Quantity discounts are available for use in workshops and for
staff development.
Call 1-800-232-0223

First Edition, 2017

10   9   8   7   6   5   4   3   2   1

In the first edition of Working Virtually, *I thanked Marianne Weidlein as one of my "abiding earth angels." She was a prolific writer who kept me focused on being a teacher and illuminator. She passed in the summer of 2015 while I was writing this new book. I dedicate this edition to Mari and so many dear friends, mentors, family, and teachers who have passed recently.*

—Trina Hoefling

CONTENTS

FOREWORD

It is a testament to the forward-thinking of its author Trina Hoefling that the first edition of *Working Virtually* was published almost 20 years ago. Back then the idea of "telecommuting" was a new and unfamiliar concept, so the fact that a book existed that explored a model to make it work—and saw it for all its benefits, as well as challenges—was actually quite a profound achievement.

Today a lot of organizations have remote employees. Some companies like Automattic, who built the hugely successful WordPress platform, are made up entirely of people who work virtually from all around the world. This second edition of *Working Virtually* succeeds in highlighting concrete actions that managers can use to engage virtual teams. It's one thing to allow your people to work remotely, and quite another to engage them in the shared mission and values of your company.

I am CEO of Culture Amp, a company that helps other organizations measure and improve how they engage their employees. I was surprised to discover that not much has changed in the past 20 years when it comes to engaging remote workforces. Building and developing a strong company culture is an increasingly important concept, and it's a very powerful one—it's the *only* competitive edge that any company has. If you aren't engaging your remote employees in that process, you are failing them. Further still, they will be failing you. It's that simple.

The remote workforce is one that is here to stay. As Trina wrote when she first published her book in 2001, "Virtual work was a 'novel idea' employed to retain that exceptional employee."[1] These days, having flexibility is one of the key drivers—and expectations—that attracts and retains talent. She notes that "people will work for less or are less willing to leave for a job that offers more, if they are able to work from home." I doubt there is a CEO or manager out there who does not have to address this.

So how do we make sure that today's virtual managers are effectively engaging their remote employees?

There were two things that really spoke to me in the book, mostly because I saw them so clearly reflected in the values we have at Culture Amp. Of course, I was pleased to see validation of those core beliefs in the work of a respected authority on building engaged remote employees.

The first thing to speak to me was, as Trina points out, we have to "change ourselves first" if we expect the same of others. Meeting the needs of virtual workers can often be seen as something they have to initiate and own, *but that really is the wrong way to think about it.* It takes two parties to make a worker remote. Trina quotes Bill Jensen, who says, "If you want to lead others into a strong future, you need to be keenly aware of how your own inner truths, biases, fears, courage, values and dreams do or do not impact the daily work of others."[2] At Culture Amp, we have a value that I believe encapsulates this idea—and seeks to live it out in our working life: "Have the courage to be vulnerable." Don't pretend to know what you don't. Be open and honest about your limitations and shortcomings.

If you are struggling to connect and collaborate with a remote team or individual, stop and think about what it is that you can change, and openly let your remote coworkers know how you are struggling—chances are they are feeling the same way. Unless you identify issues in an open and transparent way, it becomes hard to address them. As Trina says, "Cynicism and judgments often limit our ability to learn and change, or at least slow us down because we are convinced something won't work (cynicism) or is a poor choice (judgment)."

The lesson here is to try, and try without fear of failure. And when you fail, seek to understand why, learn from it, and improve.

The second thing to speak to me and that I felt was so nicely articulated by Trina when she talks about the value of trust is: "Trust others to make decisions." This can be especially hard when a team or person is remote, but the benefit to individuals and companies is huge. Unfortunately, as Trina reminds us, "In a virtual environment with technical monitoring, a sense of Big Brother watching increases tenfold." When you trust your people to make decisions you unblock a lot of bottlenecks that exist in organizations. We're all familiar with scenarios where to get something approved it has to cascade through three different teams and managers to see the light of day. Companies that trust their employees benefit from smarter, quicker decisions; better morale; and more engaged employees.

The same benefits exist for both remote and office-bound workers, though building up that trust can often be harder when you work across times and locations. Again, the change starts with you. The more you trust your remote people, the more likely they are to live up to that trust. The same for distrust: When people don't feel trusted, they are likely to act that out.

Some other key takeaways for me were the following:

- "Technically enabled people can work virtually and still have a seamless connection to the team. In 2015, telecommuting was named the top desired employee benefit. No organization wants to lose its best people because of a long commute, a spousal relocation, or child care conflicts. Organizations experience 20% reduction in turnover when virtual work is an option."

- "Bring people together digitally and face-to-face, synchronously (live) and asynchronously (when they work best). Organizations add value when talent is supported and well deployed."
- "The real purpose of virtual work is not to allow distance but to create synergy without limitations of time or space."

Anyone who wants to build stronger relationships across time, space, and teams will find value in reading this book.

Didier Elzinga
CEO and cofounder of Culture Amp

Notes

1. Trina Hoefling, *Working Virtually*, Stylus Publsihing, 2017.
2. Bill Jensen, Future Strong (Melbourne, FL: Motivational Press, 2016), www .goodreads.com/book/show/26583278-future-strong. Also, see Jensen's TED talk: "Are You Future Strong?" Tedxtalks.ted.com, added May 29, 2015, http://tedxtalks .ted.com/video/Are-you-Future-Strong-Bill-Jens

ACKNOWLEDGMENTS

It took a virtual team to write this book. When I first committed to a revision, I thought it would be easy because so much of what underpinned the book in the late 1990s is still true today—to help people work together better in an increasingly distributed work world.

People are brilliantly complex and amazingly consistent in how we relate to each other and adapt to a changing world. The principles of virtual teaming haven't changed much. The work world of 2016, however, is transformed.

Telecommuting was a concept more than a practice 20 years ago. Early adopters successfully led the way, but working virtually was still mostly in a pilot phase. The technology was tied to the desktop. The user interface wasn't seamless yet, let alone integrated. The Internet of Things was science fiction. Today people understand the concept of mobile work, but I underestimated how challenging a book update would be.

Generous flexwork and telework colleagues contributed richly to this book. I'd like to thank the book's team, even though I'm the only named author.

Charles Grantham helped with ruthless cutting and generous reminders that we write the next book only because we forget the pain of writing the first. His early and progressed wisdom about virtual work is astounding.

Eddie Caine has been a colleague since the 1990s, a champion of public-private partnerships that enable companies to bring work-life balance through telework initiatives. As a content reviewer and subject matter expert, his client examples and observations were invaluable. Always pragmatic, Eddie kept me focused on what most matters—the virtual leaders and their teams.

Kathy Kacher, a respected researcher, consultant, and trainer in flex work, shared tools and assessments, research reports, and thoughtful conversations that raised my standard.

Susan Krautbauer, a woman of many talents and strategic genius, developed graphic images.

Kevin Ward, colleague and friend, nudged me to start writing again.

Judith Light, Lisa Rice, and Erik Otto called up their copyediting skills.

Allison Kessler and Steve Dorn added examples, hacks, and perspective as content reviewers. Their insight and clarity elevated the book.

I'd like to acknowledge all who responded to my survey and interview requests. I can confidently say this book is grounded in real virtual teamwork practices.

John von Knorring, my publisher, was patient during a year of unexpected events that took me away from the manuscript too often.

I'm blessed with earth angels and tribal drummers who support me. To all those named and unnamed, here and passed, who have emboldened and supported me as I traveled this writing path . . . thank you.

Trina Hoefling

The Network Is the New Workplace

"There is no end to education. It is not that you read a book, pass an examination, and finish with education. The whole of life, from the moment you are born to the moment you die, is a process of learning."

—Jiddu Krishnamurti

Work—and How We Are Compensated for It—Is Changing

Work is a collection of activities we undertake to add value to an enterprise or community for which we are compensated. *But we're just not working in the same old way.*

Smart technology applied to enterprise solutions has changed the way we work and manage. It has also impacted the traditional employee contract. Though the U.S. tax code and much of our societal mind-set haven't changed as quickly, much of the U.S. workforce is already doing transactional work that is provided by contract workers—freelancers, contract employees, consultants. U.S. political rhetoric speaks of job creation with little understanding that many U.S. workers (forecast to be half by 2020) are working independently and often virtually.[1]

The nature of the employment contract has a direct impact on how virtual teams are managed and led. Virtual leaders are managing alliances more than controlling work or managing individuals.[2] Organizations with flex-work options attract a more agile workforce from a bigger talent pool.

This book applies best practices to working virtually in the context of this changing workplace landscape. More of us are collaborators with portable skills. We see ourselves as companies of one, navigating our own career path, no longer following one laid out for us by our employer. In 1989, Charles Handy wrote about the emergence of *portfolio workers*—individuals who reject the notion of a single, permanent job. Today's millennial workers think as portfolio workers. In 1997, Daniel Pink started the Free Agent Nation when he became an independent contractor himself.[3] Flexible work options and telework are no longer an emerging trend. We've surpassed the tipping point, and they have become normal.

1

This book provides a clear road map to navigate today's work realities while producing team results and working virtually. *This book is for the executive* who focuses on integrating networks of teams, working with information services to set up real-time information networks, connecting more and controlling less, and adapting performance management processes to be more team driven and technology leveraged. For those just beginning, *Working Virtually* has practical advice for leading changes in an enterprise that is preparing for virtual work.

You're reading this book because you want to learn more about virtual work. Maybe you're looking for a permanent job offer or promotion. Maybe you are like a lot of us, a little collaboration technology intimidated and afraid to look dumb. Maybe it's simply a way of remaining employable. Or like the traditional reader of the first edition, perhaps you work or manage virtually.

This book is for the professional who works from an office, a home, or a hotel. You need to know about the process of getting your enterprise, your teams, and yourself enabled for virtual collaboration. This is not a technology how-to book, though you will learn something more important—the principles and guidelines to select and use tools well.

This book is written to and for the virtual leader. It shows managers a clear path to develop, support, and lead high-performing virtual teams. *Working Virtually* provides an understanding of the context in which we all work, as well as the roles and responsibilities that go with a career in the mobile workplace.

Worker: Brings Talent to an Organization, Exchanging It for Money

Worker is a lowly term. *Work* isn't an exciting word. A Wikipedia search of "worker" redirects to "laborer."

Regardless of label, however, *we work for hire.* Therefore, for convenience as a reader of this book, *you are a worker.* I mean great respect. Workers bring their talent to work—often virtually. You are also a leader. Today's teams collaborate, and the best ones manage themselves. If you're a virtual worker, you are a coleader for bridging virtual distance, a responsibility that is seldom formally defined in the contract.

Virtual Workers

Most people think of virtual workers as telecommuters, but that is only one type. Eddie Caine, a nationally recognized and oft-quoted expert with more than 25 years' experience, defines *virtual workers* as not only teleworkers but also

- nontraditional workday extenders who work evenings and weekends,
- part-time or occasional teleworkers,
- job sharers, and
- remote employees from a satellite office or traveling employees.

Leaders work collaboratively with human resources, information technology/information services, and facilities departments to determine the equipment, real estate, and policy requirements for each type of worker. Office and digital network design warrants some systemic thought.

Network: The Vehicle *and* Platform of Work

We are in a relationship with technology. We are nodes on vast interlocking networks across work and home. We must navigate the changing work habitat *and our careers*. If you think of yourself (and your team) as connectors (or nodes), your value grows as you forge stronger ties with your professional networks—all enabled digitally.[4]

We can't talk about work without referring to the network. Work is built on networked technology platforms, even if team members are not working virtually. The leading dictionary definition of a *network* is a group of two or more computer systems linked together.[5] Networks in virtual organizations are *the structures we use to connect and communicate*.

Professional and social media networks are increasingly part of work life, too. They include *the people and groups with whom we stay connected*. These are purposeful relationships we develop face-to-face and online through social media, such as LinkedIn.[6]

The network has expanded to embrace the technical *and* human, and they are inseparable.

Professional relationships inside and beyond organization boundaries are essential to career success. Many service firms expect their people to develop a robust internal network, taking an active role in sourcing projects for themselves under the organization umbrella. More organizations are considering the value of a candidate's professional network in hiring decisions, *leveraging the node that is you*.

This Book Is for You If . . .

You are reading the right book if you work with, lead, or support teams who aren't always together at the same time. Human resource, information technology/information sciences (IT/IS), and facilities professionals will benefit from reading this book.

Executives will see their organization differently if they read this book. Organizations coordinate work through networks of teams, and any who read this book will see the power of a technology network built for relationships.

Team managers are the obvious audience and beneficiaries of *Working Virtually*, as are virtual team members. Everyone influences the team's success and, therefore, is a virtual team leader. Here are some of the key questions answered in this book:

- How will virtual teams affect the organization's culture? *Our* team's esprit de corps?
- How will I know people are working? How will my manager know I am working?
- How will I coach people and support a team I don't see?
- Can we trust each other?
- How will I get what I need and not feel isolated?
- Am I using the technology correctly and using all the capabilities my team needs?
- How will working virtually affect my career?

At the core of these questions is one answer: *Learn how to maintain strong, trusted relationships, digitally and in person.*

Everyone must build and nurture relationships across time and distance, even the traditional office employee. Understanding today's work realities helps map a strategy to thrive in today's mobile work world. *Working Virtually* provides a guidebook that works today. In reading, discover what works for you and your virtual team.

Why Working Virtually Now? Because It Matters

The way we connect has evolved since the first edition of this book was published at the turn of the twenty-first century. Virtual connection mattered then, but it was a limited set of options, usually blended with in-office team time. Virtual connection is easier now as technology has transformed. It matters even more since many teams are virtually full-time.

People Matter

Technology is an indispensable team enabler, but people are still the key. To adapt President Clinton's famous quote, *"It's about the people, stupid."* Despite the changing employer-employee contract and rapid increase in work auto-mation that eliminates some positions, *people are essential.* Many of us have looser ties to our employers, but we still want to do work that matters with people with whom we work well. In a virtual work world, team members need support, whether traditional employees or contracted experts. Everyone needs to be enabled to collaborate virtually and motivated to perform well. As this book will reveal, teams won't get that support without competent leadership. Many organization and virtual team leaders stifle productivity without knowing it. This book shows how to unleash talent, and how to do it virtually.

The Virtual Leader Matters

The virtual manager is *the key influencer* of work satisfaction and employee retention. The team leader is key to knowing how our work contributes, and that we are valued. The manager greatly influences how committed people will remain to the team and the organization. In a mobile work world, lead-ers must reexamine how to reward and lead through virtual influence, reach-ing out so people want to bring their intelligence and creativity to the team. Leaders who genuinely connect virtually with their people are, simply, better.

Technology Matters

Technology is a disrupter and an enabler; we are virtually mobile *and* organi-zationally connected. We must master relationships with people *and* tech-nology, using the network and collaborative tools to come together. Today's executives are rightly focused on redesigning organizations to be digitally integrated and network based—a network of teams.[7]

What You Will Be Able to Do After Reading This Book

Unleash your own and others' talent, clear obstacles, and collaborate with people face-to-face and virtually. Lead engaged virtual teams, whether you are a team member or manager. Learn to develop and nurture authentic, trusting relationships across the digital divide. The role of technology has grown dramatically since publication of the book in 2000, and it continues to drive the *way* we work and manage. Performance management is more auto-mated—for example, by leveraging task and project management tools. You'll learn when and where to use technology to manage people and to collaborate.

What has not and cannot be automated, however, is the team. When people come together as one, they hope to form a team that comes to think of itself as a dynamic force. Teams don't just coordinate intellect and skills. They open themselves to the potential of doing something together that none could do alone. The organization's integrated technology facilitates collaboration, *but the virtual leader and team members make it happen.*

Evolve your practices from what you learn in this book. Use and adapt technology and tools that support the *people part* of virtual teams—the uniqueness only you and your team can be.

Go to the book's information website (www.WorkingVirtually.org) and download additional tools and assessments to improve your virtual work and team, available free for book readers. Start building your tool kit.[8]

Included as a thank-you gift is a FREE BONUS CHAPTER: *Virtual Meeting Management.*

How to Navigate the Updated Edition of *Working Virtually*

I have curated workplace flexibility experts' experiences, sought client input, and interviewed all levels of the organization, exploring what has changed in the last two decades, not wanting to rely on just my own client work. This second edition incorporates shared wisdom into a road map for virtual mastery. This book travels a Threefold Path to team performance, as shown in Figure I.1. This edition also introduces the Fourth Path to a successful professional career. The team leader begins the team on the development path, launching or repositioning the virtual team to work together well. The support path begins while forming the team and continues throughout the life of the team, closing the distance that comes with virtual work. The outcomes path produces results that bring it all together for the team. Mission accomplished.

The book is laid out so you can go directly to the section or chapter you need most, though a front-to-back read is obviously what I hope you choose to do. Table 1.1 provides a quick reference of each part.

Part One speaks to how the workplace is mobile and the current state of flex work, telework, and virtualization. It also warns where to shift mind-sets to thrive in a mobile work world. It defines drivers and blocks to virtualizing their operations for collaborative work, including cost savings and effectiveness statistics.

Part Two assesses an organization's virtual effectiveness. You also have access to free downloadable resources, a virtual readiness assessment and

Figure I.1. The Threefold Path for high-performance teams.

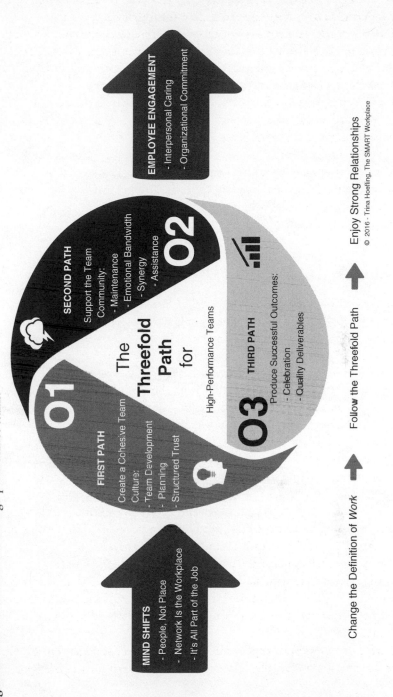

MIND SHIFTS
- People, Not Place
- Network Is the Workplace
- It's All Part of the Job

O1

FIRST PATH

Create a Cohesive Team Culture:
- Team Development
- Planning
- Structured Trust

O2

SECOND PATH

Support the Team Community:
- Maintenance
- Emotional Bandwidth
- Synergy
- Assistance

The
**Threefold
Path**
for

High-Performance Teams

O3

THIRD PATH

Produce Successful Outcomes:
- Celebration
- Quality Deliverables

EMPLOYEE ENGAGEMENT
- Interpersonal Caring
- Organizational Commitment

Change the Definition of *Work* ➤ Follow the Threefold Path ➤ Enjoy Strong Relationships

© 2016 - Trina Hoefling, The SMART Workplace

TABLE I.1
Navigating the Book's Reading Path

Part One: Virtually Mobile, Organizationally Attached	Vital mind shifts, virtual drivers and blocks
Part Two: Will Virtual Work Here?	Redesign of the workplace systems and processes to leverage mobility
Part Three: Essential Virtual Competencies	Virtual team leader and member competencies, team qualities
Part Four: The Threefold Path of High-Performance Virtual Teams	Virtual team leader and member competencies; team qualities; and team development, support, and results management
Part Five: From Me to We	Technology, tools, and communication for collaborative teamwork
Part Six: Expand Emotional Bandwidth	Having relationships based on trust and generosity, engaging virtually, and navigating the fourth path to a successful career

sample opportunity profile matrix, so you have a point of comparison for your own organization.[9]

Part Three provides the information you need to be, hire, and develop competent team leaders and virtual professional team members. It discusses stages of development for new virtual workers and teams, and how the manager can respond. It lays out the Threefold Path for high-performance virtual teams.

Part Five steps through many pragmatics to build a virtual toolbox for the team. Communication and tool choices impact relationships and trust and team results.

Part Six focuses on the interpersonal dynamics that build trusting teams and expand the emotional bandwidth in relationships. We examine what it takes to have a virtually engaged workforce and set up professionals for lifelong career success. The book ends with a chapter on my thoughts about what's next.

Why Am I Your Pathfinder and Guide?

I've been at this for a while. I developed an early remote management training program in 1984, before telecommuting or virtual work had a name, in an effort to help engineers in a global corporation manage matrix-based project teams built on expertise, not geography.[10] They were separated by culture, continents, and language, but they were connected by a shared team mission. We didn't have a word for virtual team management then. I still help individuals and organizations work together better after all these years, often virtually. I wrote *Working Virtually: Managing People and Organizations for Virtual Success*, first published at the turn of the century, while I was Telecommuting Success, Inc.'s vice president of training programs. I've continued to grow as I provide strategic organization transformation to organizations seeking to retain an engaged virtual workforce. At the same time, too little has changed when I work with people. Good people struggle to help people work together, especially virtually, prompting me to curate what I've learned. I sincerely hope my update is helpful for today's mobile workforce.

Notes

1. Dan Schwabel, "10 Workplace Trends You'll See in 2016," *Forbes*, November 1, 2015, www.forbes.com/forbes/welcome/#6bbe75a4456e1fe51497456e

2. Reid Hoffman, Ben Casnocha, and Chris Yeh, *The Alliance: Managing Talent in the Networked Age* (Boston: Harvard Business Review Press, 2014).

3. Daniel H. Pink, "Free Agent Nation," Fast Company, December 31, 1997, www.fastcompany.com/33851/free-agent-nation

4. "Node (computer science)," *Wikipedia*, last modified July 2015, https://en.wikipedia.org/wiki/Node_(computer_science)

5. "Network," *Webopedia*, www.webopedia.com/TERM/N/network.html

6. Trina Hoefling, "Making Your Net-Work," public workshops, 2006–2015, various locations.

7. Deloitte University Press, "Global Human Capital Trends 2016: The New Organization: Different by Design," https://forms.workday.com/us/landing_page/webinar_deloitte_global_hcm_trends_report_lp.php?camp=70180000001EaaM&campid=ussm_lip_c_hc_no_15.151

8. www.WorkingVirtually.org

9. Go to www.WorkingVirtually.org for additional resources and assessments. Download a free bonus chapter on how to manage virtual meetings!

10. Team managers in the U.S. Midwest were managing engineers in Japan.

PART ONE

VIRTUALLY MOBILE, ORGANIZATIONALLY ATTACHED

"We are all virtual leaders, whether we have the title or not. We are all virtual team members, whether we're in charge or not. We all work from wherever we are, digitally connected, whether we telecommute or not."

—Trina Hoefling, *Working Virtually: Managing People for Successful Virtual Teams and Organizations,* first edition

VITAL MIND-SET SHIFTS IN A MOBILE WORLD

"Learn how to see. Realize that everything connects to everything else."

—Leonardo da Vinci

"It is not the strongest of the species that survives, nor the most intelligent that survives. It is the one that is most adaptable to change."

—Charles Darwin

"The most dangerous place to make a decision today is in the office. I run most of my business from my phone. . . . Everything is connected, collaborative, and mobile."

—Ulrik Nehammer, CEO, Coca-Cola

How we think defines what we see and how well we lead. Our mind-set limits or opens us to adapt. In 1996 Atlanta, Georgia, hosted the Olympics. Coca-Cola brought my company in to prepare for traffic congestion since their offices were located near Olympics events and hotels. We developed a temporary telecommuting work plan. Concurrently, we conducted a Telecommuting Readiness Assessment to see if this could be a pilot program from which Coca-Cola Corporate could implement a fuller virtual work solution.

The Olympics initiative went well, but they were not ready for telecommuting. The infrastructure, job analyses, and capabilities were in place. *The culture, however, was not.* In the mid-1990s, status and prestige were obvious at Corporate. Office grandeur, tailored suits—image mattered culturally as well as implicitly; it was a reflection of status.

No change plan could quickly change the hearts, minds, and egos of upwardly mobile managers. It was too much to go against a cultural norm that was, quite literally, grounded deeply in that building. Instead of saying no to telecommuting, however, leadership decided, *"No, not now."* Culture, especially perks such as large offices, had to change first to break a strong career incentive that was deeply woven into their way of being. Once perks began to decouple from office spaces, mind-sets changed, followed by cultural shifts. As years passed, Coca-Cola changed. It got virtual. CEO Nehammer, quoted at the beginning of this chapter, is a global leader, not in downtown Atlanta. The CEO is a virtual worker.

Visionary Leader or Nineteenth-Century Executive Mind-Set?

The German Post Office held the first management conference in 1882, for CEOs only. The conference was for one purpose: to help CEOs not be afraid of the telephone. Nobody showed up. The invitees were insulted; the idea that they should use telephones was unthinkable—telephones were for secretaries.

The same story applies to executives not long ago about the personal computer. Today, everyone has multiple devices—computer, tablet, smartphone, all backed to the cloud—that simplify our smart lives. Technology is no longer science fiction; we've become the Internet of Things. The iPhone broke through in record time, an indication of the pace with which we adapt today. It took 76 years for the telephone to reach half the population. The smartphone did it in less than 10 years.[1] The iPad penetrated even faster. Ninety-six percent of workers use the Internet, e-mail, and mobile devices to work; 81% of employees spend an hour or more on work-related e-mail during the workday.[2]

Our behavior has shifted individually, and so has the virtually mobile, smart organization. The way Coca-Cola used the Olympics to explore a more virtual workforce is laudatory. It adapted its culture to fit the mobile workplace. Despite its entrenched incentives, Coca-Cola's leadership saw what needed to happen—shift mind-sets to fit today's world—and it successfully changed. How much has your mind-set shifted to match a virtually mobile work world?

TABLE 1.1
Mobile Work Mind Shifts

1. "Best Fit" Environment
2. The Network Is the Workplace
3. The Paradox of Meaningful Work and Looser Employment Ties
4. Reward Collaboration Over Individual Expertise

Organizations and leaders who are ready to thrive virtually adapt to create the best fit workplaces that support their people in achieving the organization's mission. As Table 1.1 shows, best fit considers the virtual and colocated work environment, organization culture, and teams structured in ways that fit the work being done.

Mind Shift #1: "Best Fit" Environment

In a virtually mobile organization with collaborative capabilities, the work space is decided on "best fit" environments. Offices and team spaces are resources, not status symbols. People don't think of a designated work space (except their computers and devices), and work is an ongoing event based on responsibilities, not a physical place. Organizations are learning to do the following:

- Transform a virtual workforce into a functioning virtual organization with viable teams who find meaning and satisfaction from the work and colleagues—across time and distance—while producing results.
- Design business operations and work spaces to be more collaborative and responsive to what workers need.

It may seem counterintuitive that groups can link more cohesively across time and space than happens typically in person, but it is counterintuitive only if you believe face-to-face interaction is essential to develop team trust. Face time can quicken relationship development, but it is not essential and potentially not even best, depending on the work performed. Many organizations function in a matrix today, meaning that managing multiple relationships is a core competency for everyone, not just managers or executives. Team members belong to multiple teams simultaneously—based on function, project, and customer initiative. Showing up for multiple team meetings by web conference, without leaving one's workstation, is a significant time-saver. Talent availability and bandwidth are, more than ever, less limited by a physical workplace.

"Best Fit" Organizations

"Best fit" organizations integrate operationally. Enterprise solutions enable people to work together in many ways, such as face-to-face conference rooms (colocated office space) that are web enabled (allowing virtual participation). This means an equal opportunity for integration of a distributed talent pool. Some teams are obviously virtual, fitting their organization structure to accommodate distance, but other teams are less obviously so. In today's global marketplace, for example, most executive teams are virtual already, made up of leaders based on value, not place. Even if executive offices are colocated, executives usually have little face time, but connect virtually on a frequent basis. Department teams may be wholly colocated, blend office workers with telecommuters, or be completely virtual. When organizations realize how integrated and virtual we already are, redesigning office space and business processes for best fit happens naturally with little curve.

"Best Fit" Teams

How a team structures itself depends on the team's purpose. One structure does not fit all. Traditionally, employees were members of one "fixed" department and perhaps on committees, maybe stretch assignments. Today, multiple team memberships are common. Organizations are made up of networks of teams, and team members are connectors in those networks.

Agile teams form and reform readily. The proverbial revolving door of rolling entry and exit needs leaders to jump-start team relationships. Seldom does a team begin and end together. You know you're a twenty-first-century worker when you've worked for five organizations in two years without changing desks! Team members are recruited for their expertise and influence, not based on hierarchy. Teams often share leadership and are somewhat self-directed. And most teams are, at least partially, virtual.

The First Path of virtual teams facilitates the fast formation and agility of high-performance teams because it follows the principle of best fit. Members fit a team based on multiple factors, such as expertise, functional (perhaps political) representation, professional fit, or simple availability. Team membership may shift based on project stage or assignment to a customer or value stream. The team may include workers who go to a traditional office, telecommuters, and traveling employees.

Teams are also increasingly made up of members who cross organizational boundaries, including customers, strategic partners, contract specialists, or vendors. Cross-organizational alliances require "fitting" knowledge-sharing infrastructure to be secure while encouraging open sharing and protection of organizational boundaries, such as intellectual property and proprietary processes. Fitting includes facilitating easy cooperation across permeable organization boundaries while managing risk and learning to quickly fit together and be effective fast.

All this serves to increase team and organizational leaders' need to manage, onboard, and coach differently, enabling people to work where and how best fits them. In the coordination of team activities, the team members develop a way of working together that "fits" them.

Do you think Best Fit?

Mind Shift #2: The Network Is the Workplace

It is no longer necessary to go to a *place* to perform basic functions—buy, sell, train, collaborate, or recruit. LinkedIn has virtually replaced the long-form resume. Organizations can distribute organization learning fast through knowledge-sharing networks and online learning platforms. Integrated organizations leverage intellectual capital, making it available through the digital network. Virtual work gives organizations the agility to increase speed, expand expertise, and access strategic opportunities to better meet customer demands—with less expense.

Design thinking is evolving as business leaders rethink how to structure the organization into a network of collaborating teams. Virtual work is no longer a last resort to keep a good employee; it's not a compromise when people can't meet in person. It is not an overlay, a replication, or a poor substitute. It is our way of working. IT has transformed intranets to be more than a place to store our data and files; we connect there.

What Is the Network?

A company network is the culmination of basic virtual work processes and systems, and the people. It is the road, the car, and the map. Think of the network as how:

- Work is done.
- Teams are built.
- Knowledge is shared.
- Complexity is managed.
- Relationships are developed.
- Agreements are solidified and trust is maintained.

The organization is literally built around the interconnectivity of virtual, human, and electronic networks, not a physical workplace. We are hyper-connected already; we can watch *The Voice* on broadcast media, smart devices, and the Internet, all available 24/7. Why not leverage that hyper-connectivity at work? Why add 20% to the average person's workweek in commute time? Whether Samantha drives 10 miles to an office or walks down the hallway at home, she will be logging into the network, checking e-mail, handling correspondence, and responding to people—probably without talking to anyone. She is a virtual worker, regardless of whether she telecommutes.

Where do you work?

Mind Shift #3: The Paradox of Meaningful Work and Looser Employment Ties

This is a time in work history when we are less tied to our employers and not tied to a desk. The trend continues to loosen organization ties with shorter contracts. At the same time, we seek more connection with others. We're in a paradox in this increasingly virtual work world, where team members are more geographically and physically isolated not only from their team but also from their organizations. The isolation of virtual work along with a short-timer mentality makes the virtual leader's job challenging.

Since the Industrial Age, managers have tried to motivate employees, so creating a motivating environment today is nothing new. Unfortunately, when surveyed, employees continue to say that we are failing to engage their hearts and minds. Many report feeling isolated from their teams, disengaged and unmotivated. Many hope to change to a job where they can engage and make a difference. The good news is managers and workers want to be part of committed, high-performance teams. The virtual challenge is that distance can slow down the onboarding and enculturation process if the organization isn't designed for inclusion and virtual collaboration, and if the manager isn't prepared to lead talent virtually.

Are you connected to your team and organization?

Mind Shift #4: Reward Collaboration and Openness Over Individual Expertise

Esko Kilpi, founder and principal of a leading research and consultancy firm working with the challenges of knowledge work and digital work environments, says, "The focus should now be on cooperation and emergent interaction based on transparency, interdependence and responsiveness. It really is a fast-and-loose world."[3] Organizations are often well-connected digital networks, yet results prove teams aren't fully maximizing collaboration. One leading inhibitor is the organization's tendency to define a person's value by how much expertise she holds. Hiring contingent workers encourages skill-based hiring, and it makes sense. At the same time, a competency plug-and-play approach to team formation is only one facet of hiring a well-balanced team. It implies our unique expertise increases our value because of what we alone know, more than sharing our wisdom does. It's actually a disincentive to collaborate with the team. If a team member's value depends on unique contribution, peers become competition, not allies. Workplace reward systems, compensation, and performance appraisal need to reward information sharing, not hoarding, and team performance as well as individual results. Examine and structure your systems for collaboration, not vicious, hidden cycles of built-in internal competition.

Two Tenets to Enable Generosity and Openness

Colocated work environments facilitate knowledge sharing, accidentally and simply by being present. Even in a mobile work world, knowledge is often shared due to proximity, timing, mentoring, or intentional alliances. Virtual work can create literal distance between knowledge and the people. Workers are left out and disengaged; performance is at risk when vital information isn't flowing and people hesitate to ask for help virtually. Accidental communication is and always will be a part of how people learn and collaborate.

Tenet 1: Look for Spontaneous Connections With Your Virtual Team

Intentional knowledge sharing should be formally structured and rewarded, of course, but there is power in informal sharing. In the emerging and boundary-crossing global workplace, with the hyperconnectedness of "smart" devices and shared apps, it's easy to capture and share intelligence. It's easy to start team chatter and cross-team conversations by facilitating informal and accidental learning while helping people get to know one another. Currently, most knowledge sharing is reliant on the manager to facilitate (and sometimes learning and development departments). Having managers be the conduit to the team is just too slow, unreliable, and costly. Does your organization rely on managers to cascade organization communication? For the informal manager, virtuality may have introduced new constraints to cascading organizational news. Are your virtual teams as well informed as those who work at a corporate office?

Tenet 2: Structure Knowledge Sharing and Information Dissemination

Time is of the essence to shift organizations toward open collaboration, rewarding team success over individual excellence. Corporate America is vulnerable. As far as I can tell, most companies are not managing knowledge sharing and organization wisdom capture well, even though they could. I facilitate in the board room and engage and listen in the trenches. I "hear" into executive thinking while also "seeing" into the belly of the operational beast. What I see is unsettling—scary misalignment between a networked organization's strategic thinking and what gets rewarded in their everyday systems, processes, and management practices.

Simply put, if performance management, appraisal, and pay remain individually focused (and, therefore, competitive at its core), all the best collaboration tools and training won't be enough to get people to become part of high-performing teams. Authentic collaboration comes when people not only are technology enabled but also are connected to their team and care about team results as their first priority. They know if the team wins, everybody wins.

Open sharing, passing wisdom on to others, fundamentally changes a culture. It won't happen if it's not mapped to how people are paid. Traditionally, people were rewarded based on rugged individualism, on their proprietary wealth of knowledge. Today, hoarding expertise is a barrier to virtual teams and organizations. Unintentional virtual worker ignorance because of poor virtual communication risks performance. If a networked collaborative mentality is to emerge organizationally, generous sharing must be rewarded.

Boomers Are Taking Knowledge With Them When They Go

Another organization issue is a frightening vulnerability. People are retiring, letting organization knowledge leave when they do. Right now, one-third of baby boomers, the organization wisdom keepers and experts, are eligible to retire.[4] If not actively managed now, much organization wisdom retires with them. I see strategic conversation, but not enough action.

At the least, encourage people to generously pass along the wisdom. Much "work" contribution is primarily mental, not muscle.

People Will Share What They Know—If

It shouldn't "cost" workers to cooperate; rather, they should be rewarded for being nodes in the network, connectors and coaches. Financially reward it. Social network analysis can directly and objectively measure who is a valuable node in the organization.

A robust knowledge management infrastructure also quickly enables people to access help when needed. Just as anyone can access a universe of knowledge through Google search, so should a virtual team member be able to access a wealth of organizational knowledge without leaving the workstation. Organizations that fail to technically integrate and culturally collaborate will never fully engage the workforce or unleash all the intelligence available. Too much will leave with the boomers.

How organizations address training also changes in a collaborative organization, and more so when virtual. Training is no longer reserved for "learning events." Information-rich employees become valued resources in the network—coaches and teachers. While classrooms and other synchronous training opportunities still have value, so does the need for continuous and readily available modular learning on demand, anytime, often online. MOOCs[5] and other on-demand learning portals[6] are primary learning resources, cutting T&D budgets or redirecting budgets to strategic leadership and talent development, while providing vast resources to employees.

Open, collaborative cultures unleash potential for dramatic expansion of organization capability. Learning happens anytime through many modes.

How does your organization encourage sharing and collaboration?

How Do We Work Together if We're Working Apart?

Disengaged virtual workers are not only isolated but also dangerous.

At the management level, if distributed team members do not have a clear sense of how their work "fits in" with the overall plan, they risk disengagement and missed performance metrics. Individual efforts run a greater risk of being misaligned with strategic priorities and team goals, regardless of how hard individuals may be working. I've facilitated heart-sinking conversations when the worker and manager both realize that the worker was not laying off work, but feverishly working in the wrong direction. Communication had broken down.

Virtual work demands everyone's commitment to communicating—listening and speaking up. How else will the team ensure everyone is working on the right track? This isn't optional. The team depends on each other. Individually and collectively, the "virtual job" creates outputs that come from coordinating work, managing each other, negotiating competing priorities, and delivering team outcomes through coordinated efforts. Lead and communicate actively. Be a role model. Teamwork supports the adage that two brains are better than one. Workers who want to be part of high-performance teams also want a voice in defining the quality of their work lives and organizations. They want more than "just a job." In order for any collection of individuals to function as a team that is able to respond, barriers need to fall between managers and employees, among the network of teams, across geography and culture, and within operations seeking efficiency while flexibly serving the customers. We're in this together, communicating and connecting.

What Makes an Organization Come Alive and Take on a Life of Its Own?

A healthy organization community is a collective of what is held in common by its members, a "creation of some jointly imagined possibility."[7] A company is not a thing that preexists, which people join to merely contribute "outputs." It is a living organism that changes based on the collective beliefs and actions of its members. I've been with virtual organizations that are alive and buzzing, more like a beehive of collective focus. The air almost vibrates across the airwaves; nothing can disrupt enthusiasm and belief. And I've more often seen the opposite (it's often why I've been called in). It's so simple that most miss it.

It's About Us!

Whether colocated or distributed, team members are more committed to the organization when they see how they contribute to its very existence, even if they contribute for only a short time. Their commitment may be to be reliable workers, and not to seek ambitious careers—to be engaged employees, happy when they are contributing.

Distance does not need to create distance. The virtual environment appears to risk increased disconnection and isolation, and it may, if the organization leaders do not do the following:

- Shift toward a more systemic, integrated view of the organization, and communicate with everyone to know how they fit into the whole.
- Support the network infrastructure that facilitates hyperconnection.
- Actively support a culture where workers share in the rewards of team collaboration.

Leaders should encourage and help people develop relationships across and beyond organization boundaries, and bring people together digitally and face-to-face, synchronously (live) and asynchronously (when they work best). Organizations add value when talent is supported and well deployed.

In a virtual environment, traditional status barriers disappear, or at least become less visible—such as office size and other status perks—and unconscious cultural biases and even some office politics become less relevant. With fewer barriers to keep us apart, collaboration can thrive.

Don't Wait for Them

You may not be in a position to affect operational priorities, and your organization may not have shifted mind-sets yet. You can do something. One leader had a "corner office status issue." He proposed a plan to remove the status barrier by mandating work away from the office. People were to use the office as an exception, and be there less than a certain percentage of work hours. This unusual move lowered the barrier to having conversations across status because of office floors, posted titles, or doors. The temporary mandate forced people to shift their habits, and, perhaps most importantly, it was applied fairly. Even executives agreed to the mandate. In this example, distance created togetherness.

Collaborative work cultures are often thought of as an organizational ideal—a value, not an operational requirement. Social time in meetings gets pushed aside for urgent agendas, for example. If people interacting is the actual process of work, and collaborative technology platforms are set up to help us function as a network of teams, then isn't now the time for us to get good at collaborating virtually?

As you read this book, ask yourself how you can better create the beliefs, habits, systems, and processes that develop teams you want to lead.

Notes

1. Bob Moritz, "Global Annual Review 2014: Technology Breakthroughs," *PWC.com's Annual Published Review,* New York, 2014, p. 10.

2. Shane Ferro, "Virtual Labor Organizing Could Be How the Next Generation of Workers Get Unionized," *Business Insider,* June 10, 2015, www .businessinsider.com/the-century-foundation-wants-the-unionization-movement-to-go-online-2015-6

3. Stowe Boyd, "Esko Kilpi on the Architecture of Work," interview published by Work Futures Institute on Medium, https://workfutures.io/esko-kilpi-on-the-architecture-of-work-1b35f9fb4bc0#.n7ix4bqla

4. Dr. Tasha Eurich, "Generational Leadership," Rocky Mountain Human Resource Professional Society, Denver University, Denver, CO, April 16, 2015.

5. MOOCs are massive open online courses, such as MIT's EdX online learning.

6. Lynda.com is currently popular.

7. John Niremberg, *The Living Organization* (New York: Irving Professional, 1993), 29.

2

VIRTUAL ROADBLOCKS AND ESSENTIAL DRIVERS

"We have modified our environment so radically that we must modify ourselves in order to exist in this new environment."

—Norbert Wiener

"There is no lostness like that which comes to a man when a perfect and certain pattern has dissolved about him."

—John Steinbeck

*"The barn has burned down!
Now, at last, I can enjoy
The sight of the moon."*

—Mizuta Masahide

Distributed Work Is Here to Stay

Technology makes workplaces intelligent, connecting virtual workers easily. Three-fourths of all office workers believe smart technology makes them more efficient and productive, with half believing their company should invest more in integrated collaborative tools. Global Workplace Analytics, an emerging workplace strategies research firm, estimates that 64 million U.S. employees, fully half the workforce, hold jobs compatible with part-time telecommuting.

Two Remaining Virtual Roadblocks

Roadblock 1: Lack of Support for and From Middle Managers
Kathy Kacher, president and founder of Career/Life Alliance Services and coauthor of the 2014 National Workplace Flexibility Study,[1] finds companies are moving ahead with flexwork options but aren't following accepted

principles of change management or providing much managerial support. "Organizations continue to believe that the culture will just come along once they have rolled out a policy or redesigned their technology platform."[2]

The most frequently cited reasons for poor organizational adoption of flexwork options were the following:

- Poor communication from corporate about initiatives and upcoming changes
- Lack of urgency from senior leaders *and middle managers* regarding the people impact
- Fear of career penalty by out-of-sight virtual and flex workers
- Lack of manager training to effectively lead mobile teams[3]

Managers Aren't Intentionally Throttling Their Team's Success

Virtual managers and their teams struggle without training. Metrics reveal that *organizations do not adequately train their managers, if they provide any training at all.* A recent workplace study found the greatest barrier to successful program rollout was getting middle manager buy-in. When trained, they get on board.[4] Managers consistently list three concerns about virtual and flex work. Each is easily addressed with training. Managers have expressed the following:

1. Staying connected to the team is harder when I don't see them.
2. Managing employees on flex complicates my job.
3. How do I know they're really working?

Remove the Roadblock

In a controlled study, managers completed training in managing flex workers, which included formulating a draft of their team plan—the First Path of team development. *While implementing flex work*, they experienced significant improvements in team performance and functioning, and even more improvement once teams adjusted to the new environment. They achieved the following self-reported skill and confidence gains after training (notice how dramatically their confidence grew):

- Understanding of flex improved 75%.
- Comfort discussing flex options improved 68%.
- Team interaction improved 53%.
- Team communication improved 55%.
- Understanding of performance goals improved 41%.

- Customer service improved 24%.
- Productivity improved 20%.

After training, 85% of the managers stated they felt more prepared, which was up from 60% readiness prior to training. They also were more confident that their employees were *really working*. Almost half the managers felt they could easily measure performance after training. It's only half, but it's significantly higher than the 34% confidence prior to training.[5]

I hope this book helps today's virtual leaders until they have access to skill development.

Roadblock 2: Human Nature's Comfortable Habits

Untrained managers are more comfortable managing by habit. Many workers worry about isolation and career invisibility. Organization leaders worry about company culture. People are slower to change than technology because habits slow us down. Neuroscientists show us how our brains build neural networks that develop into habits. We have to be able to challenge our habits to deepen and broaden our skill sets. How easily we do that *is* limited by *our willingness to experience discomfort and stretch ourselves, and whether learning resources are available.* People run from discomfort, even though it's necessary for growth. We're more open to discomfort when we understand *why* we need to change, *and when we can learn safely.* Mistakes are learning opportunities, not career risks, and training is available to initiate better habits.

Removing the Roadblocks

Train, coach, and communicate the hows and whys of virtual team leadership.

Virtual Drivers

1: Workers Expect Smart Collaboration

The millennials are an educated, technically savvy generation that has expectations, like *full* digital integration of the workplace. They already collaborate digitally, so a Facebook-like user experience is a minimally acceptable standard.

Dated technology isn't the only contributor to poor collaboration. When older workers don't feel comfortable in a digital workplace, or are unsure how to use the collaborative tools, organizations aren't attractive to millennials. In a virtual environment, collaboration platform and tool training brings fast return on investment (ROI) for the technology averse, teaching practical skills and removing mental roadblocks.

As boomers are retiring, millennials are moving into leadership positions faster than any previous generation. They are the most educated workforce in history. They were raised with technology and interface with it easily. As workers, they expect digital collaboration; as leaders, they'll demand it.

2: Meaningful Work Bridges Distance

Millennials are motivated differently than boomers were in their early careers. Millennials' top priority isn't making money or reaching a certain status—it's being engaged at work.[6] More than ever, leaders need collaboration competence built on real relationships—not just for productivity and workflow but to keep people engaged. With looser ties between professional and employer, loyalty is earned, and the manager is key to earning that loyalty.[7]

A 2015 survey sponsored by the *Economist* was revealing. Over one-third (35%) of millennial respondents confirm that the manager is key. The manager's ability to support the team through facilitating a sense of shared purpose and common corporate culture drives millennial loyalty. One-third also say they value meaningful work over pay.[8] Seventy percent plan to change jobs soon and half are confident they will do so successfully. Meaningful work has turned out to be the most significant recruitment and retention tool.

3: Flex Work Leads Recruitment and Retention

When I first published this book in 2001, virtual work was often a "novel idea" used occasionally to retain exceptional employees. No longer novel, it's becoming a worker expectation. A flexible workplace attracts and retains top talent. A Society for Human Resource Management (SHRM) survey discovered that four of five employees *crave* flexibility, which includes the ability to work from home.[9] A strong word, *crave* shows the strength of worker desire. People will work for less—or are less willing to leave for a job that offers more—if they are able to work from home.[10]

People want and need flexibility for a variety of reasons—lifestyle choice and work-life-family balance being common. Technically enabled, people can work virtually and still have a seamless connection to the team. In 2015, telecommuting was named the top desired employee benefit. No organization wants to lose its best people because of a long commute, a spousal relocation, or child care conflicts. Organizations experience a 20% reduction in turnover when virtual work is an option. *Virtual work has become a leading recruitment benefit.*

4: It's Socially Responsible

Half of American workers could work virtually. Even if people worked from home half the time, greenhouse gas emissions would reduce by 54 million metric tons annually, the equivalent of taking almost 10 million cars off the road. We would consume 640 million fewer barrels of oil annually.[11] While this isn't a leading driver currently, perhaps executives should follow the lead of companies like Dell and Xerox that are striving for a 50% virtual workforce by 2020 as a strategic commitment to the environment.[12]

5: It Saves Money—Big-Time

Real estate savings. Telecommuting delivers real estate savings. IBM and American Express turned around in the 1990s largely by shedding real estate costs through telecommuting. Real estate is expensive, so if a company can disperse its employees, having them colocated in less geographically expensive places or as teleworkers, tremendous savings fall directly to the bottom line. Corporate real estate is being rebudgeted from long-term, fixed assets to provisioning dispersed *networks* of workplaces to support flexible, mobile work. Real estate is becoming a variable cost. Facilities and IT are the strategic partners in redesigning the physical/digital workplace for full integration and collaborative cultural impact.

Productivity gains. Managers continue to worry about production on a virtual team. "*How do we know remote employees are really working?*" When it's actually measured, however, it's a needless worry. Virtual performance measurements indicate an average productivity increase of 20%. Virtual workers have fewer distractions, and virtual workers also work more hours. More work is being done virtually than we know, often off the clock. Telecommuters are almost twice as likely to work more than a 40-hour workweek. Only 28% of nontelecommuters work more than 40 hours a week, while 53% of telecommuters do.[13] The higher the skill level of the virtual worker, the greater the productivity gain.

Lower overhead costs.[14] The Productivity, Innovation and Entrepreneurship program at the National Bureau of Economic Research monitored one home-based call center virtualization. The company saved $1,900 per employee in overhead reduction while per-employee productivity increased by 13.5%. Also, virtual call centers spent less in retraining because turnover reduced by half, with employees stating increased job satisfaction as their reason for staying.[15] *That's not a typo—half.*

Sun and Cisco share virtual work ROI—undeniable! The rewards to the organization are undeniable, as evidenced in this chapter and elsewhere. In 2006 Sun Microsystems, an early adopter of virtual work, published metrics of its telecommuting initiative, including cost savings directly attributed to virtual and flexwork environments. This was before integrated technology was robust, suggesting even greater gains if implemented today. At that time, 20,000 Sun employees from 33 countries telecommuted at least 2 days a week, and 1,760 of those employees telecommuted 60% to 100% of the time. This was half the workforce. Fourteen drop-in centers were used by 5,000 telecommuters, and 127 physical locations were defined as *work spaces* by global telecommuters. The results?

- 6,600 "work seats" were eliminated without losing employees
- $63.9 million was saved in the first year
- $319 million was saved over five years
- $24 million was spent on technology[16]

Cisco not only offers market solutions for virtual work but also does what it sells. It shared ROI metrics gathered from virtual workers who used a touch-down office in one San Jose campus. It provided Cisco workers the option of working from anyplace and provided a physical work space for anyone who needed to touch down or hold a meeting. The benefits were irrefutable:

- Real estate costs were reduced by 37%
- New facility construction costs were reduced by 42%
- Workplace services (infrastructure and support) costs were reduced by 37%
- Furniture costs were reduced by 50%
- IT capital costs were reduced by 40%
- Cabling costs were reduced by 60%
- Equipment space requirements were reduced by 50%[17]

These are typical results when organizations measure virtual work effectiveness.

Virtual work is not unusual anymore. With a bit of organizational support and training, managers release old habits, removing two major virtual roadblocks. We have many ways to come together once the barriers are removed. Platforms and integrated tools have evolved. It's human nature to connect, so *we* don't need to evolve. Some of us just need to learn, and organizations just need to virtually connect.

Notes

1. Kyra Cavanaugh, Jennifer Sabatini Fraone, and Kathy Kacher, "National Workplace Flexibility Study," 2014, www.bc.edu/content/dam/files/centers/cwf/research/highlights/pdf/NWFS-Report-012014.pdf

2. Kathy Kacher, interview by Trina Hoefling, personal notes from an interview with author in 2015.

3. "Survey on Workplace Flexibility," October 2013, Worldatwork.org

4. Ibid.

5. Cavanaugh, Fraone, and Kacher, "National Workplace Flexibility Study."

6. Dr. Tasha Eurich, *Bankable Leadership: Happy People, Bottom-Line Results and the Power to Deliver Both* (Austin: Greenleaf Book Group Press, 2013).

7. Deloitte Consulting, "Mind the Gaps: The 2015 Deloitte Millennial Survey," 2015, www2.deloitte.com/content/dam/Deloitte/global/Documents/About-Deloitte/gx-wef-2015-millennial-survey-executivesummary.pdf

8. The Economist Intelligence Unit, "Automated, Creative, & Dispersed: The Future of Work in the 21st Century," *Economist*, May 20, 2015, p. 5.

9. Donna Fuscaldo, "Why Your Company Should Offer a Flexible Work Environment," Glassdoor.com, October 7, 2013, http://employers.glassdoor.com/blog/why-your-company-should-offer-a-flexible-work-environment/

10. "Flexibility or Salary: Which Do You Value More?," Free Money Finance, February 6, 2012, www.freemoneyfinance.com/2012/02/flexibility-or-salary-which-do-you-value-more.html

11. For current data on telecommuting and other work environment statistics, see "Latest Telecommuting Statistics," Globalworkplaceanalytics.com, August 14, 2015, http://globalworkplaceanalytics.com/telecommuting-statistics

12. Sara Suton Fell, "How Telecommuting Reduced Carbon Footprints at Dell, Aetna and Xerox," Entrepreneur.com, April 22, 2015, www.entrepreneur.com/article/245296

13. Jennifer Parris, "New Statistics on Telecommuting and the Workforce," Flexjobs.com, August 21, 2013, www.flexjobs.com/blog/post/new-statistics-on-telecommuting-and-the-workforce/

14. Phyliss Korkki, "Yes, Flexible Hours Ease Stress: But Is Everyone on Board?," *New York Times*, August 23, 2014, www.nytimes.com/2014/08/24/business/yes-flexible-hours-ease-stress-but-is-everyone-on-board.html?_r=0

15. Nicholas Bloom, "To Raise Productivity, Let More Employees Work From Home," *Harvard Business Review*, January/February 2014, https://hbr.org/2014/01/to-raise-productivity-let-more-employees-work-from-home/ar/1

16. "Sun Microsystems," *Smart Commute*, 2006, http://smartcommute.ca/more-options/telework/sun-microsystems/

17. Charles Grantham and James Ware, "Measuring the Business Value of Distributed Work," White Paper, The Work Design Collaborative, Prescott, AZ, February 2006, used with permission.

PART TWO

WILL VIRTUAL WORK HERE?

"Whatever you can do, or dream you can, begin it. Boldness has genius, power, and magic in it."

—Goethe

"We have it in our power to begin the world again."

—Thomas Paine, *Common Sense* (1776)

3

REDESIGNING THE WORKPLACE FOR THE HUMAN NETWORK

"We're not just talking about the computer network anymore. We're talking about the human network, and having an impact on the way people work and live. . . . It's about tapping into a brand new collaborative business process to accelerate the pace that business is done."

—Don Proctor, SVP, Cisco Networks, leader of Cisco's Cybersecurity Task Force

"A single orchestration platform is effectively the brain and is an absolutely fundamental requirement for a smart workplace. . . . The more connected things you want to coordinate, the more likely it is for the whole network to become a cluttered mess if not orchestrated properly."[1]

—Mark Furness, CEO, Essensys

Jeffrey, the CEO of Fast Growth Company Inc. (FGC), meets with a key strategic partner. They have an opportunity but are nervous about the turnaround time. Jeffrey calls the office from his car—powwow, conference room, 15 minutes. All priorities are realigned. Jeffrey walks in, coffee brewing, whiteboard wiped clean, the team assembled minus Marianne (still at lunch). The meeting begins. Thirty minutes later, COO Joan takes over the huddle, mind mapping and negotiating tasks. Marianne returns, reviews the whiteboard, rolls up her sleeves, and dives in. Jeffrey leaves for a customer meeting.

Two hours later, Jeffrey finds the team scattered, on the phones and computers. With the meeting scheduled to reconvene at 5:30 p.m., Jeffrey stops in Marianne's office to make sure she's fully briefed. He then remembers that Cranton needs some figures to run a forecast, pulls the data, and carries hard copy over to Cranton's office after uploading the file to the shared drive. Cranton isn't there, so Jeffrey writes a quick note and leaves the material on his MacBook Pro.

At 5:30 p.m., everyone scurries to the conference. Packets are distributed, everyone with a tree's worth of paper. Everyone takes notes. The next assignments are relegated based on agreed adaptations. A writing lead is assigned to compile the pieces into one flowing proposal. Because of the company's fast growth and similar events, the team agrees to the short-straw method. It will require someone pulling another late night to meet the deadline. All agree it's worth it, the payoff's spectacular, and everyone secretly hopes they get to head home. Because of past experiences, a second straw is to proofread, in by 6 a.m. with a rested eye.

Everyone works in parallel. All input their revisions and notify the short straws. Many offer availabilities. Jeffrey has to catch a plane to make a key presentation for additional funding and will be unavailable after noon, so the document has to be in his hands by 11:15. All nod their heads, look at their watches, and count stock options in their heads instead of sheep in their beds.

And so it goes.

FGC is fast growth, fast paced. The culture is highly collaborative out of necessity, habit, and choice. Meetings, paper, more meetings, more paper, and long hours at high speed are the norm; people are energized.

How might virtuality change this company culture? Would it improve efficiency but interfere with the focused energy? How can FGC redesign its workplace to keep the good going but coordinate more efficiently?

Organization Design, Culture, and Virtual Team Synergy

Designing the workplace means to simplify, entering information into context and facilitating conversations with interdependent team members in a way that gets work done. Because time and place have been separated from the work, design isn't limited to buildings anymore.

This chapter explores how to help an organization develop virtually without sacrificing the culture and team synergy. *Virtual work does bring change, however.* It is naïve to think that virtual work does not impact organization design, or that culture won't impact both. For example, a previous client is a large global manufacturer, private and family owned. The face-to-face, family feel was deeply valued. Voice mail was used often, an age-old habit of talking even when people aren't available (though an e-mail would be a better choice for many messages). The business-to-business sales division was unprofitable because its product distributors were often small retail stores in rural areas. Account representatives lost time driving every day.

When leadership decided to have account managers do more virtual account management, account representatives were hesitant, understandably. This was not their way to build and maintain accounts; they had face-to-face relationships. The company implemented the change anyway.

After implementing a partially virtual solution, replacing drive time with phone time, these same account representatives were convinced, becoming advocates. They had watched their sales figures grow exponentially (in some cases 100%), and their customers were thrilled with the arrangement. Virtual account management was a success, occasional face-to-face visits were cost-effective, and everyone was happy.

Because of the productivity and financial gains, plus increased employee and customer satisfaction, the strategic decision, naturally, was to expand the initiative to other departments. Luckily, we conducted a Virtual Readiness Assessment.[2] It uncovered that, culturally, they were not ready for significant virtual work expansion beyond account management. The in-person communication patterns were so entrenched that people needed to transition, not jump, into virtuality. They began adjusting systems and habits culturally so that the close-knit, family culture could be preserved while building readiness.

Telework was not abandoned. Its implementation schedule was adjusted so that the culture could adapt with the shifting work environment. Virtualization can be done without paralyzing the organization. If moving in a more virtual direction is strategically intelligent (and it is), intentionally nudging your organization onto the virtual path is the only reasonable choice.

Technology has already changed the way we work, with organizations designing work around the network. If virtually connected by more than a shared storage drive, how might Jeffrey's company have achieved the same synergy, met the same turnaround target, and allowed more efficiency and work-life balance? What if the team's meeting was captured on a digital white-board, and one master document was shared by all contributors, structured for consistency across sections for better flow, available outside the conference room digitally? What if one instant message notified all team members when a member's section became available for review? What if Cranton could go into the network to pull what he needs? What if Jeffrey could check in on document progress anytime?

Organizational Paradigms in Recent History

We've gone through major transformations regarding work, beginning with the farm, and we are going through one now. Work was where the farm was, the market was local (until refrigerator trucks made distant markets viable), and the tools needed were the horse and plow or tractor. The primary asset was land, tying the worker to the workplace.

From Farm to Manufacturing

The Industrial Age came with the factory, also local, and the technology was machinery and assembly line. The primary asset was capital equipment. Work was standardized, and factories focused on Frederick Taylor's model for efficiency in repetitive work, leading to high productivity and quality control. Workers were location bound, based on where the manufacturing line was.

Certain unexamined "beliefs" defined *work* because we went to a place to work. Work happened there. The more successful the organization, the bigger and better the work space (like acreage on a farm). Manufacturing is still a strong workplace-reliant sector of the economy today, though the mind-set has broadened toward the digital age. R&D, marketing, sales, and customer support are digitally connected functions that have redesigned manufacturing into an integrated ecosystem with fewer location-dependent aspects to the business. In fact, service worker roles make up more than one-third of manufacturing workers, linking designers, developers, production, and customers across the globe.[3]

From Manufacturing to the Knowledge Worker

In the late twentieth century, the Information Age redefined the business environment again. Technology enabled "the corporation" for unlimited growth. Work became nonlocalized, but management habits remained traditional.

Knowledge-based work is still prevalent today, though it's more complex and boundary crossing. We work in a digitally integrated, hyperconnected network with commitments to strategic alliances, public-private partnerships, and corporate and social communities. Companies are just beginning to see the need to redesign systems and processes to accommodate this complexity and interconnection. Executive surveys from 2016 reflect a growing awareness of the need, though many aren't prioritizing it yet.[4] Currently, chief information officers (CIOs) report organization network redesign is prioritized by fewer than 35% of global companies.[5]

Manage From the Network, Not Place

In a way, the future of work is a reversal of a 350-year trend. Work and home are coming back together, like the farm, only better because you can work anywhere. People don't have to go to a place to be connected. Unfortunately, our people management hasn't changed as much. Management standardizes work to measure productivity, and cultures continue to gravitate toward bureaucratic control using technology. Technology, being neutral, complies. New enterprise solutions are emerging to partner with managers for performance management. Analytics are information rich and should be used, but not in ways that keep organizations culturally stuck in old management habits. It's good to control the controllable; however, organizations need to evolve to embrace the team leader's role as fostering interdependence, innovation, and collaboration. Let the network and technology solutions assist in traditional management activities and efficiently gather and disseminate information. We must manage from the network, partnering with collaboration and management software.

The Nudge Needed Isn't Always a Big One, but . . .

Beliefs and Habits

FGC is a perfect company for partially virtual work, yet it continues to function from unexamined "beliefs" about people needing to be together for synergy. Despite its progressive actions regarding strategic alliances, opportunity response speed, and aggressive leadership, the team still revolves around meetings, paper, and parallel work flow with designated integration points.

The templates to shift habits and beliefs are available, this book being one. Many have paved the way for effective workflow collaboration. The common practice of outsourcing, for example, embeds virtual management practices just by nature of the contract. FGC, for example, outsources its human resources, digital marketing, and public relations functions. In such agreements, focus is less on physical presence and more on the agreements between the companies, clarifying clear outcomes and expectations. Providers are selected based on compatible approaches, values, and ability to represent a positive image to customers (if they will be representing the client).

Is This Anything New, Really?

Maybe not, but few organizations have fully redesigned for collaboration, and team leaders don't see what integrators and connectors they are. Today's teams are more like the movie industry. The cast and production "team" are built around a shared goal, a good movie, and members are highly interactive and interdependent—producers, director, screenwriters, actors, cinematographers, musicians, editors, and crew. Rather than a traditional organization chart, today's teams are aligned around interdependent competencies and relationships. There are no middle managers keeping everyone organized; the nature of the relationships and outcomes builds in accountabilities and collaborative management practices.

Multiple Teams in a Matrix Environment

People are often on multiple teams and have multiple alliances. Committees, task forces, and project teams often require team members to carry the additional role of "representative" to the organization as members in a network of teams. This is especially common in matrix organizations. The matrix has great usefulness and integrates beautifully with digital collaboration, but it has been mistakenly applied to organization design. The matrix isn't an organizational design. The matrix was intended as a structured communication and relationship network, and it works best when seen as the flexible network that adapts to user needs. Too often it becomes a rigid structure. In order for enterprises to evolve organization design to embrace virtual work, leaders need to further their understanding of the integrated relationships among people, technology, and process.

We're not just linked, but inseparable.

Are You a Hyperconnector?

We have work to do to become collaborative cultures. We've become bionic with our technology personally but not fully as teams and organizations. In a matrix corporate structure, there's no getting around it. In such dynamic work environments, the team members' primary alliance is to their "home" team (or profession). Other team commitments are deprioritized as less important or juggled. "Representation" often feels like protection, advocacy, and politicking. If the organization is traditional, it is encouraging a competitive culture among star performers, too. It can interfere with team members' commitment to and identification with their teams.

This is an organizational design issue as much as it is a culture issue. Many organizations still evaluate performance traditionally. Virtual team leaders must learn how to evaluate the effectiveness of team collaboration, coach for collaboration, and help people manage multiple commitments. Team members will need to negotiate competing priorities.

Teams are part of larger systems, and team members have to be able to manage the pull. They must be able to network not only with their own team but also with the larger organization and its alliances.

You cannot build networked organizations on electronic networks alone; the culture must encourage human networking. Workers and leaders benefit from using network tools as relationship management vehicles, though collaboration is sustainable only when people are willingly open and communicating. Communication is, in fact, where most of the actual process of work gets done. A Harvard study examined complex and dynamic businesses that were undergoing radical changes, often unsuccessfully. It concluded that an organization is fundamentally a social structure. It may be motivated for various reasons and designed in various ways, but the workflow to achieve strategic objectives is always driven by social interactions.[6]

Are Executives Missing the Mark?

The Harvard study also found that "despite this clearly relational nature,"[7] an increasing preoccupation with structural control has resulted in executive teams focusing on centralization, decentralization, and formalization. In other words, research proves that social relationships are the fuel of organizations, but organizations continue to seek control through metrics, which usually hinders collaborative social relationships. This is the organizational equivalent of shooting yourself in the foot, missing a design opportunity to better match organization structures to the way work really gets done.

I recently reviewed a job opportunity for a coaching client, clicking through on what seemed a perfect fit based on the job title—Employee Engagement Coordinator. Talk about missing the mark! Rather than a job to help link people and teams to the technology, this position was an IT analyst job to design the digital network, but with no involvement with the users themselves. The strategy was to design a foolproof network path where employees would follow digital pathways so well built they would be "forced" through a prescribed pathway to the information needed. That's a start, but it's an attempt to control behavior, not design systems around workflow. *Where's the user engagement in the design?*

If social interaction in your organization flows through hierarchy and permissions, expect a challenge in becoming collaborative.

Begin with assisting people, teams, and departments to create "habits" of digital interaction and knowledge exchange. Help your team's new habits seep into the social design of the organization. You will be preparing the organization for a virtual environment. Virtual work is helping weave a sustainable, invisible fabric of collaboration into company cultures and the design.

Tighten Loose Relationships

Many workers begin as loose-tie contractors who eventually become more strongly tied to an organization. Time and multiple projects create bonds between the worker and the organization, creating stronger ties of trust. Smart executives develop high-performance workers, including contractors. Reliable talent redeployed knows the organization, making it more valuable. By doing so, the relationship, while still based on a contract, is less transactional, more durable.[8]

Buildings That Support Virtual Teams

The physical design of a building can support or deter virtual collaboration. As more employees are off-site, the physical office changes to accommodate teams more than individual work spaces. Facilities take on a different look and feel, more like gathering places and drop-in work sites. Not everyone needs to be a virtual employee, but many will, and facilities adapt. When people gather face-to-face, they still want a place to put their "stuff," so smart facilities managers provide lockers, for example. In addition to teaming rooms, have workstations that are plug-and-play—a docking station, whiteboard, and shared printer. Ask employees about little touches that make a difference for them.

Have rooms of various sizes, grandeur, formality, and privacy. Buy furniture lines designed for on-the-fly redesign. Lightweight tables can be joined together to form a conference table and pulled apart to form smaller table groups. Web conferencing is available in all teaming rooms. Whiteboards are electronic and app enabled for digital storage and display. A room may hold a training session in the morning and a project team in the afternoon.

Build your organizational design on the network and adapt buildings to encourage a flexible, dynamic teaming environment, amorphous and connected. Use the collaborative tools whether sharing a visual on a wall or over the network. As your organization plans, facilities morph to support hyperconnected collaboration.

Cultures of Independence, Competition, and Control

Having teams collaborating together requires a shift in the emphasis from "me" to "we." Train people to use the collaborative technology, though tool competence is only part of the solution. Developing collaborative environments is easier said than done. Competition is baked into the way we do business and is part of how people are typically rewarded. Recently, a global consulting firm examined its own culture for evidence of collaboration, knowledge sharing, and effective use of technology. It found embarrassingly little cooperation among staff until it reached the partner level. Instead, it found an extremely competitive, individualistic operating norm. Upon investigation, compensation and career opportunities rewarded competition, even though the firm had invested heavily in tools to improve communication, which were used as personal organizational tools. Its investment added no more value than the simplest personal productivity apps available on smartphones and tablets.

The firm's mantra for years had been team cooperation for the customer, but the unspoken culture was lone ranger heroics and fighting for a seat on the next team. Recruitment policies and compensation packages reinforced this culture. Performance appraisal processes often reinforced it.

What does your organization reinforce?

The Emperor Has No Clothes

Very few organizations stand up to the scrutiny of being culturally open and collaborative. Very few individuals stand up to the scrutiny. Business is built on capitalism, which has taught us to stand out, to have a unique value proposition that helps us compete professionally and in the marketplace. Since business organizations compete in a capitalist, competitive society, everyone holds beliefs, habits, and past experiences that interfere with our ability to be fully open and collaborative. So which comes first—changing your culture to fit the virtual environment, or implementing virtual teams that lead the charge to a more collaborative culture?

BOTH. They feed and support one another.

Making Virtual Work in *Your* Culture

Organizations have to incorporate virtuality into their current cultures. The challenge is greater or less, depending on the gap between an organization's current culture and a virtual, collaborative one. Most organizations are not going to wholesale redesign themselves overnight, so start where you are. All organization cultures are more and less conducive to virtual work and virtual teams. It's not about what's better—it's about identifying what in the culture supports virtual work now, what is ready for intentional change, and where total transformation is needed.

Virtual Leader Responsibilities

Regardless of an organization's core culture, strive for the following responsibilities, shared by everyone regardless of status, longevity, or experience:

- Build trust instead of suspicion, and value sharing over secrecy.
- Achieve the end product together; no one "hands off" responsibility until the goal is achieved. Everyone is responsible.
- Seek knowledge. No one is excused because they "didn't get the memo."
- Create meaningful work.
- Leverage learning across the organization.

How Naked Is the Emperor?

To know how big the gap is between a virtually effective culture and your current state, conduct a top-down/bottom-up assessment of virtual work as a viable workplace strategy. Look at current organizational, strategic, operational, managerial, employee, technical, facility, and performance management readiness. For organizations already partially virtual, assess the consistency with which virtual work is being implemented across divisions, departments, facilities, and teams. An honest examination identifies issues and opportunities for expanding a virtual environment.

Culture is maintained through communication, connection, and shared agreements about *"how we really do things around here."* Technology has always played a role in creating and maintaining organizational culture. The technology of the pen and paper were predominant connectors prior to the typewriter. The telephone was dominant prior to e-mail. Previous technologies do not go away; the cadre of available tools merely expands. At first, a technology seems unnecessary, and then becomes indispensable. The more we use technology, the more it becomes a transparent, necessary tool, like a flipchart or whiteboard. The iPad seemed ludicrous to me until I got one. Who remembers having only the telephone and U.S. Postal Service? Our organization cultures are already interdependent with the technology tools.

One can certainly argue about tool misuse or overdependence, but one cannot argue against the tools themselves. Smart-tech competence is hardly an option. We now view virtual communication as being as vital as face-to-face (often superior). Where asynchronous communication is needed, virtual tools serve well, and keep people connected between live, synchronous meetings.

It is one thing to connect teams with tools; it is more powerful to integrate organizations. People and technology are merging into integrated partnerships. Networks are human systems that rise from the "people parts." Cisco calls itself "the human network." The technology is a powerful enabler, better every day, and affects organization design.

Real collaboration is still about people working together to fulfill their intentions and commitments. Good organization design supports interaction; the tools become the mechanisms to perpetuate a collaborative culture. When a company is a truly networked organization, it's the quality of relationships and conversations that make it so. It's the people who matter most. When relationships are strong and communication is good, the organization is also better able to respond to a market that's constantly on the move.

It's all about the people.

Notes

1. Internet of Things/Smart Technology Blog, "Single Orchestration Platforms Are Key to Smart Office Set-Up—Here's Why," *Computer Business Review*, April 18, 2016, www.cbronline.com/news/internet-of-things/smart-technology/single-orchestration-platforms-are-key-to-smart-office-setup-heres-why-4867647

2. You can download a free Quick Check Organization Virtual Readiness Assessment at www.WorkingVirtually.org or see it in more detail in Chapter 4, this volume.

3. Sarah Miller Caldicott, "Steve Case Predicts Four Keys to Success With the Industrial Internet," *Forbes*, March 31, 2015.

4. Josh Bersin, "Predictions for 2016: A Bold New World of Talent, Learning, Leadership, and HR Technology Ahead," Bersin by Deloitte, Deloitte Publishing, 2016, http://marketing.bersin.com/predictions-for-2016.html

5. Leading Edge Forum, "There's a New Digital Drama Unfolding in the C-Suite," *Virtual-Strategy Magazine,* June 15, 2015, www.virtual-strategy.com/2015/06/15/there%E2%80%99s-new-digital-drama-unfolding-c-suite#ixzz3dEaglNEi

6. Christopher Bartlett and Sumantra Ghoshal, "Beyond the M-Form: Toward a Managerial Theory of the Firm," *Strategic Management Journal* 14 (1993): 23–46, doi:10.1002/smj.4250141005.

7. Ibid.

8. Reid Hoffman, Ben Casnocha, and Chris Yeh, *The Alliance: Managing Talent in the Networked Age* (Boston: Harvard Business Review Press, 2014).

4

SYSTEMS READY, PEOPLE WILLING, ORGANIZATION ENABLED

"What could be more important than doing unimportant things? If you stop to do enough of them, you'll never get to where you're going."

"But why unimportant things?"

"Think of all the trouble it saves. . . . For there's always something to do to keep you from what you really should be doing."

—Norton Juster and Jules Feiffer, *The Phantom Tollbooth*

"The real basic structure of the workplace is the relationship. Each relationship is itself part of a larger network of relationships. These relationships can be measured along all kinds of dimensions—from political to professional expertise. The fact is that work gets done through these relationships."

—Michael Schrage, *No More Teams*

We are currently in the middle of a fundamental transformation in the way organizations function. "Integration" is not just hardware, software, applications, and platforms. Integration means networking people, work, communication—the very structure and systems of organizations.

Yet people resist letting go of old ways of thinking and doing: *"Virtual work leads to chaos." "I'd get so lonely." "It's okay for those high-tech companies, but it won't work here."* These are direct quotes from professionals interviewed in 2015.

In virtual organizations, well-developed systems help alleviate such fears. Each organization needs to take an honest inventory of current readiness for virtualization. If you have a road map to get from here to there, you will avoid chaos and disjointed efforts.

Teams can work virtually as systems evolve, but their success will be hampered if not connected through an integrated network. This chapter discusses requirements and considerations for networked, collaborative systems that support a network of virtual teams.

At its broadest level, systemic soundness is a manifestation of a connected organization. Influential forces are part of a common process that informs the system. Patterns and cycles become obvious when we look at the whole system.[1] The behavior of an organization follows common principles that have been widely studied, so we have a solid body of knowledge to inform us.[2] An organization functions organically, not as a machine. The networked databases and collaborative applications need to integrate in order to facilitate the processes people use naturally. Just as we humans are more than the sum of our parts, so are organizations.

Organization Realignments and Considerations—New Vistas

Building community in the workplace is viewed by many as ideal but unrealistic. *It doesn't need to be.* Connected teams utilize the digital network better. They are part of larger organizations, team communities within an organizational community, nodes within the network. Rather than creating distance, collaborative tools enable organizations to build connections within and among teams by facilitating *relationships*.

If team relationships are where work really gets done, and if people want to be part of a work community, then virtual teams open opportunity to redefine relationships within the organizational system as a whole.

The key to successfully expanding virtual work is integrating the following four critical success factors (CSFs):

1. Collaborative tools and systems
2. Intranet and networked infrastructure
3. Business processes
4. People and inspiring leaders

All four CSFs are part of an enabled organization. Relationships among teams are organic, like a living body. People and communication are aligned around strategy more than they are limited to functional departments. The network, rather than hierarchy, forms the backbone of the operation, and team tools are linked if not fully integrated.

Sound Like Too Much?

Not every organization needs to leap into full virtualization. Telecommuting and other flexwork options are steps forward that don't require major system overhauls. Let's examine how to get a sense of your organization's readiness to leverage virtual work.

Ready, Set, Jump?

Unless you are truly virtual—and few are—assess the readiness, willingness, and ability of your organization to work virtually. Assess technology, facilities, culture, systems and processes, and management practices. The speed of adoption (and level of employee satisfaction while undergoing the change) depends on organization readiness. It goes faster and easier when the change plan is built from a solid analysis. You will also discover how quickly and in what areas of the company to initially execute. You'll discover where to change now, where to begin preparation, and where resistance and challenges remain. *You'll have hard data to inform your plan.*

What You Have to Assess

Readiness is the organization's preparedness. Like a runner that is posed at the starting line waiting for the gun to go off, be ready for the race. *Willingness* is the desire to step into change. *Ability* is just that—infrastructure, systems, processes, and people *capable* of operating virtually.

Organization readiness, willingness, and ability across the four CSFs may not be uniform; the assessment results will vary across the organization. For example, one client assessment showed IT was ready, willing, and able. Affected systems and processes could be ready with few revisions. Growth had created a cramped office; the organization needed to expand without walls through telework or lease more space. Legal resisted due to security and liability concerns, but these concerns were easily remedied. The discomfort of cramped quarters had increased people's willingness to try something new. Many employees wanted more flexibility in their work/home balance. *Yet people were still reticent.*

The company's culture was a face-to-face habit—birthdays and anniversaries celebrated in break rooms, in-person meetings, and friendships formed that extended beyond the workday. The worry was, "How will virtual work impact this culture?" People are seldom prepared for dramatic change. This does not mean virtual work won't work; it does mean you need a clearer picture of how, when, where, and how fast to change hearts and minds. Their assessment indicated a need for work on people's readiness.

Organization Virtual Readiness Assessment

Take the time to conduct an honest organization self-assessment.[3] Start with focused questions. Table 4.1 shows a full set to consider.

Most questions can be answered with a little research, asking, and listening. The greatest resource for *real* answers lies with the workers themselves, so include a cross section of surveys and interviews in your analysis.

Condense your gathered information into a profile of the organization's readiness, willingness, and ability to work in a virtual, mobile work environment. A simple opportunity profile provides concise data and a way to communicate with decision makers. Table 4.2 shows an example of one client's opportunity profile matrix (OPM) using a scale.

As you can see from this client profile, they met the baseline requirements to initiate virtual work after addressing readiness and willingness. This culture's organization isn't fully ready to transform its work environment, nor is the employee career path and talent management process, *but there is enough to begin.* The organization is structured adequately to move forward, enabling processes to be readied for virtuality fairly easily.

Feel free to download the Organization Virtual Readiness Assessment, data-gathering instruction, and this real client's OPM summary as examples to follow. Use the assessment to help your leaders prioritize how you proceed with business virtualization.

Tooled Up and Trained

People's virtual collaboration comfort ranges from fearless to terrified. If team members view virtual tools as a challenge, they approach warily. I know a colleague who was a vocal opponent of virtual work until she accepted a position recently not realizing it was 90% virtual. Because it was her new employer's *"way of doing things around here,"* she changed her mind. I laughed when she declared enthusiastically how much she loved telecommuting and her teammates, and she couldn't imagine working any other way.

This was a complete mental turnaround in less than three weeks *because she had no choice* (and had a great virtual team leader). Executives and team leaders must *use the collaboration tools as an operating practice* and train people to use the tools well. Encourage new ways to use tools to discover what works for what kinds of team activities. Without integrating them into the way the team works together, tools will be used sporadically and primarily as personal organizational tools. While this is helpful, it falls far short of the team's potential.

TABLE 4.1

Organization Virtual Readiness Assessment

	Technology	Work environment	Work systems and processes	People
Readiness and willingness	How effectively does the current information technology infrastructure support remote access and collaborative tools? Does the organization's budget support equipping and supporting remote team members? How does the organization handle security and network issues now? How might security policies need to change in an electronically connected environment? Is bandwidth adequate everywhere it will be needed?	What is the attitude toward virtual work here? (Seen as mainstream, special circumstances, exception, perk?) How do the organization's culture and values support or contradict virtual work? Will virtual work have any impact on the customer? How is the organization's core culture conducive to virtual work? What is the overall management style? Communication style? Meeting style? How are teams currently being used? How might that change if virtual teams are implemented?	Which job families and functions are virtually conducive? How do remote locations communicate and report to the rest of the organization? How is productivity measured? Effective results? How will that change virtually? What systems are set up that support and measure virtual work? What beliefs does your organization have about compensation and incentives? Do these change in a collaborative team or virtual environment? Do reward systems recognize collaboration across boundaries? How are employees guided on their career path? How will that change in a virtual environment? How well do current business processes support virtual work flows?	What are the management constraints? Supports? At what levels or divisions? What are the human resources constraints or supports? Training/learning and development? Overall, what do people like about virtual work or teams? Dislike? What are their fears and concerns? Desires? How engaged are employees now? How will that need bolstering in a virtual environment? How committed is the organization's leadership to virtual work as a strategic initiative?

	Are mechanisms in place for knowledge management access and sharing?	Does the union support virtual work? What is your competition doing with virtual work? How well designed is the office to accommodate more team meeting spaces? Drop-in cubicles?	Are human resources, organization development, corporate communications, and other functions able to adjust their delivery mechanisms and policies or procedures to support virtual work? How does training currently get done? How is that impacted by remote employees?	What are the organization challenges that a virtual team member faces? A virtual manager? How can leaders address challenges?
Ability and training needs	Do the collaborative tools function in a way that supports business processes and people's needs? Can information be shared quickly and fully enough, regardless of location? Do all have equal access to tools and training? Do team members know how to fully utilize the collaborative communication tools available, and are they comfortable sustaining relationships through tool usage? Will any additional long-term support be needed?	What communication plans, educational campaigns, and other change management strategies need to be implemented? Are resources (time, facilities, budget) set aside for virtual team development and project planning activities?	Can delivery systems get resources and tools to the people when needed, regardless of location? Can training, product updates, and mentoring be delivered virtually, or in combination with face-to-face?	Do people know how to fully utilize collaborative software tools? Can team leaders and members rally a team around a common purpose, and maintain commitment and productivity, regardless of dispersed team members? Are people trained in remote operations, netiquette, and voice mail etiquette?

TABLE 4.2

Virtual Opportunity Profile for XYZ Company, a Financial Services Company

Factors	Assessment items		
Division level	Capability	Readiness	Willingness
Environment (average)	3.67	3.17	3.00
By locations	3	3	3
Number and status of management levels	4	3	2
Security policies	4	3	4
Ease of implementation:			
Technologically	4	4	4
Geographically	3	3	3
Management decision-making ability	4	3	2
Technology (average)	3.33	3.17	3.33
Environment	4	3	4
Decentralization	3	4	4
Ease of implementation:			
Technologically	3	3	3
Geographically	3	3	3
Facilities	3	3	3
IT decision-making ability and user engagement	4	3	3
Culture (average)	3.50	2.33	3.00
Compensation and incentives	4	3	4
Performance management system	3	2	3
Motivation for telecommuting	3	2	3
Risk-taking	3	2	2
Telecommuting empowered by managers	4	2	2
Communication channels	4	3	4
People (Average)	3.89	2.98	3.55
Training	4	4	4
Teams	4	3	4
Career path dynamics	4	2	3
Average OPM	**3.57**	**2.90**	**3.19**

Note. 1 = low probability of success; 3 = baseline; 5 = high probability of success.

Tribal Walls to Open Collaboration

As discussed in the design chapter, workers today are often members of multiple teams and connecting nodes in the organization network. Even when the organization is designed for connection, organization systems such as performance management and reward systems may be misaligned. If not adapted for team collaboration, old management practices and appraisal systems reinforce, for example, an individually competitive culture at the expense of collaboration.

When salaries and other rewards are based only on individual contribution, no organization can design a network well enough to change behavior. Generally, a minimum of 20%–30% of base pay should be tied to team performance in order to reinforce a collaborative culture. Please note that the organization should do this only if team members have influence and real impact on team results.

Structure performance appraisal and reward systems to support well-developed relationships and generous knowledge sharing if you want a collaborative culture that adapts quickly. It takes time to dissolve tribal walls, competitive behaviors based on self-interest, and information hoarding. Be patient and immovable about the virtual collaboration commitment, and align systems to support the emerging culture.

Embed Openness and Virtual Connection

Obviously not every system, process, or work flow has to be perfect to collaborate virtually. The Organization Virtual Readiness Assessment questions help you identify where the greatest supports and obstacles are.

Let's look at specific systems and processes most impacted by virtual work, and that most impact people's readiness, willingness, and ability to collaborate virtually.

Is the Job Virtually Viable?

Some activity is not amenable to virtual work, such as manufacturing parts assembly (though 3D printing may change that), food service, and some on-the-job training. Other functions are already partially or fully virtual, such as online training and human resources (HR) employee and benefits administration. Here are some pointers for virtualizing job roles and functions:

- Be sure that job descriptions become less about task responsibilities and more about building the integrated "web" of expertise, experience, and collaboration the team or department needs.

- Make sure that everyone's job description clearly states expectations for virtual collaboration and knowledge sharing, regardless of whether working virtually.
- When planning team assignments, balance skill competencies and collaborative mind-sets, discounting location as a critical variable.

How Are You Measuring?

A later section focuses on virtual management, but a few guidelines for the organization are worth noting:

- Remote performance management cannot be any more effective than current on-site management practices. Virtual work is an opportunity to look at current practices and intentionally move to a more collaborative, shared responsibility approach to team performance leadership. Project and task management tools do a lot of the individual activity management, collecting much information for the manager.
- In a collaborative culture, individual *and* team-based results matter. Both the team member and the team are held accountable for commitments.
- More structure and planning are required. Management and team leaders need to become more thoughtful and organized. Disorganization confuses virtual teams.
- Less structure is also required. Command-and-control management doesn't work well virtually and interferes with synergy.
- Managers need training in virtual leadership and tool use. The good news is managers can use this as an opportunity to "brush up" on basic management and team leadership.
- With virtual teams, poor managers usually show up, while good managers get better. The same holds for teams.

Getting There From Here (Virtually)

HR and line managers work together to assist individual team members to navigate the organization, as well as to source opportunities for employees. In a collaborative culture, people are valued for their competence and knowledge, but they are also appreciated for their collaborative approach and influence on their teams. When team members are virtual, career opportunities are widely communicated and fairly distributed throughout the organization so virtual employees know they're on the career track as much as their in-office peers. If 75% of all promotions come out of Chicago, for example, what message does that send to other regional offices?

HR systems are becoming digital and analytics driven. A new generation of talent management and learning and performance management systems is available for today's workforce. New HR support tools designed to accommodate complex, mobile workforces integrate the talent management cycle, from recruitment to training. "*Design thinking is impacting every part of HR (including performance management, onboarding, and employee lifecycle programs),*" confirms Josh Bersin of Deloitte.[4] People analytics are part of the emerging talent management support tools, objectively assessing individuals' current value and development opportunity.

Invisible Learning

Learning is a social phenomenon above all. Integrated networks and collaborative tools enable people to learn from each other through just-in-time coaching and training. Informal learning happens in everyday interaction, invisibly. Formal learning is channeled through systems like online training libraries.

Informal learning is at risk virtually. Isolation and disconnection are more likely, lessening the opportunity for accidental learning. Virtual workers *need* to be connected to their teams and larger organization, so they are part of *this* culture and laying groundwork for peer learning. We learn about resources and shortcuts in casual conversations. The more virtual, the more connection is needed, especially to become a high-performance virtual team. Virtual team leaders get tongues wagging and fingers keying about many topics throughout the day.

How Does Work Flow?

Flow will vary from team to team depending on the team's work. Some high-level business processes may need to adjust to be virtual, but most are ready. Obviously, document flow is digital, fully virtualized already. Team work flows include work done:

- Simultaneously (parallel work, may require coordination)
- Serially (sequential work completed in assembly-line fashion, may require cooperation)
- Together (integrated or cocreated, requires collaboration)
- Independently (does not need to be integrated with other work in a significant way)

Some changes aren't big. Work that doesn't need to be integrated can be accommodated through simple management tools, easily virtualized. Coordinated work comes together at designated times in the process. To coordinate, virtual teams utilize templates for easy handoffs, chat rooms or instant messaging, web conferences, document sharing with publisher and review protocols, and good old-fashioned in-person meetings.

Fit the communication and collaboration tools to your work flows. Technology aids are just that—aids, not tyrants. Train teams to use tool functions that fit their virtual work processes.

For example, in early weeks of virtual teaming, have teams structure templates from current and previous work cycles (if they are not already standardized or built into the collaborative tools). Improve little things to better support virtual work, but no more than is necessary. *Simple, easy integration is the overriding guideline.* Try not to add layers of bureaucracy. Use tools already in place as much as possible.

What structures will your team agree ease work flow, coordination, and cooperation?

Everything's Going to Change!

Working virtually is strategic and practical, but will change the way people work. This entire book is a road map to manage the transition, starting with an examination of how your team currently works to deliver results. The mind shifts discussed earlier help virtual leaders see ways to adapt that won't disrupt business. For example, if an employee relations manager currently holds coaching sessions in his office because that's traditionally how he has built trust, he can "change" to web conferencing for virtual employees. If minds have shifted and the network is enabled, little changes yield fast results with less resistance.

How Do I Get My Stuff?

Centralized purchasing makes financial sense because of economies of scale and ability to harness and distribute resources efficiently. However, how does virtual work—especially for home-based teleworkers or traveling road warriors—impact such a simple delivery system as office supplies? If virtual workers are part-time virtual, the delivery system is not significantly impacted; people just pick up supplies while on-site. If they are mostly virtual, does Purchasing set up master accounts with office supply stores and courier services? Virtual workers need to be as fully supported as their in-office counterparts with a simple system for getting supplies.

Help! My Network Is Down and It Won't Come Up!

When all equipment was in one or a few locations, a maintenance program was easy. When equipment is literally all over the globe, different systems need to be created. Some devices are company owned, some worker owned. Who is responsible for maintenance and security? Many options are possible, as long as Information Services sets clear policies and support systems, ensuring the organization isn't adding duties to the virtual worker. The fact that one becomes a virtual worker does not mean one becomes a technical expert. Basic troubleshooting and maintenance make sense, but what does the virtual worker do when basic strategies fail? If your workers are distributed globally, that may mean 24-hour support.

To Whom Can I Turn?

People learning to work differently want to know they have a lifeline that won't let the new *way* they work get in the way of the work they need to produce. Set up multiple support systems, especially if the organization is actively virtualizing or expanding its flexwork program. Create a corps of "helpers" who are experienced and committed to virtual teaming. Create virtual buddy systems. Provide online access to real virtual coaches. These can be internal or external resources. Perhaps the training department outsources virtual management training, subscribing to a virtual university that provides immediate access to training in, for example, setting up a home office, managing stress on the road, or quickly realigning a troubled team.

Train to the Tools

You can't leverage technology if you don't invest in training. When team and manager train together, they are developing protocols and agreements while learning. Even if only some team members work remotely, the entire team is a virtual team, so collaborative tool training helps everyone. *By the way, collaborative tools are best learned with others, using the tools while learning.* Meaningful use of the tools increases the likelihood they will be fully utilized. Little learning happens by seeing a demonstration without engagement.

Classroom training still works as long as learners are using the tools they're learning with each other. Try to have some components of collaborative tool training be virtually delivered. If virtual workers are expected to conduct virtual web-based meetings using collaborative tools, for example, they must actually work with the tools before facilitating. In many ways, online learning *as a team* is ideal for tool training. Give people time to experiment and play. Provide exercises that use the team's actual work whenever possible so that learners see immediate application. Otherwise, deadlines and other work pressures preoccupy people's minds, and training falls by the wayside. Teams learn on the fly, and bad habits develop.

As you virtualize your team processes, systemically review and adapt other areas, too. New employee orientation would include, for example, an introduction to the virtual team environment and collaborative culture.

Connecting People to Virtual Work

"We underestimated the technology needs. We corrected that the first year. However, our single biggest mistake was not understanding the people issues. If we were starting over we would spend more time and resources emphasizing training and communication." So states Robert Egan, director of global mobility and virtual work at IBM about its early adoption of telecommuting. This book *is* about the people part of working virtually. As I frequently say, *technology is the enabler, but people are the key.*

All organization systems should serve the needs of the people and be structured for virtual work when possible. Improvements and innovations focus on *making work easier for people.* If workers have to adapt too much to fit organization requirements, virtual work will always remain an initiative. For smart companies, it's a way of life. Integrate technology, culture, systems, and processes to sustain an innovative, collaborative culture.

Maintain Engagement in a Virtual Organization—SMART Guidelines

It's good to connect through common tools; it is better to become a network of teams. Remember these guidelines as you lead your organization's changes:

- **S**tructure teams as interlinking nodes in a network of teams and alliances, rather than as a hierarchical chain of access and reporting.
- **M**ake conversations happen, rather than "cascading" information down and out.
- **A**ctivate robust (push, post, and pull) communication systems.
- **R**each learners and develop leaders in many ways (face-to-face and online, live and self-paced, individual and team learning).
- **T**ap people as knowledge-rich nodes in the network.

Manage System Changes—Verifone's Advice

Verifone, a well-known early virtual success story, followed four core guidelines during its virtualization. These principles can guide *your* virtual rollout while also summarizing this chapter:

1. Be eternally vigilant, build on success, remedy glitches, and support virtuality. Prototype and build out without hesitation. *Notice they did not pilot whether it worked—they prototyped to learn* **how it worked for them**.
2. Constantly communicate at all levels of the organization.
3. Operate based on clear and unambiguous value statements. In a dispersed work world, core values guide behavior and decisions, and provide identification with the organization.
4. Focus on *all* elements of success, not just the technology budget or real estate savings.

Notes

1. For those wanting a valuable primer, Stafford Beer's work is a good grounding. "Stafford Beer," *Wikipedia*, last modified September 7, 2015. http://en.wikipedia.org/wiki/Anthony_Stafford_Beer

2. Peter M. Senge, *The Fifth Discipline Fieldbook: Strategies and Tools for Building a Learning Organization* (New York: Currency, Doubleday, 1994).

3. For your convenience, you can download this Quick Check Organization Virtual Readiness Assessment set of questions at www.WorkingVirtually.org

4. Josh Bersin, "Predictions for 2016: A Bold New World of Talent, Learning, Leadership, and HR Technology Ahead," Bersin by Deloitte, Deloitte Publishing, 2016, http://marketing.bersin.com/predictions-for-2016.html, p. 31.

5

BUILDING BLOCKS FOR
VIRTUAL TEAM LEARNING

"In times of change, the learners inherit the earth while the learned find themselves beautifully equipped to live in a world that no longer exists."

—Eric Hoffer

"The human individual is equipped to learn and go on learning prodigiously from birth to death. Man has at various times been defined as a building animal, a working animal, and a fighting animal, but all of these definitions are incomplete and finally false. Man is a learning animal, and the essence of the species is encoded in that simple term."

—George Leonard

Teams Leave Contributions on the Table

Interestingly, the aspirations of my team have become quite homogenous over time. Still, we have incredibly high standards for what we do, but within the context of what we already provide. This also connects to our personal embodiment of purpose. Our team is very committed to the excellent outcomes we produce for our clients, but this now tends to be held together by our traditions, not by a sense of creating an expanded future that better serves. There is respect for the contributions people make to each other and the broader body of knowledge we work from. This contributes to the products we develop for our clients, but our team's learning tends to be peripheral and accidental. (Global services [virtual] manager and virtual member of a network of teams, personal communication)

The purpose of knowledge management is not to store information, but to build knowledge across the organization.

The real purpose of virtual work is to prevent distance from isolating team members and instead create synergy without limitations of time or space.

This global service manager's experience is typical. Individual learning is peripheral; the team is functioning because everyone is professional, *but they are not excelling*. This limits the organization's potential. I'm guessing this global company's leadership is unaware of the problem.

Another Retention Tool

Learning opportunity is also growing as a desired employee benefit, impacting employee retention and engagement ratings, according to Deloitte's 2016 HR Trends report.[1] Employees want to access online learning when they have a need, in addition to having access to professional and leadership development programs. Learning management systems are evolving to be mobile, highly focused, interactive, and user friendly. They are able to help the learner choose what and how best to learn, often with just-in-time learning modules available anytime online.

It's Alive!

"Knowledge" is not a collection of static facts. It is alive—forever changing, growing, and evolving. It often requires *un*learning to enable innovation, making room for new possibilities. Every nugget of knowledge won't be fully captured. Knowledge becomes nested within other knowledge, and not all events are recorded or even remembered. Real learning happens in relationships outside any "training" environment.

Knowledge Management—Learning From the Past

Structured knowledge management, simply put, is a way to capture and organize information so we can find it, learn from it, and use it. The structure can't fully capture abstract thoughts, but systematically managing information is an integral part of enterprise architecture. Its purpose is simple—help people find what they need when they need it to do their work. The type of information stored hasn't changed much in 20 years,[2] but how it's done has transformed. Employees can access information through powerful enterprise search engines immediately, leveraging captured organization wisdom. Today's learning organizations are those who shift to interdependent wisdom, the collective captured knowledge of the organization.[3] Most organizations have excellent knowledge-sharing architecture in place; it's just often underutilized.

Innovation—Learning From the Future

The heart of a virtual team is its commitment to each other and the members' shared vision of what they are creating. Virtual leaders continually manage teams with a future focus. Without a reason, little innovative learning occurs naturally. Teams may learn from the past but not have an eye on what's coming. In a fast-changing world where past learning is insufficient, future-focused learning is imperative. High-performance teams learn and adapt however needed to achieve the goal.

The Best Learning Happens When . . .

Organizations learn when people share insights, knowledge, concerns, and experiences. Project management tools and search engines are excellent resources for learning, but they seldom yield the kind of insights that come from conversations. Breakthrough thinking comes from people talking, from hearing others' thinking. We learn how to learn from one another. Learning organizations leverage team learning across all areas of the business, often opening conversations to include strategic allies and collaborators from all sides.

Learning teams and organizations depend on the virtual leader to open the team to the collective mind.

People search to find solutions, to confirm their knowledge, or to improve an approach. That specific focus is helpful, but people often don't recognize information that is available, but not where they're looking. Information becomes invisible because we have tunnel vision. People who don't think systemically are more prone to myopia and, therefore, limited learning.[4] The best team learning connects formal learning with coaching and lots of informal conversation. Knowledge gets shared, captured, cataloged, and posted to be available.

Learning Is Individual and Collective

Learning and development departments have traditionally trained individuals. Training to the individual is a limiting paradigm that doesn't always reflect good learning theory in today's collaborative and distributed team environment.[5] While learning is an individual responsibility, it is also a group activity. Coach teams as you would individuals. Regularly reflect on a simple question: *What does the team need to learn in order to produce successful outcomes while maintaining the well-being of its members?*

Facilitate conversations that look toward what's coming. Ask people to share reasons for positions they take, to learn from each other's logic and perspectives. Expect people to ask for help and offer peer coaching. This spontaneous, free-flowing team communication is as important to team learning as are formal systems.[6] Virtual communication tools provide many ways to capture knowledge, especially when coupled with robust conversations.

Building Blocks for Virtual Team Learning and Innovation

1. Train Together on the Tools

Learn collaborative applications as a group, letting the team be the learning lab. Adapt as the team discovers better solutions.

2. Give Forth, Don't Hold Back

Generosity is not a common business term, yet isn't a spirit of generosity an essential part of sharing knowledge? In the past, experts became indispensable and highly paid because they held knowledge. A historical culture of "information as power" doesn't dissipate overnight.

Building cultures that support and reinforce knowledge sharing over hoarding, however, can be done when it's supported and rewarded. Every team member is a node in a virtual information network; communication pathways connect us. Catalyze team learning by asking provocative questions and inviting dialogue. Ask members to consider other perspectives. Acknowledge experts who freely give forth advice. Seek creative ideas in the inexperienced person's questions. Reward mentoring and coaching, and reinforce learners, too. Help your team discover the whole really is more than the sum of its parts.

3. Reinforce Synergy

Some teams perform together quite easily, almost breathing together while running down the virtual path. They exude generosity and excitement. They trust the team framework they cocreated, which guides their behavior and team culture. They're a cohesive community of high-performing learners who developed into a synergistic team. They have a natural and informal information flow that is fast—pushing, pulling, and posting information constantly. They know when to work with the tried and true, and when to innovate.

Why doesn't this happen for all teams?

People do what they get reinforced for doing. If you want to support generous knowledge sharing across individual competencies and functional or virtual boundaries, reward it. Do not acknowledge unique expertise unless the experts develop others by sharing their knowledge. Make learning and teaching an ongoing goal for the team, especially if innovation is a core value or team requirement.

4. Build Commitment, Not Control

Team and organization learning works better when it is facilitated. In a team, technology rules and organization controls will never replace the virtual team's need to think for itself. Managers naturally want to control the controllable. However, with performance-tracking tools, managers can easily impose too much structural control, perhaps unintentionally, which can have a demotivating impact. Instead, develop team protocols using project management and collaboration tools to facilitate easy work coordination and metrics. Helpful tracking is less work for the team and supports sharing knowledge, which adds to everyday learning.

5. Onboard Rolling Team Members

Team members often roll on and off teams and need to quickly learn how to find information that helps them contribute fast. The team with published team agreements and onboarding resources is welcoming. They make it easy to learn team protocols. Peer coaching and scheduled conversations provide opportunities to ask questions. The team's culture is assimilated quickly.

6. Virtually Coach and Mentor

Mentoring is a long-standing tradition for sharing knowledge and developing the wisdom of star performers. Without intentionally planning for emerging leaders' development, mentoring suffers in a virtual environment. Spontaneous coaching happens less often because accidentally observed opportunities aren't obvious or frequent. Just as books don't teach us under our pillows at night, specialized knowledge isn't transferred by osmosis in a virtual environment. (It isn't really transferred by osmosis in a colocated environment, but informal and natural conversation is an invisible "learning forum" that isn't replaced virtually without intention.)

The Magic Word Is . . . *Network*

Encourage people's networking. A collaborative culture encourages relationships at many organizational levels and across teams and boundaries. Smart virtual leaders encourage team members to invest time with their networks to exchange information, find expertise, and pool resources and talent. These networks also cross-pollinate organization learning.

Every team member is a rich "node" connected to a network of human beings loaded with knowledge. Mapping organization networks reveals who talks to whom about what kinds of issues. Social network analysis maps the digital communication of a team or an entire organization. Social network analytics show how information flows, quickly identifying people who are information-rich nodes—important go-to people—or who are bottlenecks—important information blockers. Use analytics to improve team communication pathways. Where are the information gaps, redundancies, people who are bottlenecks or valued advisers? Who's being left out or not responding regularly?

Know Whom Your Team Relies On

People need people. We form alliances because that's what we do. Onboarding team members come to your team with existing networks on which they already rely. You want to help onboarding team members to quickly rely on their new team, too. If they don't, individuals may remain overly reliant on their outside network, taking needed emotional bandwidth away from the team. Be a virtual connector, a sort of people resource search engine. Consider how to support your team's relationships with each other. Expand the team's access to needed resources.

Also, watch to see if team members are overly dependent on one person (often the virtual leader), which creates bottlenecks (and possibly perceived favoritism). As the virtual leader, encourage cross-pollination and nurture the team's interdependence. Unless your team functions more like a work group that isn't reliant on each other, this may be your primary responsibility. (In part three of this book we'll talk about how a manager leads different types of virtual teams.)

Some teams learn well together but insulate themselves from the rest of the organization. They are overly reliant on each other, not linking enough to other teams, forming a semiclosed system. Closed systems are not learning teams and often become misaligned to the organization's priorities, so keep the team connected to and reliant upon the larger organization.

A Learning Team Is a Performing Team

Until a team comes together to do more than perform a job, it's not a performing or learning team. The team functions normally, but it will not perform to potential, as the global services manager's experience demonstrated. Teams need to talk about more than project updates. People learn from one another by talking, watching, and imitating. Virtual teams have to reach out to do that, which may not happen without the virtual leader. Soon people will naturally continue conversations and want to engage when they see the benefits and rewards to themselves and the team. Lead by initiating. Partner a millennial "digital native" with a Luddite boomer and what do you get? A chance to encourage the cultural value of mutual coaching. Deliberately create learning opportunities if reasons to talk are not in place already. Begin by looking at how you currently share new information. What are you doing now, however informal? Can this be used or adapted when you are leading the virtual team? Embed sharing as a habit on your team.

Innovation Events

Pharmaceutical company Novo Nordisk developed a collaborative culture of innovation with a colocated and virtual workforce. Its approach shows how easy it is to engage people virtually in a way that invites disruption and innovation without having to change the culture. Leaders held a virtual innovation process to engage all employees through crowdsourcing.[7] They posed a current organization challenge to "the crowd" for a limited time. Employees participated in two ways. They submitted ideas of their own, and they evaluated others' submitted ideas. Co-innovators posted comments and voted for best ideas, and they worked in temporary teams to hone and submit the best one based on predetermined criteria. They learned how to develop ideas into businesses cases and then prototype quickly. The first event was so successful they did it again. More employees participated than expected—job titles ranged from chief medical officer to administrative assistant, reaching across the whole organization.[8] Talk about a team-building experience!

A team can host its own innovation event. For example, find hacks, or shortcuts, to speed up a project dynamic that interferes with high performance. Try hacking business issues in multiple collaborative forums, and see what works best for the team—workshops launched from a presentation, a posed question, or a targeted focus that launches a web conference dialogue, brainstorming asynchronously in discussion forums, coming together for colocated discovery labs.[9]

Whatever the desired outcome, build in social time, too. Much learning happens informally on scheduled event breaks. If virtual, plan for continued connection to keep the learning going.

Innovation is critical for most organizations to stay competitive. Innovation and learning are inseparable. Rosabeth Moss Kanter researched innovative organizations for years.[10] She summarized a critical differentiator between innovative organizations and the rest. The results are surprising: The innovative organizations reward people who maintain multiple and overlapping networks, both inside and outside the organization. These valued workers cross-pollinate ideas, with the organization being beneficiaries of that network. The more expanded the team's collective web of networks, the more likely the members have access to everything and anyone they may need.

Fortunately, the same cultural and structural commitments that build successful virtual organizations also produce a learning environment for strong innovation. A vital knowledge management process then leverages team learning across the organization.

Embedding an integrated approach to team learning significantly increases engagement, too. Teams that take the time to learn together record higher employee satisfaction and performance.[11] The team becomes a valuable asset to itself and others thanks to a well-networked knowledge management process. In short, strive for networked teams, share responsibility for open and lively communication, encourage boundary crossing, facilitate access to people and information, and connect teams to their mission and organization for useful learning and necessary innovation.

Notes

1. Josh Bersin, "Predictions for 2016: A Bold New World of Talent, Learning, Leadership, and HR Technology Ahead," Bersin by Deloitte, Deloitte Publishing, 2016, http://marketing.bersin.com/predictions-for-2016.html

2. Alan Frost, "Knowledge Management," Knowledge Management Tools, last modified 2015, www.knowledge-management-tools.net/#ixzz3bpq08beM

3. "Learning Organization," *Wikipedia,* last modified September 1, 2015. Peter Senge defined the *learning organization* as one that features systems thinking, personal mastery, mental models, shared vision, and team learning. These are tenets consistent with the principles of this book. For a primer and as a link to more information, begin with https://en.wikipedia.org/wiki/Learning_organization

4. Gerald C. Kane, Doug Palmer, Anh N. Phillips, David Kiron, and Natasha Buckley, "Strategy, Not Technology, Drives Digital Transformation: Becoming a Digitally Mature Enterprise," *MIT Sloan Management Review Research Report,* Deloitte University Press and MIT, 2015, www2.deloitte.com/content/dam/Deloitte/cr/Documents/audit/documentos/auditnews/151106-Strategy-not-techonology-drives-Digital-Transformation.pdf

5. Albert Bandura, "Social Learning Theory (Bandura)," Learning-Theories Knowledge Base and Webliography, 1971, www.learning-theories.com/social-learning-theory-bandura.html

6. Jane Hart, "Learning & Collaboration: The Difference Between Social Learning and Social Collaboration," Learning in the Social Workplace, C4LPT blog, March 18, 2015, www.c4lpt.co.uk/blog/2015/03/18/the-difference-between-social-learning-and-social-collaboration/

7. "Crowdsourcing refers to a wide range of activities, providing different benefits for its organizers. Crowdsourcing in the form of idea competitions or innovation contests provides a way for organizations to learn beyond what their 'base of minds' of employees provides (e.g., LEGO Ideas)." "Crowdsourcing," *Wikipedia*, last modified September 8, 2015, https://en.wikipedia.org/wiki/Crowdsourcing

8. Lorri Freifeld, "Novo Nordisk's Ideastream," *Training Magazine*, May 12, 2015, www.trainingmag.com/novo-nordisk's-ideastream

9. "Hackerspace," *Wikipedia,* last modified June 27, 2015, https://en.wikipedia.org/wiki/Hackerspace

10. Paul S. Meyer, ed., *Knowledge Management and Organization Design* (Boston: Butterworth-Heinemann, 1997).

11. Andrea Foertsch, "The Innovative Corporate Workplace: Incorporating Coworking, Makerspaces and Accelerators," Agile Workplace Conference, Washington, DC, September 15, 2015.

6

LEARNING FROM THE LAST 20+ YEARS

"'You'll find,' he remarked gently, 'that the only thing you can do easily is be wrong, and that's hardly worth the effort.'"

—Norton Juster and Jules Feiffer, *The Phantom Tollbooth*

"The thing with high-tech is that you always end up using scissors."

—David Hockney

What Have We Learned?

In the mid-1990s, I was a founding executive in a company dedicated to virtual work implementation and training. We asked dozens of executives and telecommuting program managers to identify what implementation components helped or hurt their success. Most initiatives were begun internally without external assistance, and the champions were usually workhorses and advocates. All had been working virtually for at least one year, most much longer. We asked about lessons learned as an organization. Common themes recurred.

I was curious to update lessons learned 20 years later to see what had changed. I talked to many, including flexwork and business design experts and clients. In some cases, I was able to find the same people.[1] I reached out to previous and current clients (at all levels, teleworkers through executives). Much had changed, as expected:

1. People had more comfort and familiarity with and willingness to do flex work, particularly part-time telecommuting.
2. Everyone used web conferencing and some version of SharePoint[2] or other virtual back-office solution (e.g., Redbooth) that enabled networked digital coordination.[3]

3. Policies no longer required only company-owned equipment (for risk management and security). Work was done through a combination of worker-owned (bring your own device) and company-provided equipment.
4. Security remained a concern, though it was no longer a reason not to implement telework.

Lessons in Hindsight

Here's the updated summary of lessons learned.

Then: *The Culture Wasn't Considered*

Overwhelmingly, most organizations had failed to give adequate consideration to the cultural impact of distributed work. It slowed their ability to quickly adapt to a virtual environment.

Now: *Unfortunately, Nothing Has Changed*

As one flexwork expert admitted,

> Organizations continue to believe that culture will come along once they roll out policy. The greatest barrier to implementation is getting middle managers to buy in. One flexibility study[4] shows that only a small percentage of companies do any type of formal training when it comes to virtual work or workplace flex.

Then: *Pilots Were the Thing*

Organizations found limited success when they took a temporary or fragmented approach. Looking back, most agreed they should not have "piloted" virtual work because it sent a message that

- this is another management fad,
- we don't know if it works, and
- we're taking a risk with your career.

This wasn't the message they wanted. When participants volunteered to become virtual employees, pilots were hugely successful. When expanded to less enthusiastic employees, the resistance became obvious. Employees were fearful that their career visibility would suffer because the organization did not fully embrace virtual work. Nothing was in place to support virtual worker visibility, for example.

With hindsight, organizations realized they were not piloting virtual work. Rather, they should have been *prototyping how to make it work in this organization*. This sends the right message about organization commitment while acknowledging a period of time to accommodate this culture.

Now: *It Still Takes Organization Support to Launch Right*

Executives underestimate the importance of getting departments that support the organization and employees on board with virtual work. Eddie Caine, an expert in telecommuting solutions for public and private enterprises, advises,

> Virtually every support department (except the champion) views telecommuting as more work—Human Resources, Information Technology, Facilities, Risk Management, Legal, *and especially middle managers*. They have to be given little choice and some motivation. By focusing on best practices during change with the employees and managers in the conversation, we help create smoother transitions.

Digital work space expert Charlie Grantham agrees:

> Eddie is spot on. They do much better with a scalable plan for rollout. Learn from prototypes, modify, expand. Without total collaboration across HR, IT, facilities management, and the business unit, you don't get adoption. Work on that collaboration *first*.

Kathy Kacher, a flexwork expert, recently completed a report on current flex/virtual work.[5] "Transparency is key to success, instead of an under-the-radar pilot approach. Organizations need to leverage their workforce, get feedback, and find ambassadors who can tell the real story before the rumor mill starts churning." For resistant organizations, Kacher proposes what she calls "a pulling rollout." Restrict teams that want to try virtual work until all team members agree and cocreate a communication strategy. Not everyone needs to telecommute, but the whole team must agree to become a virtual team. The result? Motivated teams lead the way, getting everyone on board and navigating barriers. As Kacher shared, "It takes longer, but the transition is smoother because the hard work is done in advance."

Then: *Training and Organization Support Was Underdeveloped*

Organizations often provided inadequate support and training to the virtual workers. Organizations that provided training in change and virtual management achieved sustainable success faster than those that didn't. When provided support—technical help desk and virtual coaching, for example—virtual employees rated virtual job satisfaction higher than those who did not receive targeted support.

Nothing dampens enthusiasm more than having a whole new "job" called virtual work. Provide training and support because their productivity and job satisfaction are more likely to be higher than not.

Now: *Sad, but Still True*

Eddie Caine on reviewing virtual work installations today:

> We find the same thing. At the heart of the problem is a lack of understanding as to why virtual work pays off for all. Seldom do organizations measure the impacts—when they do it's typically for a pilot. Too seldom is actual management development training provided, especially in leveraging collaboration tools. They finish the pilot and stop measuring the impacts because they proved it works. Once they stop measuring, they forget how valuable the program was to begin with. Priorities change and . . . because companies seldom manage virtual work holistically, causing issues to arise. Issues become problems; problems that are resolvable and unnecessary if they had received basic support.

Then: *Trial-and-Error Learning Slowed Team Formation*

Interviewees recalled reinventing the wheel when virtual teams didn't learn from each other. Virtual teams "discovered" their own habits and protocols, but little was in place to help other teams learn from them so they could become productive quickly. When individuals changed teams they had to learn completely new team habits. Smart organizations learned to provide sample team agreements, templates, and communication protocols applied consistently across all teams.

Now: *Finally, Some Progress!*

We've gotten better at managing change when the commitment is real and determined not to be a fad. Here is a summary of the best advice I can share from my experience and conversations with seasoned leaders about how to ease the transition to virtualization:

- "An effective communication campaign is invaluable."
- "You need a formal marketing campaign beginning way before you start implementation. Position what's upcoming so people are ready. That means social media and short training videos also."

- "This change in work patterns needs to be taken as seriously as a product development process and/or rollout. The same business principles apply."
- "Align, align, align to the mission and vision. Then create a brand, communication strategy, and ongoing plan to keep it alive. Champion an internal advisory team that commits to support virtual success."
- "Keep fresh views on the team. Celebrate success. It reduces burnout."

Notes

1. I'd particularly like to thank Charles Grantham of Community Design Institute; Eddie Caine of Eddie Caine Consulting, LLC; Kathy Kacher of Career/Life Alliance Services; and Steve Dorn of Pivotal Resources for their ongoing conversations beyond my initial interview. They especially helped solidify the results and opinions I heard in my interviews.

2. "SharePoint," *Wikipedia*, last modified September 13, 2015, https://en.wikipedia.org/wiki/SharePoint

3. Established all-in-one work stream collaboration and communications platform that makes teams more productive and accountable with a seamless integration of chat, file sharing, search, task management, and video and voice, centralized into an intuitive virtual work space. Founded in 2008, Redbooth is a pioneer of team collaboration and communication solutions. "Redbooth," *Wikipedia*, last modified September 10, 2015, https://en.wikipedia.org/wiki/Redbooth

4. Kyra Cavanaugh, Jennifer Sabatini Fraone, and Kathy Kacher, "National Workplace Flexibility Study," 2014, www.bc.edu/content/dam/files/centers/cwf/research/highlights/pdf/NWFS-Report-012014.pdf

5. Ibid.

PART THREE

ESSENTIAL VIRTUAL COMPETENCIES

"Collaboration isn't about being best friends, or even necessarily liking everyone you're working with. It is about putting all and any baggage aside, bringing your best self to the table, and focusing on the common goal."

—Meghan Biro, *Forbes* contributing writer

7

VIRTUAL LEADERSHIP
DIFFERENTIATORS

"If you want to awaken all of humanity, then awaken all of yourself. Truly the greatest gift you have to give is that of your own self-transformation."

—Lao Tzu

"The major barrier to developing a sustainable virtual organization is a polity that lacks basic competencies to pull organizations forward in the direction of societal evolution. That direction, by the way, is towards continuously greater connectivity, harmony of relations among different groups and the recognition of unity of purpose. But most leaders today don't know what they don't know."

—Charles Grantham, designer of Talent Integration Ecosystems

Poof! You're a (Virtual) Manager

You no longer gather in a conference room on the spot. Your team stretches around the globe. You are the link between the team and the organization.

Regardless of how virtual the organization is, the virtual manager is always the primary link between team and organization. *If even one team member is virtual, you are a virtual manager.* Regardless of whether you are virtual yourself, you are leading remotely. Leading virtually means managing a network of interdependent relationships while keeping the team focused on mission accomplishment. It is active management through relationship, communication, and coaching, skills critical to a virtual manager.

Colocated teams are no longer the ideal, with distributed team members a compromise. High-level interaction, interdependence, and performance occur in multiple work environments. With available technology tools, you have a full spectrum of connection vehicles. Business virtualization has enabled teams regardless of where they work.

75

It's team communication that changes most virtually, creating challenges for virtual managers. Virtual teams usually meet virtually *and* face-to-face, work independently *and* interdependently. It's not either/or. This chapter defines competencies most critical for leading in a virtual and continuously changing environment, which can be daunting when moving to virtual work. The virtual leader is the change manager and face of support during the transition. *What must you do differently? What changes as you move to mobile work?*

Change Ourselves First

Stop believing today's managers are effectively engaging employees. *They are not.* We are wasting far too much human intelligence. Multiple talent reports tell us repeatedly, and have for years, that the biggest change leaders need to make is surprisingly simple.[1]

In *Future Strong*, Bill Jensen writes, "If you want to lead others into a strong future, you need to be keenly aware of how your own inner truths— biases, fears, courage, values and dreams—do or do not impact the daily work of others."[2]

In other words, *know yourself.* Others see us. We show ourselves in our communication. We learn about ourselves when we listen to the language we use. Most people typically focus on the past, a habit that limits us to learning only from what we already know. Cynicism and judgments often limit our ability to learn and change—or at least slow us down because we are convinced something won't work (cynicism) or is a poor choice (judgment). One coaching client shared this realization simply: "Logic, rituals, and habits can stand in the way of thinking about a future where I *can* learn and innovate."

Managers of first-time virtual workers are asking them to change, let go of the familiar, and embrace the new. It might help to remind the team this is new for the leader, too. When leaders are open (and make it safe for others to be as well), teams are more inclined to allow new habits to emerge and be patient with themselves while they find their new work rhythms and flows. *What assumptions, fears, and past experiences are preventing you from opening to what's new?*

Distrust Is the Natural State

Let's be honest, though. Distrust is natural in corporations. If management hovers, appearing to distrust, team members are self-conscious and more careful. In a virtual environment with technical monitoring, a sense of Big Brother watching increases tenfold. Career caution is built right into the fabric of organizations and isn't overcome by exhortations to trust.

If management hovers digitally, trust will not increase or decrease in a virtual environment. Old habits get re-created virtually, perpetuating a climate of *dis*trust. Instead, *build* trust through supporting people while managing team results.

I interviewed an influential virtual leader who manages several global, virtual teams. She described what happens when organization culture fails to support virtual teams, as is the case with this young leader. She asked to remain anonymous.

> There is no question that we have used tools to effect operational improvement, and our team is on purpose and shares principles. Encouragement and support are not strong values in my company, though, so having practice with tools to use them more effectively is not a focus for the company.
>
> Instead, mistakes are seen as grave errors in judgment, rather than learning and growth opportunities. Coaching is not freely given; it is something that has to be sought out, and can be intimidating to ask for.
>
> I think people start out wanting to give to the organization, but with time and the lack of appreciation of intellectual capital, many people "check out" and give the bare minimum because there is a lack of motivation or clear goals and mission.

Is it any wonder that distrust is the natural state? Unfortunately, this cultural state limits the opportunity for collaborative learning.

For the remainder of this chapter, reflect on your management strengths and areas for improvement. You are the only person who decides whether the past repeats itself or a new future can emerge. Unexamined assumptions about people may be limiting your potential. Be open to examining your assumptions about how to manage and lead.

Be willing to reconsider your understanding of power and influence in work relationships.

Navigating the Threefold Path

As Figure 7.1 shows, we begin on the First Path for high-performance virtual teams: team development.

The virtual manager launches the team by facilitating its members getting to know each other while clarifying the team charter, team scope, and expected deliverables. The First Path also includes team decisions about

Figure 7.1. The Threefold Path for high-performance teams.

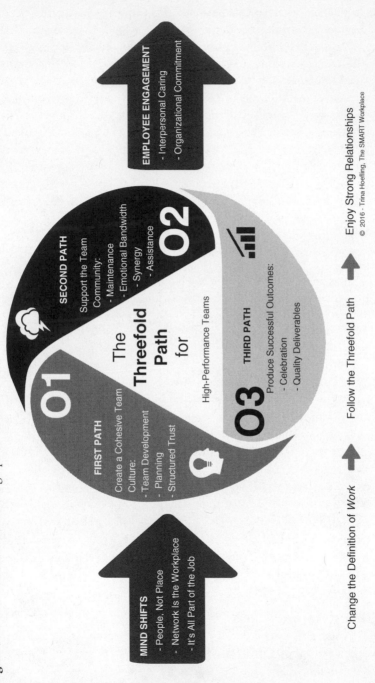

MIND SHIFTS
- People, Not Place
- Network Is the Workplace
- It's All Part of the Job

01 FIRST PATH
Create a Cohesive Team
Culture:
- Team Development
- Planning
- Structured Trust

02 SECOND PATH
Support the Team
Community:
- Maintenance
- Emotional Bandwidth
- Synergy
- Assistance

03 THIRD PATH
Produce Successful Outcomes:
- Celebration
- Quality Deliverables

The **Threefold Path** for
High-Performance Teams

EMPLOYEE ENGAGEMENT
- Interpersonal Caring
- Organizational Commitment

Change the Definition of *Work* ➤ Follow the Threefold Path ➤ Enjoy Strong Relationships

© 2016 - Trina Hoefling, The SMART Workplace

communication and work agreements, timelines and quality expectations, and team processes.

The virtual manager spends most of her time navigating the Second Path. The Second Path may be, in fact, the driving success factor for virtual team success, collectively and individually focused on team support. *An effective virtual leader clears the path that builds trust and sustainable performance.*

The Third Path actually begins before and continues throughout the life of the virtual team's charter. It's the production path to successful outcomes. Performance management has changed, with smart virtual managers partnering with the collaborative tools. As a virtual manager leading your team through the Threefold Path, use and adapt work tools that help you track and measure performance. Today's technology functions as a reliable management partner, so the manager spends less time tracking activity because project management tools automate much of it. This opens more time for engaging with people and connecting resources.

Conversation and attention to relationships have to be scheduled into the virtual manager's day. Use the collaborative tools to develop trusting relationships with your team. They can be highways for trust and communication that inform you about how to facilitate team processes and work flows, leverage metrics and analytics, and ensure outcomes around a clearly defined strategy for your team.

The Manager Matters

Over one-third (35%) of U.S. employees say managers need to be better at nurturing talent and connecting people.[3] Research, employee surveys, and exit interviews confirm that the manager is the main reason people stay or leave.[4] People will work for up to 10% less money for someone they like and respect.

Leadership effectiveness research shows us that *virtual managers must do four things better*:[5]

1. They must effectively *communicate* and facilitate others' communication face-to-face, virtually, in writing, and audiovisually through web/audio conferences.
2. They must *manage by results* with a focus on coaching and development.
3. They must *trust* employees and provide coaching based on team members' stages of virtual effectiveness.
4. They must *facilitate introductions* and career growth opportunities.

These require strong relationship management skills and social intelligence—influencing people across the organization and within the team. The virtual leader advocates for the team. This means he needs to build and maintain his own network in order to widen available support for the team. Understanding the power and politics of the business operation is like having a private invitation to the party, and you bring invitations back to your team. And remember, as the geographic boundaries that define organizations fade, the virtual manager *is* the face of the organization to the virtual team.

The Language We Use Confines Us or Opens Us

Virtual competency is more than web conferencing. It requires self-awareness and ability to express ourselves clearly. Begin to listen to how you—and your team—talk. Listen to examples, stories, metaphors, and images used. Are you imaginative, inviting new possibilities? We are unaware of how mechanical many of our business metaphors are. Business processes are compared to an assembly line since work flow seems straightforward. What really happens is usually more organic, flowing through people. A metaphor from nature may be a more accurate description, such as the root system of an aspen grove. If you and your team are still "thinking" with unevolved metaphors, it limits your ability to learn and innovate quickly.

Leverage Complexity

Virtual managers often work in a complex work environment, such as a matrix. A matrix is not an organization structure so much as a set of reporting relationships that tie the organization together laterally. Complexity always increases interdependencies, requiring communication and cooperation by more parts of the whole. Mechanical metaphors limit a leader's ability to see the potential of such a rich, dynamic environment. Leverage complexity by thinking more in terms of relationships:

- Handle multiple relationships across lines of power, politics, and authority.
- Collaborate virtually to manage competing resources across lines of business.
- Influence to find needed resources for the team.
- Practice patience (within limits).
- Navigate power struggles and find wins for everyone.
- Be authentic and communicate with sensitivity to others.

Relationship management can be planned, supported, and even measured. As you plan your virtual team's interaction with the larger organization, think of relationships you need to develop. Help your team members have access to needed influencers. Facilitate access so that all stakeholder perspectives are considered by your team. Issues are resolved faster because people have better information. Virtual communication protocols can be cascaded into organizational rhythms, habits, and flows.

What About When It Doesn't Go According to Plan?

Team members face a number of predictable barriers to performance. Virtual teams more so. Predictable barriers (and common complaints) encompass the following:

- Reliance on other teams who don't prioritize your team's needs
- Organization politics and cultures of cynicism
- Geographic, temporal, language, and cultural differences
- (Un)reliable technology
- Difficult people

A proactive leader anticipates barriers, opens doors, and coaches team members to navigate barriers. A proactive *virtual* leader uses technology to help. Of course, the objective of a virtual team is to complete the work. The virtual team *leader* is focused less on task and more on relationships on and beyond the team.

Virtual Coaching and Support

For newly formed teams or teams that are newly virtual, the virtual leader must focus on virtual competencies and team development. Some virtual team struggle is normal, especially as members move through team development stages.[6] Teams adjust as they discover how to navigate conflicts and differences, becoming high functioning as a unit.

As a virtual leader, do not shy away from team frustration, irritation, member withdrawal, or disengagement. The team should expect rough spots at first and learn to talk about and negotiate challenges. Expect to facilitate evolving team agreements, adjusting as needed when it's clear something must change. The performance of a newly formed team improves as fast as its members. Learning comes from addressing confusion and disagreement. As people get to know each other better, they begin to self-manage to talents and strengths.

If the team doesn't do this, the virtual manager must step in. The virtual leader keeps everyone actively engaged and speaking up. Most teams will not reach optimal performance. Too many "diplomats" or "peacemakers" may prevent a virtual team from reaching its full potential. In a virtual environment, it's easier to become disengaged because team members can more easily disappear. The virtual manager is a facilitator who holds the team together until members develop their own bonds and healthy practices.

Developing New Virtual Team Members

Managing a virtual team does not require a magic pill. It does require more planning, thought, and organization, as well as clear communication and proactive coaching. With time, the attentive virtual leader becomes more in tune with team challenges and member motivations. As team members adjust to a virtual environment, managers facilitate the team's successful progression to full productivity as quickly as possible.

Typically, virtual workers will go through four stages of personal adaptation to the virtual work environment: excitement, disappointment, confusion, and synergy. (Visit www.WorkingVirtually.org to download a free job aid describing the stages with management responses.[7]) Virtual leaders help improve virtual worker competence *in the new virtual environment*. Everyone becomes personally effective, working and collaborating virtually. You will coach on the following:

- New and adjusted work habits
- Communication and cooperation
- Emotional support while team members adjust to the remote work environment
- Virtual office setup, if needed

You are *not* coaching to job competence; that is assumed and remains unquestioned, especially if the virtual workers performed the same job competently prior to moving to a virtual work environment. If performance falters when it was up to standard before, it is a virtual work environment or team issue, not a job competency issue. *Coach to the real issue.*

Virtual work is common but not pervasive, so team members will have varying virtual competence. For seasoned virtual team members who have had good experiences, the development stages of virtual competence are complete. These team members can be recruited to help move newer virtual workers up the learning curve quickly.

Every virtual worker joining a new team goes through an adjustment period. Teams are living organisms, each unique. Watch for indications of a virtual team member's confidence with the virtual work environment, and respond situationally. Some frustration is natural for new teams. Knowing it's normal helps everyone get through it.

Managers should remind themselves and team members that structure is the servant of the team, not the ruler. All procedures and rules are servants themselves. They are in place to serve the delivery goals, not enslave people to unnecessary rules.

The First Path of high-performance teams begins with involving the team in setting its own rules, protocols, agreements, communication rhythms, and collaborative flows. These guidelines can and will adjust as everyone settles in.

Often challenges come from outside the team. Helping the team handle challenges may require assertive advocacy. Do you need to solicit additional budget to bring the team in for a confab? Challenge operational routines? Push for more robust and integrated collaborative tools? Your networking and influencing skills are more critical than ever as you advocate for high performance in a virtual organization.

Managing virtually may be new to you as well, meaning you are going through your own developmental stages. It's not just the team that is learning and adjusting; you are, too. Accept some emotional ups and downs but don't get lost in them or question the validity of virtual work.

Eight Virtual Leader Competencies

Leading adaptive, virtual, fast-paced teams is exhilarating and challenging. "Old" competencies don't become defunct. Bring the best of the past into your virtual management practices. Become a leader who commits to continuously improving eight competencies that shift team management to a shared responsibility for performance.

1. Build Commitment, Not Control

Command-and-control management methods simply do not work in a virtual work environment. The organization is too complex. There is obviously a place for structure, but not stricture. Virtual teams look to the virtual manager to keep an eagle eye on how the team coordinates with the rest of the organization. They want to know for what—and whom—they are working.

Gain the team's commitment by modeling and expecting consistency, fairness, and trustworthy action. Commitment is given fully only when trust is present. Otherwise, a transactional agreement is struck, but not true commitment.

Never confuse the two. Accept that until trust is present, transactional agreements are as good as it gets, and engagement will be limited. As it relates to the team's work, the virtual leader has to pull everyone into the project vision *enough* for team members to suspend their distrust, minimally agreeing to meet their obligations. Build commitment in small steps until the team stops transacting and begins cooperating.

Commitment builds more commitment, so start small if that's where people are. Be scrupulously fair and begin the team engagement with the trust glass full. Show *you* trust first and set up team agreements that support the trust glass staying full. Expect commitments to be honored, and do not settle for excuses.

As a virtual manager, face your own discomfort with managing in a less controlled environment. Negotiate with yourself and others to find that personal edge—that place where discomfort pushes you to new learning but where loss of control isn't pushing anyone over the edge into chaos and panic.

2. Focus, Coordinate, and Communicate—Don't Authorize, Command, or Plan

The old joke goes, *If you want to hear God laugh, tell him your plans.* An antithetical saying says, *Failure to plan is guaranteed failure.* These are not contradictory; they are both absolutely true. The virtual leader needs to focus and flex, coordinating all the pieces of the game plan without becoming entrenched in how it has to go. If a plan is too structured, it will not be able to keep up with fast-paced demands. If there is no plan, the fast pace of change will whip the team around much like a loose garden hose with the water gushing, nothing to "hold the direction." It's hard for a team to hold its focus when reacting.

Virtual workers expect strong leadership—someone to "hold the direction" of the garden hose. They will not tolerate, however, rigid commandeering or entitlement authority. Today's workers want and need structure but do not perform well with onerous rules and invasive oversight.

A significant twentieth-century contribution has been productivity mechanisms that collect, manage, and measure data. For repeatable work, control by measurement makes sense. The work product structures productivity, in a sense. Software tool builders continue to respond to executives' cries for more controls and oversight, producing useful enterprise solutions in HR, finance, and operations. Solutions produce analytics that inform and direct operational behavior. For traditional production work, this is great.

For collaborative virtual work, solutions also prioritize coordination and open communication. It makes the manager's job easier to share information through dashboards to keep the team informed. Performance feedback enables people to course-correct. People like to know how they're doing, so why *not* let the tools help you inform them? When we *know* where we are with a team, a project, or a deliverable, we can focus on moving the work forward instead of wasting time wondering and seeking answers.

3. Connect, Don't Gate-Keep

A team leader's credibility is directly related to her ability to obtain resources across the organization. Networking, keeping people informed, and soliciting input from team members, stakeholders, partners, and customers are an integral part of a team leader's job, virtual or not. In a virtual environment, it is critical, especially if team members are virtual full-time, reducing their visibility to executives and influencers.

Virtual team leaders open doors to information, resources, and people. Ensure that your team members are known by upper management and have the opportunity to work in high-profile capacities. Make your virtual team "visible" to the organization to guarantee that virtual status does not derail your team's career paths.

This involves networking up, down, and across organizational boundaries, sometimes outside the organizational walls. What would make your virtual team and members visible in the organization, regardless of location? When a team member's role on a project is coming to an end, for example, a virtual leader scouts for the next opportunity and advocates for and positions team members. Successful career connectors will never want for professional workers willing to serve on their virtual teams.

4. Manage by Results, Not by Sight

It's true that managers can't manage what they can't see . . . using old techniques. Old performance management techniques may work, but only if they translate well to an electronically networked environment. Call center managers, for example, can manage agent performance electronically much more easily than a new product launch team leader. Available technology opens managers to rethink how to manage performance. For example, when is the individual the right focus for performance evaluation, and when is it the team that should be evaluated based on collective results?

One of the bigger barriers to virtual work has been managerial fear of the answer to the following: "How do I know they're really working?" The better question is, "How do I know they're working now, in a traditional office?" If you can answer that question, you can usually extrapolate how to know people are working in a remote environment. If you don't know how they're working now, then what difference does it make? You have some first steps to improve your performance management. (We'll look at that more closely in chapter 12.)

The question "How can I manage virtual team performance?" is better reframed as "How do I support collaboration and teamwork so that we reach our targets?"

Along with enterprise collaboration tools, virtual leaders also rely upon team agreements and feedback loops built by the team during the First Path of development. These and the team's goals are the basis for performance and results management. At the very least, a virtual leader must stop being preoccupied with clock time and start thinking about outcomes. Focus on communication and facilitating team processes. Let the team know the lengths and limits of their authority, how and in what ways to involve you. Reward collaboration, knowledge sharing, and team learning explicitly. Help the team honor those who meet commitments. Celebrate results and compensate accordingly.

5. Coach, Don't Manage

One of the bigger challenges for the virtual leader is developing team members without the traditional face-to-face interaction and observation. Typically in a colocated environment a manager would observe a coachable moment, and use that as a reason to approach the team member.

Observation looks different virtually; it isn't as easy to detect frustration and casually intervene or see someone putting in long hours and ask what you can do to help. Virtually, the leader seeks the subtle cue: sharper than usual e-mails with an almost staccato feel, e-mails spread throughout the day from 7:00 a.m. until 10:30 p.m., a curious drop in communication from someone. Become sensitive to the subtle cue. Sometimes it's nothing—the team member is splitting her day in order to spend time with her children after school, hence the early and late correspondence. Sometimes, however, behavior change signals a warning—a client was unhappy with a milestone deliverable, and the team member doesn't know how to ask for help or feels overwhelmed.

While *how* you observe behavior changes, the basic coaching skills do not change virtually. Effective coaches guide team members into increasingly effective performance without doing it for them. They anticipate problems and conflicts, intervening before they get too big. An effective coach is the person to whom a team member goes to get alignment on a project or for advice. This is no different virtually.

How and where you give feedback change. Face-to-face is not always an option in virtual organizations. The coaching axiom is to praise publicly and through all media; give constructive feedback privately and in person. The axiom holds true virtually with the exception of "in person."

One "virtual reality" to keep in mind: One-way feedback is critically important to deliver with care. The poorer the context, the fewer "clues" to meaning (e.g., facial expression or voice tone), the higher the likelihood of misunderstood meaning. A simple piece of advice via e-mail is more easily misconstrued as harsh criticism than that same advice delivered over lunch in person. A telephone conversation conveys more meaning but is still missing the smile that softens the words.

When in doubt, go with the "richest" medium that is possible and practical. Videoconferences have become acceptable for performance feedback since the video streaming is almost like being in person. A genuinely involved manager facilitates coaching conversations and schedules ongoing follow-up. She ensures the situation is improving for everyone. A perfunctory manager handles the situation by talking to the involved parties. The difference is small but significant. Take the time you and the team need to hold full, vigorous conversations that end with improvement plans.

6. Dialogue, Don't Dictate

Many businesses must innovate quickly, meaning they are learning fast. Learning organizations require facilitative managers who help people interact with an inclination toward fast adaptation. Teams are more likely to be innovative when they freely share experience and knowledge through intentional conversation. Being able to innovate as a team requires the team to hold challenging, creative conversations that unearth new possibilities. Collaborative work needs *healthy conflict* and active debate in order to generate ideas. Generative thinking comes from debate. As the team's manager, facilitate vigorous inquiry and advocacy by everyone, encouraging differences of opinion.

Facilitate your team's ability to test and experiment quickly through prototype, reflection, and adjustment. Work-focused conversations should lead somewhere—a decision to try something before analysis paralysis sets in, a creative resolution to a stubborn problem, combining multiple opposing ideas into a better option. Help the team reach majority agreement, if not consensus, coming back together after robust debate.[8]

When people don't see each other daily, actively facilitate discussion opportunities. Teams need practice talking before they need to solve tough problems together. As fast as the work landscape changes, virtual managers must be able to move their teams from initial idea to execution or prototype with little time to adjust. The better the team discusses together—debating, exploring, assessing, deciding, designing, trying, adjusting—the more agile it can be.

High-performance team leaders have more than a good plan, an effective process, and team eagerness; they facilitate teams that quickly and intelligently think together. Conversations are the equivalent of teams thinking out loud. Everyone's hearts, wills, and minds are, ideally, engaged in an ongoing commitment to create solutions and find improvements.

Provide "sacred spaces" to talk. Some conversation is simply downloading information so everyone has shared knowledge. Many business conversations function at the level of debate, essential to assess the value, risk, and potential of options. Healthy conversations expand perspectives and invite questions. Healthy disagreement enables teams to question current "truth" in search of a more fitting, generative "truth."

Dynamic conversations are most likely to be transformative when they flow freely. Workers are often unwilling to challenge the status quo. Many work experiences leave people disinclined to respond to emerging needs, especially without encouragement. One of the greatest gifts you can offer your virtual team is to encourage them to ask deeper questions, explore, and take time to reflect. Questioning is legitimate and important and accesses more of the team's brilliance. The tone of the conversation becomes one of shared curiosity. Invite people into virtual conversations, both synchronous and asynchronous, who bring different perspectives. Let new ideas emerge from the team, often thoughts that would not have occurred to anyone if everyone had not been talking.

Get people in the habit of discussing their findings and exploring what comes. Let the group determine relevance. Encourage team members to have wide-ranging conversations with their networks. Capture learning as a group, and seek larger implications for future projects. This creates true synergy and shared responsibility for continuous improvement rather than allowing team members to delegate up the organization, relying on you.

7. Blend Technology and People

People versus technology is a false choice. They are not mutually exclusive. Virtual managers do need to be technology competent, but the focus is still on the *people connection*. Most tools are user friendly, so learning to facilitate using collaborative software does not have to demand technical expertise. The real power of a virtual leader is in understanding the nature of people and teams, and applying the collaborative capabilities the tools bring.

In its original meaning *intimacy* did not mean emotional closeness, but *the willingness to pass on honest information*. Team intimacy can be created and enhanced through multiple vehicles, and the team needs to decide which technologies are best for it. Anonymous polling functions, for example, are great for getting a sense of the group around sensitive issues without asking people to declare a position. Chat rooms allow group interaction and casual, more reflective conversation. An audioconference is a terrible vehicle for reflective dialogue; the silence appropriate to dialogue is confusing on a phone—was the team member unintentionally disconnected from the call or quietly thinking? Videoconferencing enables fast movement. The energy you want to build, the pace you want to move, and the container you want to create are all influenced by the medium you use.

8. Integrate, Don't Comply

Develop and adapt guidelines, processes, and infrastructure to meet the team's needs. Include connection to the larger organization. Virtual team members can be confused and feel cut off from the organization if there isn't enough visceral connection. They can collectively or individually drift off or become renegades. They may lose their sense of value if they lose track of how they are mission-critical to the organization. A virtual manager needs to help the team feel "embedded" and integrated into the larger community. Help team members integrate their work with the team, and the team's work with the organization. Be the duct tape—the sticky factor—for your team.

Walking the Talk of the Threefold Path

With strong virtual competency, you are creating and sustaining a cohesive team culture, supporting your team community, and doing your part to ensure that team goals are met. Walking the Threefold Path to manage high-performance teams is more an art than a science, so find ways to make your management style your own. All virtual managers need to be involved in the work, but more often they facilitate team functioning, clear obstacles, or rally resources. Sometimes a leader's daily activity is less with the team and more in the organization—networking, advocating, and leading change.

Your commitment, as a virtual leader, is clear: *to purposefully and intentionally support your team and the organization in achieving meaningful strategic goals.* Team leaders always attend to that and facilitate continuously for effective flow. All structure, technologies, and systems serve to support results. When in doubt, ask, *"How can I support and sustain a virtual community so that everyone feels included, clear, involved, and responsible? How can I tear down silos and walls that interfere with that?"*

Notes

1. Kyra Cavanaugh, Jennifer Sabatini Fraone, and Kathy Kacher, "National Workplace Flexibility Study" and "Global Workplace Flexibility Pilot," 2014, www.bc.edu/content/dam/files/centers/cwf/research/highlights/pdf/NWFS-Report-012014.pdf, 2014. Many current research reports and survey analyses are referenced elsewhere also. To avoid redundancy, I'll cite one insightful study: http://clalliance.com/CLASEL/docs/global%20flex%20pilot%20ppt.pdf

2. Bill Jensen, *Future Strong* (Melbourne, FL: Motivational Press, 2016), www.goodreads.com/book/show/26583278-future-strong Also, see Jensen's TED talk: "Are You Future Strong?" Tedxtalks.ted.com, added May 29, 2015, http://tedxtalks.ted.com/video/Are-you-Future-Strong-Bill-Jens

3. The Economist Intelligence Unit, "Automated, Creative, & Dispersed: The Future of Work in the 21st Century," 2015, www.futureofworkhub.info/allcontent/2015/5/1/automated-creative-and-dispersed-the-future-of-work-in-the-21st-century

4. Again, so many reports say the same thing. A few highlighted conclusions that make the case: Employee Benefit News reported 70% of employees are poised to leave because of their manager; Gallup ESat confirms 75% are disengaged; Carnegie Institute states virtual team issues are 85% people problems, 15% technical challenges; Microsoft (UK) finds communication, performance management, and trust named as biggest virtual challenges.

5. Among others, Jonathan Whited, "Virtual Team Leadership Skills Delphi Method" (DBA diss., University of Pheonix, 2007).

6. "Tuckman's Stages of Group Development," *Wikipedia*, last modified September 6, 2015, https://en.wikipedia.org/wiki/Tuckman%27s_stages_of_group_development

7. For more detail on developing new virtual team members, download a free job aid, "The Virtual Manager's Guide to Developing New Virtual Team Members," at www.WorkingVirtually.org

8. Linda A. Hill, Greg Brandeau, Emily Truelove, and Kent Lineback, *Collective Genius: The Art and Practice of Leading Innovation* (Boston: Harvard Business Review, 2014).

8

HENHOUSES AND JAZZ MUSICIANS

When Is a Team a Team?

"May your adventures bring you closer together, even as they take you far away from home."
—Trenton Lee Steward, *The Mysterious Benedict Society and the Perilous Journey*

"It takes two flints to make a fire."
—Louisa May Alcott

"Five guys on the court working together can achieve more than five talented individuals who come and go as individuals."
—Kareem Abdul-Jabbar

What are the differences between work groups and teams, and why should you care? Whether you're a virtual leader or a team member, you need to know the difference in order to do the following:

- Leverage your team's careers by finding best fits.
- Build teams with the kind of open and collaborative team dynamic that attracts high-quality team members.
- Produce successful team outcomes.

How a group works to accomplish the team purpose should be driven by the work itself. Team relationships develop through coordinated work, but how much of an authentic, nontask-focused relationship does the manager need in order to lead team members? I believe the deeper the interdependence required of team members, the stronger the connection. More dynamic, complex work will, by its nature, demand more cooperation on the team.

Sometimes, however, work is simpler. Before selecting your team, answer the following:

- How much cooperation does the team need?
- How often will the team need to work together?
- In what ways must the team cooperate for the work to get done right and timely?

From these answers, you begin to know how connected you need team members to be and how important virtual collaboration competency becomes in your hiring. When colocated, work friendships come naturally, sometimes becoming work-intimate strong. When teams seldom or never see one another, the virtual manager has an additional job responsibility—to facilitate friendly work relationships until they develop on their own, especially if the work itself doesn't require it.

Team Competence, Cooperation, Consideration

Obviously, candidates meet professional skill requirements before consideration for team membership. An equally important consideration *virtually* is the candidate's desire to cooperate with others and support the team as a whole. Look at how effectively a potential team member can work the way *this* team functions and fill the role that *this* team needs. For example, I worked with a colleague who was strong at building on others' ideas but unable to design from scratch. She would be a poor candidate on an innovation team that needed to develop new possibilities. On a continuous improvement team, however, she would excel.

Two people with the same job competencies can bring dramatically different energies to your team as well. Someone who does exceptional work but won't share credit with others can leave virtual teammates feeling unappreciated and derailed.

Who is a good choice for your team?

Ensuring Diversity and Team Balance

The virtual leader facilitates the fast formation of aligned high-performance teams through facilitating cohesion. You want a cohesive team culture that grows out of shared values, beliefs, negotiated agreements, and behaviors of the team. Every team's culture strongly influences how people behave— hopefully, they're engaged.

At the same time, cohesive teams can come to think *too* similarly over time. When a team values harmony and alignment over accurate analysis and critical evaluation, a phenomenon called *groupthink* can set in. Groupthink truly limits any team's ability to respond to its environment quickly, if at all. Groupthink leads to individual team members unquestioningly following the majority. It discourages disagreement.[1] If a team prone to groupthink makes one false assumption in a decision-making process, it means the team is acting from faulty foundational thinking, thereby putting its results at risk.

To avoid this risk, you want your team members to see the team's work from different perspectives. An analytical person will excel at finding the operational strengths and weaknesses of various options with an eye toward quality control. A people-oriented teammate will look at the impact on people with an eye toward advocacy for all stakeholders. You want both perspectives in the conversation and at the decision-making table. You want a virtual team that is aligned, but also speaks up, reaches out, advocates, and inquires. You want a team that challenges itself and each other.

Diversity on your team is like getting a booster shot against risk.

Diverse teams can harness collective intelligence because multiple perspectives are considered. Team diversity is more than culture and race. Team members come with different values, personalities and social styles, experiences, backgrounds, and cultures.

The evidence is unequivocal.[2] Scott E. Page, political scientist and economics professor at the University of Michigan, used mathematical modeling and case studies to show how variety in staffing produces organizational strength. Teams made up of similar team members consistently underperform diverse teams. One reason for this is that teams whose members have similar experience, backgrounds, and personalities tend to share similar perspectives and approaches. They enjoy working together more often because they think and work similarly. They reach consensus more easily. *They also fail more often.* Their lack of diversity creates collective blind spots for the team, increasing the risk of missing important information. Homogeneous teams think *too much* alike. Team diversity leads to broader collective thinking and better decisions.[3]

Personality profiles and temperament assessments are a popular way to ensure team diversity that is less obvious than race or culture. The Meyers-Briggs Type Indicator (MBTI),[4] for example, sells nearly two million assessments annually in the United States. Assessments like the MBTI, DiSC,[5] and others are easy to grasp and an inexpensive way to assess team member preferences with a goal of selecting team members who bring a full perspective and balance to the team.

StrengthFinders,[6] developed by Gallup, is another tool that identifies individual strengths in many areas of interest and performance. Its strength-based philosophy enables leaders to build on team member strengths. When a team is well balanced, team members don't have to be strong in every team role in order for the team to perform. Excellent performers are rarely well rounded. They have edges, but the team that comes together around its aligned work *is* well rounded.

A cohesive team will collaborate by delegating to strength.

When selecting team members, look for "best fits" based on all relevant factors, such as experience; education; functional (perhaps political) representation; organization cultural fit; and, in some cases, availability. Best fit team members complement one another to make a good fit together. A *collaborative* culture, the culture of a typical high-performing virtual team, for example, attracts team members who are naturally open, generous, and responsive. People culturally want to approach goals and deliverables with a shared focus and faster results.

Think about the kind of team balance you need in your team selection process. Plan for a diverse team before building your team. Seek team members who meet three criteria:

1. Candidates demonstrate essential and desired virtual competencies (discussed in chapter 9).
2. Candidates have a natural affinity for the vision, values, and culture of the team they are joining.
3. The team as a whole is diverse—selected team members bring different experiences and training, cultural diversity, and a balance of personality types and style preferences.

As a virtual leader, you have the advantage of a larger talent pool because you're not limited by geographic availability. Widen your search to find and build the best team you can.

You want your team to be

- aligned around purpose (shared purpose and meaning of the team's work);
- in agreement about the team's approach to getting work done (values, operating procedures, and team agreements);
- in consensus about wanting to collaborate together; and
- willing to not always agree; healthy debate and even strong opposition unearth hidden risks and innovative solutions. Diversity brings different points of view.

Are you selecting, measuring, developing, and planning careers for your team members based on strengths, balance, and diversity?

Are You a Henhouse or an Orchestra?

Many work groups call themselves teams, *but they're not.*
Maybe they don't need to be!
The first question a team leader must ask is, "Is this really a team, or is this a work group?"
Not all work groups should become teams.
Hens in a henhouse are colocated and are all expected to perform the same task—lay eggs. Their charter of laying eggs, however, does not require them to work together to accomplish that task. In fact, to charter hens with cooperative egg laying wouldn't make sense. It would take hens off their nests for team meetings, cutting into egg-laying time!
Select team members who are best fits for your team, which begins with examining how the team needs to work together. Don't force task coordination on employees who work independently. Do encourage conversations, letting people get comfortable while talking about something related to the work. You can develop team commitment, but you don't need interdependence to encourage it.
Most teams today are not henhouses, however. The work is more dynamic and complex. Virtual team leaders function more like orchestra conductors than overseers of a chicken coop. The contributions of each team member add to a collective production—the performed music, if you will.

Four Criteria of a Team

Four basics call for an orchestra instead of a henhouse. Ask the following questions, and you will know if you are developing and supporting a work group or a team.

1. *Does the group have a reason for working together?* Is there a shared purpose and vision of how to accomplish it? Are team members coresponsible for the team's product or service outcome? A symphony, for example, is chartered with creating and performing beautiful, harmonious music. If a musician wants a solo career in jazz, he or she might not be the best recruit for the conductor.
2. *Are group members dependent on each other?* Individual musicians in a symphony cannot perform musical scores without each other. Even a

virtuoso pianist cannot perform an overture alone. Working together is essential. The product is truly team created.

3. *Is the team committed to working together?* If the group is reticent to work together for any reason, start team development here.

4. *Does the team answer for its work as a team?* How people are rewarded may deter team cooperation. Many organizations make the mistake of rewarding individual performance while expecting team cooperation. In keeping with the symphony metaphor, if the musicians are paid individually based on demonstrating superior musical skills and receiving fan feedback, then human nature will seek distinction. As a result, cooperation will suffer if bonuses are based on individual virtuosity. As a virtual manager, be aware of hidden, insidious disincentives to teamwork. Table 8.1 summarizes the requirements of a team.

If these four criteria are not in place, you can still manage a very effective virtual work group (and even call it a team), but people will work more independently from one another, probably communicating more through and with you. The team may enjoy working together and will hopefully develop professional friendships, but it's not necessary for the team's success.

Teams require more collaboration than henhouses, so members also need to have good relationship-building skills. To become a *virtual* team, the leader has to find synergies and habits that work for the whole. In many ways, a virtual team is just like any other team, *only more so*. Teammates don't have to be best friends, but they need some rapport, respect, and confidence in one another.

If teaming is appropriate but your team does not meet all the criteria, strengthen your team based on the principles of this book. In a virtual environment, commitment and connection can dissipate without the virtual manager's care and feeding, so work at team connection as a virtual team priority.

TABLE 8.1
Four Criteria of a Team

Team charter	We have a purpose.
Interdependent	We can't do it without each other.
Committed	We want to be part of this team.
Accountable	Others are counting on what we do together.

Managing a Henhouse

If teaming is not necessary, a virtual work group is easier to manage virtually. It has fewer complexities. Don't let this tempt you to create virtual work groups by reducing interdependencies, however. It isn't necessarily easier to manage folks who do not need to interact with each other much. This henhouse philosophy can be good, but consider a few points carefully before choosing the henhouse option.

- *More falls to the virtual manager.* A work group manager is primarily responsible for the workers' connection to the organization and its mission. As more people see their jobs as temporary, the virtual manager is the key connector for people to feel part of the larger organization. Less interdependence on the team will usually mean more one-on-one coaching and support from the manager. Plan for more individual time with virtual workers.
- *Autonomy doesn't encourage cooperation.* If virtual workers are too independent, they may not support a collaborative culture, such as working with other departments.
- *Cooperation increases commitment to the company.* How much team members must rely on each other to get things done correlates positively with how committed they are to the organization. This challenges some virtual managers' tendency to want to decrease the amount of cooperation required by virtual workers. If high commitment to the organization is desired, a teaming environment is preferred. Design your business processes to increase interdependence when possible.
- *Cooperation increases commitment to the team.* Virtual teams cannot be any more cohesive than a traditional, colocated team, of course. If a virtual manager wants to manage individuals instead of a team, complete task autonomy is appropriate but may not be smart. Job satisfaction is higher when we like who we work with and interact with teammates often. Studies of workplace behavior prove that the more team members naturally work together, the greater their commitment is to each other and the team.

  If the work doesn't demand team interaction, the virtual manager will need to intentionally facilitate team bonding. In virtual work especially, business process and workflows should support frequent and ongoing interaction and cooperation when possible.
- *Cooperation increases people's desire to help.* How regularly and enthusiastically the team engages affects individual members' willingness to help each other. In other words, the more team members *have*

to rely on one another, *the more likely and willing they are to do so.* Whether the motivation is enlightened self-interest or the satisfaction and expanded emotional bandwidth that comes from knowing people better, it is what it is. Use it.[7]

Motivating Today's Team

David McClelland's human motivation theory teaches that every person has one of three driving motivators: the need for achievement, affiliation, or power. McClelland's need theory was the basis of twentieth-century management theory.[8] None of the three motivators are inherent; we develop them through culture and life experiences. The old management model underpinned managerial behaviors by determining that for most people, the need for power and achievement drove motivation in the workplace.

Power and achievement are not what motivates most workers today, particularly with the influx of millennials into the workforce. Their life experiences give rise to the driving motivator of affiliation. Workers are motivated when they work with an organization that is contributing "meaningful work." We want to be part of something bigger and more important than ourselves, communities we are proud to be part of.

Regardless of whether you manage hens or conduct a symphony orchestra, you want to hire the right people to do the job. Find people who like what they do and see the value they provide, whether it's a call center employee helping customers with technical challenges or a scientist joining a team hoping to solve a major health issue. Once you've determined whether you need a team or a henhouse, it's time to select the right team members, the focus of the next chapter.

Notes

1. "Groupthink," *Psychology Today*, www.psychologytoday.com/basics/groupthink

2. Claudia Dreifus, "In Professor's Model, Diversity = Productivity," *New York Times*, A Conversation with Claudia column, January 8, 2008, www.nytimes.com/2008/01/08/science/08conv.html?_r=1; Natalie O'Toole, "Diversity Leads to Stronger Outcomes," Cornell Chronicle, August 26, 2016, www.news.cornell.edu/stories/2015/04/diversity-leads-strongeroutcomes-says-lecturer

3. Scott E. Page, *The Difference: How the Power of Diversity Creates Better Groups, Firms, Schools and Societies* (Princeton, NJ: Princeton University Press, 2007).

4. "MBTI Basics," The Myers and Briggs Foundation, www.myersbriggs.org/my-mbti-personality-type/mbti-basics/

5. "What is DiSC?" DiscProfile, www.discprofile.com/what-is-disc/overview/

6. www.gallupstrengthscenter.com

7. James Wallace Bishop and K. Dow Scott, "How Commitment Affects Team Performance," *HR Magazine* 42, no. 2 (February 1997): 107.

8. "Need Theory," *Wikipedia*, last modified July 26, 2015, https://en.wikipedia.org/wiki/Need_theory

9

MORE THAN SMARTS— VIRTUAL TEAM MEMBER COMPETENCIES

"It's very important in a restaurant to do the right hiring, because there's no restaurant that you have one cook and nobody else in the kitchen."

—Wolfgang Puck, restaurant owner

"Actually," [Wax] said, "we came here because we needed someplace safe to think for a few hours."

Ranette: "Your mansion isn't safe?"

Wax: "My butler failed to poison me, then tried to shoot me, then set off an explosive in my study."

Ranette: "Huh . . . You need to screen these people better, Wax."

—Brandon Sanderson, *The Alloy of Law*

Virtual leaders do their job best when they focus on communication and interpersonal relationships combined with simple and carefully chosen team tools. Managers are faced with and measured by two main tasks—their ability to do the following:

1. Make sure the job gets done.
2. Help the team members trust the team's ability to function as a unit and that the organization will keep its promises.

The virtual roads have been built and well traveled by virtual leaders that have paved the road for virtual teams. Three roads, in particular, are now well traveled enough that best practices are available and continuously improving. This chapter helps the virtual team know how to do the following:

1. *Start together*. The First Path develops teams that are aligned and prepared.
2. *Continue together*. The Second Path is one of support and attends to relationships and resources.
3. *Finish well*. The Third Path ensures successful outcomes so that teams accomplish their goals.

Current research on high-performing teams confirms that all managers actively manage the Threefold Path, virtual or not.

Structure serves productivity *and* relationship. The First Path (Develop the Team) structures the team's ability to start, continue, and finish well within the virtual work environment. The Second Path (Support the Team) is where the virtual manager spends most of his or her time. It may be, in fact, the driving success factor for virtual team engagement. This is the path of virtual leader and peer support. Virtual managers have help with the Third Path (Produce Successful Outcomes), thanks to technology-enabling tools. The first two paths will put the team on the third path of producing successful outcomes with help from you, the virtual leader.

Before any virtual team pathfinding, however, you want to consider team selection as you prepare for the additional complexity of working in a virtual environment.

Virtual Team Member "Employability"

The leadership competencies delineated in Chapter 7 may actually be *employability* competencies for all workers, not just leaders. Every skill and competency is essential for the virtual manager *and* the professional worker.

Talent managers are beginning to seek what they call *sustainable employability*.[1] Similar to the competencies of the virtual manager, sustainable employability means having the ability to develop and learn, adapt, and be self-reliant and self-managing. There are no hard-and-fast rules about who will best succeed in a virtual work environment, but certain qualities and competencies have emerged as essential or highly desirable. Pick team members carefully based on experience, competence, and reputation.

Select team members who have high integrity and good reputations for mutual support and team play. People who aren't team players bring a distinct disadvantage to the team's ability to perform. True sports professionals play the game well because they know how to play with others. They want the *team* to win, not just achieve personal stats.

You, as virtual leader, want to know if your team members are able to play well with people they won't see every day. Select people who are essentially honest and capable of commitment. Select people who do what they say they will do without prodding. Team members need some reasonable respect and confidence in one another in order to become a trusting team. This is even more so in a virtual environment because face-to-face interaction isn't there for reassurance.

Essential Knowledge/Competencies

Communicates Well

Good communication skills, both written and spoken, are critical in a virtual environment, which is synchronous and asynchronous. Written communication is especially prone to misinterpretation and coldness because there is no immediate feedback happening between the sender and the receiver. Clear articulation, interpersonal caring, effective listening, and clear writing are all part of today's teamwork. Choose team members who can have different kinds of team conversations, written and spoken; information sharing and factual clarification; healthy comparison and debate; *and* curious exploration and discovery. Today's virtual collaborators also often need to be able to influence and present well. Communication competence matters.

Has the Skills

An important rule of effective team making, virtual or not, is to hire competent people in the first place. Unless you intend to provide skill training, skill competency is a baseline before considering someone for the team. As a virtual team leader, you must have confidence that this person can do the job without continuous coaching or oversight of the job itself, especially when the new hire is working virtually. Trust in an individual's abilities allows you to focus on other priorities, like team maintenance, clearing obstacles, finding resources, and relationship management. Some organizations stipulate that employees cannot work in a virtual environment until they have performed their job responsibilities for a certain time or maintain average or above ratings on performance appraisals.

Leverages Technology (or Can Learn)

In order to lay the path for a productive team—performing on time, within budget, and without interpersonal fallout—all members need to be competent with the collaborative tools and comfortable functioning virtually. Decide if you want to select only candidates who are already tool competent, or if you will help transition teams systematically from colocated work habits to online collaboration through the network.

Reassure team members that you, as virtual leader, will coach them. Make training available and consider requiring it. You can't expect every candidate to be equally as prepared. Of course, many people have virtual team experience, and not all have had good experiences. Not everyone comes onto a team with the same commitment, confidence, or competence in virtual collaboration. The First Path, developing your team, is the time to align everyone to the tools as much as the goals.

Work gets done by people through the digital network. The tools are easier and more integrated, so virtual competency is not as challenging as it used to be. Online learning is familiar to everyone today, enabling just-in-time (JIT)[2] learning through on-demand tutorials, self-paced courses, or a YouTube demonstration.

One advantage of enterprise solutions is that everyone across the organization uses the same platform and tools, shortening learning curves. Team members are expected to learn and use them. Virtual work shouldn't become an employee's "other job" to figure out the technology, but today's professionals should expect some learning when they join a new organization. Training team members in the basic tools will save everyone inordinate frustration.

Is Able to Self-Manage

While this is valuable in any environment, it's indispensable in a virtual environment, especially if the team member telecommutes. Setting up a virtual office, managing home and work boundaries, maintaining two or more work spaces if telecommuting part-time, and coordinating communication and work flow require a high level of organization and time management.

Desirable Knowledge/Competencies

Is Assertive

One of the challenges of a remote work environment is that the next ready resource isn't as simple as a holler over a cubicle wall or a quick walk to an expert on the second floor. Chat functions and other real-time collaboration help, but if no one is available, you want your team member to be proactive. Deadlines may also drive a need to decide without full input. In order to get the virtual worker's needs met, sometimes that means speaking up, asking for help, or making the call and moving forward anyway.

If your candidate is the kind of person who doesn't like to reach out, the autonomy and responsibilities of telecommuting may not be for him. As much as an organization and a team leader attempt to keep remote members informed, usually the fear of "out of sight, out of mind" still happens, and for less assertive virtual workers especially. Also, initiators and solution finders are more quickly trusted by teammates. Last, the more team members assert themselves to engage with the team, the less likely the team will stall from the inertia that can come virtually.

Handles Differences Well

You want people who are able to deal directly with opportunities, issues, challenges, and conflicts. Proactive outreach is indispensable in a virtual environment where it is too easy to avoid issues until it is too late. Team agreements help avoid unnecessary conflict, but some conflict is needed to test and improve team outcomes. It helps to select team members who are able to disagree and debate—without being disagreeable.

Relationship intelligence combines the multiple intelligences of Howard Gardner[3] and Albert Bandura's[4] social learning theory and can't be overemphasized. Look for people who know themselves and their impact on others. Team players take care, genuinely feeling empathy and showing compassion for others.

Knows the Organization

Even though virtual team members will not be in the corporate office, they are, nonetheless, members of an organization bigger than themselves. Contractually, they take on the rights and responsibilities of that membership. Knowing her rights and responsibilities, plus the informal "lay of the land," increases a sense of belonging and purpose for the individual new member. New team members spend significant energy figuring out how to find what they need, who to turn to for what, and how to best fit in. If joining members are not already familiar with the organization, your team will need to bring them on board quickly. This includes helping people learn informal norms and political realities. Coach team members to navigate the organization for personal and company success.

Candidates' organization knowledge can be a value-add to your team. Connectors are skilled at and fluid in crossing boundaries and building bridges, becoming nodes of influence. Having connectors on your team broadens access to resources and synergies because of their already existing high-trust relationships.

Essential Characteristics and Qualities

Takes Initiative

Virtual employees must be able to work without the reassurance of others or constant feedback. The best virtual performers are those who enjoy working alone *and* with others. They are action oriented. You want virtual team members who confidently reach out to the team when needed and confidently act on behalf of the team when needed.

Is Open

Paradoxically, your ideal candidate is both independent and open to collaboration. It's a myth that the independent virtual team member is any less committed to the team than colocated employees who see their teammates every day. In my work, I've found people believe that introverts make the best home-based workers. What I've found in reality, however, is that both extroverts and introverts succeed virtually. In fact, extroverts may have a slight edge because they naturally seek interaction across time and distance and seek out relationships.

I've also seen extroverts and introverts fail virtually. Just because someone works independently and virtually does not mean she operates in a vacuum. There are times when reaching out is required. Virtual team members open up to the team, seeking collaboration when appropriate, not letting personal tendencies or distance isolate them.

Is Adaptable

When I wrote the first edition of this book, *adaptability* was *highly desirable*. Today it is *essential*. A distributed work environment does have its challenges that require quick adjustments. Networks go down. Technology malfunctions. Customer crises emerge while you're in the field. Plans and schedules change. You want team members who are able to anticipate, plan for, and flex with issues and delays. The more comfortable people are with the unexpected, the more comfortable they will be in a virtual environment.

Has Integrity

Doing what we say we will do is probably the biggest contributor to developing team trust, critical to a high-performance virtual team. Meeting deadlines and achieving quality standards with little supervision are essential. Teams with integrity follow through and communicate clearly when anything interferes. People own mistakes and seek solutions.

Is Committed

Feeling a sense of "ownership" in a project and the team brings a sense of belonging and shared responsibility. Being committed to and seeking achievement for self *and* the team help individuals connect emotionally. It takes an emotional connection to get past virtual isolation issues, which can be debilitating for some.

Desirable Characteristics and Qualities

Is Resourceful

There is a correlation between candidate resourcefulness and access to a trusted network. One key to career success is our ability to build a personal professional network that helps us know more, by proxy, than we can on our own. LinkedIn, for example, is not just a career-building platform; it's a place to find and engage with professional communities and continue our learning. Selecting candidates with an existing network might be helpful. Current HR big data tools are, in fact, often examining employees' social network activity as part of their talent research analytics. Ask the candidate about his or her resourcefulness specifically, and listen for whether the candidate seeks outside input, such as through professional connections.

Sets Boundaries

It is not uncommon for the telecommuter to become the neighborhood UPS and FedEx delivery stop. Until the household and neighbors are "trained," family and friends may unwittingly assume that if someone is home, he or she is available. Boundaries for household situations help virtual workers stay productive and focused. Team members who cannot say no may spread themselves too thin. I have a neighbor who still gets my voice mail 80% of the time because she calls during my workday. She sees my cars and knows I'm home, unable to grasp my world. It's okay, but voice mail has become a time management tool for me.

Virtual employees also need to set boundaries with work colleagues, household members, customers, and managers. Disorganized or crisis-driven virtual teams can pull virtual teammates into work more frequently and create more stress than is really needed.

Being available at all hours and all places is creeping into work consciousness today with smart technology keeping us connected 24/7. It leads to burnout and work addiction. Everyone—virtual or not—has the right and responsibility to be unavailable sometimes.

Self-Starts and Self-Stops

The previous quality focused on managing external boundaries. It is equally important to manage our internal boundaries. If you are the kind of person who has a hard time getting started in the morning, "going to the office" naturally helps to get into work mode. For a teleworker, that structure isn't there. Interview candidates about how they create "get-to-work" rituals, or help them create some.

What I have found more often, however, is that people have difficulty stopping the workday. Virtual workers stop distinguishing between work and home: "I just want to check e-mail one more time before we watch that movie." Two hours later . . . Workweeks in the United States have reached an average of 50 to 70 hours a week. Work addiction is at an all-time high, even though we don't often call it out. If virtual workers aren't careful, they find themselves "selling their souls to the company store." Most of us don't even recognize when we're doing it since work is ubiquitous. You don't want burned-out teams.

Is Focused

The very structure of a "workplace" is missing for the teleworker. The traditional office helps people to focus on work. Outside the traditional environment, it is imperative that the virtual team member be able to create and maintain his or her own structure and discipline.

Other Factors to Consider

Home Work Environment

Virtual team members are not all home based, but for those who are, a separate and sacred work environment is important. Making room on the corner of a dining room table is not conducive to a sustainable work focus. Virtual workers need a safe, ergonomically suited, and well-ventilated and well-lit work environment that is away from household activity. A phone- or terminal-based worker does not require much space and could even use a corner in a spare bedroom. For other workers, it may mean a room set aside with desk space, computer station, filing cabinets, storage areas, and room for peripheral devices, like printers and scanners—and a door. Help team members consider how much space is needed, what safety requirements must be met, and whether this space is removed enough from household traffic to provide adequate work focus and sufficient work-home separation.

Connectivity

Equipment, telephony, and Internet access and broadband speed requirements will vary depending on the job requirements. Virtual workers need to ensure that their virtual offices are located where reliable connectivity (at the needed bandwidth) is no barrier. The household itself needs to be able to handle increased bandwidth demands.

With these criteria in mind, you are in a better position to assess the appropriateness of each virtual team candidate.

Three Virtual Team Responsibilities

Everyone shares responsibility for the team. High-performing virtual team members play three additional roles to ensure effective collaboration and high performance. Select team members who agree that *everyone* does the following.

1. Manages the Team

All team members co-manage healthy group functioning. This is even more critical in a virtual team. For all virtual teams, spend time explicitly defining and negotiating expectations in a virtual environment, and how the team holds itself accountable.

Colocated team members don't typically think of themselves as managers. It's easier to let the colocated environment carry the burden for clarity, information sharing, and team functioning. Traditional work environments don't guarantee good communication, but the chances are greater that everyone will hear what they need to hear and share what needs sharing just by virtue of everyone being in the same place. The office environment helps facilitate the process of communication.

In a virtual environment, unless *everyone* clearly takes responsibility for communication and feedback loops, *communication will break down*. Every team member, regardless of job description, is responsible to co-manage the team's effectiveness. Luckily, because it is a virtual environment, people take the process of maintaining healthy teams more seriously. Because they don't see each other often, they are more inclined to ask, "What did you do today? What's happening in your life? What have you learned recently? What do I need to know?"

Communication breakdowns still happen, unintentionally. It doesn't change the potential fallout, however. A significant percentage of company information sharing occurs naturally and accidentally by overhearing or being in the right place at the right time.

Remove the literal "watercooler," and see how much communication occurred this way (and, by extension, how much the virtual worker misses out without informal conversation). Intentional communication channels must be re-created virtually. I know how it feels to be left out of the communication loop. I know how it feels to be angry and feel like someone let me down—my teammate, my team lead, the human resources department, the account manager. In a virtual team, it's not going to do anyone any good to withdraw or point fingers. Everyone has to take a shared responsibility for making sure to clean up issues quickly, and ensure that no one is out of sight or out of mind.

People in general, in a business environment, want to focus on the work. Teams don't need everybody to like each other, but in a virtual work environment, people need to proactively communicate and remedy misunderstandings before they lead to unnecessary conflict.

2. Coaches and Learns

Some communication protocols are needed, and they will change as the team develops. Who will manage team routines? How will audio conference notes be captured and summarized, stored, and retrieved? Who is expected to read them later? Who will onboard new team members to what aspects of the work and the team? These and other responsibilities can be assigned, delegated, and rotated based on logic, or remain with the team leader. How they are delegated is not as important as that the team learns and adapts as needed.

3. Advocates

Whether virtual or not, team members share responsibility for helping fellow team members succeed. In a virtual environment, the team leader takes on additional responsibility to advocate, especially when virtual teams are primarily temporary teams. Team leaders can anticipate and design rotation schedules and stretch projects to expose virtual team members to the larger organization. Team members hopefully want to be actively involved in creating opportunities. When a team is ending or a team member's role is ending, work with the team member and the organization to create a successful transition to another meaningful project.

Organizations are political, and if not careful, virtual team members are at a career disadvantage. Celebrate the team's accomplishments and broadcast good news. Ensure that individual contribution is recognized within the team and in the larger organization. Ideally the company's talent management process is prepared to seek and find virtual workers who aren't obviously on a visible fast track. Help find other opportunities that will progress members' careers. Advocate for your team members. High-performing teams advocate for each other willingly, especially when they see their leader doing so.

In building your team, once you've identified candidates who meet the job requirements, assess them against these characteristics and competencies. You'll choose people who fit a virtually collaborative team culture. Before your team can effectively come together, however, the individuals you have selected will still need some help to become a team. Let's bring the team together and begin walking the First Path, the development path, in the next chapter.

Notes

1. "Employers and Skills? What Does It Mean to Be Employable," Limerick Institute of Technology, accessed August 14, 2015, http://193.1.88.47/careers/units/unit-s029.shtml

2. "JIT Definition," www.wisegeek.com/what-is-just-in-time-training.htm#didyouknowout

3. "Emotional Intelligence," *Wikipedia*, last modified September 15, 2015, https://en.wikipedia.org/wiki/Emotional_intelligence

4. "Social Learning Theory," *Wikipedia*, last modified August 14, 2015, https://en.wikipedia.org/wiki/Social_learning_theory

PART FOUR

THE THREEFOLD PATH OF HIGH-PERFORMANCE VIRTUAL TEAMS

"Coming together is beginning. Keeping together is progress. Working together is success."

—Henry Ford

"To die for the revolution is a one-shot deal; to live for the revolution means taking on the more difficult commitment of changing our day-to-day life patterns."

—Frances M. Beal

"As a leader, you can't control or determine how situations occur for others, but you do have a say."

—Dave Logan, *Three Laws of Performance*

THE FIRST PATH—DEVELOP YOUR TEAM

"Talent wins games, but teamwork and intelligence win championships."

—Michael Jordan

"Don't be afraid to take a big step if one is indicated. You can't cross a chasm in two small jumps."

—David Lloyd George

Teams Work Together Differently When Virtual

Technology gets most of the attention, but it's the changes in the way teams connect when working virtually that create new challenges for team leaders and members. As enterprises learn to manage dynamic complexity, virtual and blended teams are increasingly temporary. Team membership on multiple teams is common; frequent team switching is normal. Today's professional might be on one team for years. Another professional might be on a half dozen teams in as many years for the same or several different organizations. The higher up in the hierarchy team members are, the more likely they are on multiple teams simultaneously. Perhaps they are a team leader on one team, a project champion on another, and a team member on a third.

The team you develop will be based on the cooperative principles of the Threefold Path to high performance. Member mobility across teams adds complexity to the virtual manager's job, but it also brings welcomed diversity with rolling team members. Serving on multiple teams broadens the worker's perspective about the organization. Hopefully, team members see their peers as collaborators rather than competition for the next promotion.

Team members' mobility within the same company helps corporate cultures evolve from competition toward collaboration. This critical mind shift must happen to fully leverage collaborative teamwork. Team members work best when they're complementary rather than competitive.

Traveling the First Path of High-Performance Virtual Teams

Today's work environment moves quickly, so the virtual leader has the responsibility for launching a new (or changing) team fast. Individuals go through stages of development when navigating from a traditional office to a virtual one. Teams as a group go through developmental changes as they learn to work together. The Threefold Path, as shown in Figure 10.1, provides a road map that you and your team can use to become high performers quickly.

This chapter describes the stages and decisions a team navigates in order to achieve a highly successful launch. It also defines the most important actions to take as a virtual leader that help teams launch quickly. The First Path for virtual teams is to develop your new team. Involve them right away. Whether a series of team development meetings or one launch meeting, being proactive in developing the team helps avoid unnecessary confusion and anxiety.

As one virtual team member shared in her interview:

> My coworkers all strive for good performance; they want to do a good job. Encouragement from leadership is lacking so being self-led and improving the team's work are not things that my coworkers attempt. Our team is in constant flux, so the core group dynamics are constantly changing. The composition of the core group is the only thing that doesn't change, as it is dependent on the CEO and president, who, by the way, rarely take input from us.

This virtual worker's team is underperforming through no fault of their own. Trusting that the manager is committed to the team facilitates fast development. The next section explores how to structure virtual trust and expand emotional bandwidth until genuine team relationships form. This chapter lays the groundwork for developing team agreements, structure for work flow, and communication.

Stages of Team Development

Permanent teams are often functional departments that work closely with other departments. Most organizations have project teams and

Figure 10.1. The Threefold Path for high-performance teams.

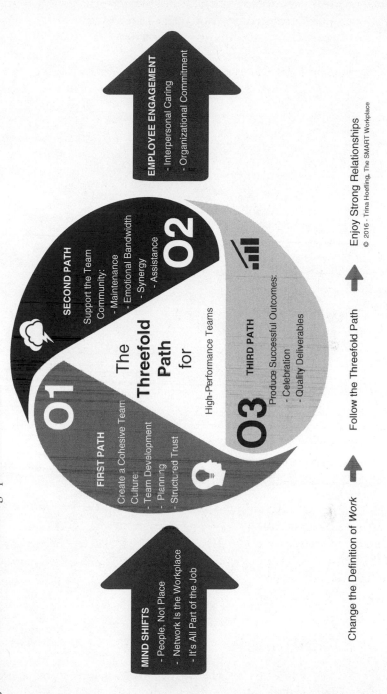

EMPLOYEE ENGAGEMENT
- Interpersonal Caring
- Organizational Commitment

SECOND PATH
Support the Team Community:
- Maintenance
- Emotional Bandwidth
- Synergy
- Assistance

O2

The Threefold Path for

FIRST PATH
Create a Cohesive Team Culture:
- Team Development
- Planning
- Structured Trust

O1

THIRD PATH
Produce Successful Outcomes:
- Celebration
- Quality Deliverables

O3

High-Performance Teams

MIND SHIFTS
- People, Not Place
- Network Is the Workplace
- It's All Part of the Job

Change the Definition of *Work*

Follow the Threefold Path

Enjoy Strong Relationships

© 2016 - Trina Hoefling, The SMART Workplace

cross-departmental teams. This means team members are moving around inside the enterprise, joining teams in different combinations.

Despite the advantages of team member mobility, the synergy of high-performing teams gets disrupted each time. This is why workers adapt better when they have professional relationships that extend beyond their everyday workmates. Professional networks are not just for job seeking, friendship, and resource finding. Fast-performance teams typically establish swift trust and team agreements more easily when members know each other by reputation at least, if not previous experience. Teams become productive more quickly because they are building on existing relationships. Temporary virtual teams go through the same predictable stages of team development and functioning. They experience end stages because they know they are impermanent.

Despite the virtual leader's best intentions, often a team will hit a wall before fully settling into performance. This happens in multiple ways—collective frustration at the perceived lack of organizational support, interpersonal conflict, task or role confusion, feelings of isolation, or some other obstacle. Good planning, an observant "virtual eye," and swift intervention as the virtual leader keep the team developing and improving. Help the team quickly settle into sustainable performance.

Teams go through up to six predictable development stages. Only high-performing teams achieve the fourth stage, where you want your team to "live" most of the time.

Forming

You chose these people to be on your team for a reason. Communicate why each team member was selected. Share strengths and passions. The team needs real agreements. Structure ways for the team to learn about each other, the team's goal and mission, the agreements and plans. This is a polite phase, so facilitate honest conversation by being a role model.

Storming

Inevitable disagreements and misunderstandings will surface. Patience can run short when the team needs tolerance to get past politeness. However, the team can become stronger, more versatile, and able to work better together. Some teams never evolve past this stage, but yours can and will. The virtual leader's focus is to hold firmly to the team's work focus while facilitating the working out of differences.

Some conflict is necessary to help the team build its muscle. Have small team deliverables due near the beginning of the virtual team's tenure.

Norming

The agreements and planning settle in as the team normalizes. Members establish their rhythms and flows, and team agreements need little adjustment. Genuine norming sets the stage for the performing stage. Most teams reach this stage of development and work fairly well. The risk to watch for is that members are so focused on avoiding conflict that they are accommodating the norms more than authentically finding team rhythms that work for everyone. This is necessary to grow to the next stage.

Performing

This is a team working well and able to course-correct. Anyone who has been a member of a high-performing team knows viscerally the difference between a normed team and a high-performing team.[1]

Renorming

Work environments will change. The team gets a new manager, members roll off, and new members join a team. Ongoing teams will go through a period of adjustment.

Adjourning

Transforming and mourning team dissolution are the last stage for temporary teams. As more teams are time-dated, temporary, or project teams, saying good-bye brings healthy closure. Help people adjourn with celebrations at the completion of the project and provide assistance for redeployment onto other teams in the future.[2]

Commit to Front-End Planning

A structured team development process is a highly effective way to get a virtual team started right. If possible, bring the team together in person, especially if these are people who don't know each other or who are unfamiliar with virtual teaming.

Combine virtual and on-site collaboration early in the team formation, if not ongoing. Conduct initial one-on-one and team meetings. Let the team know that this team will function virtually. Leave room to define together what collaboration guidelines will be critical to the team's success. You may provide training on the tools and want to reinforce their usage. Move forward steadily until everyone is clearly committed and confident, working together virtually.

Time together doing team planning saves time later, guaranteed. If it's not possible to meet face-to-face for a day or two, plan to get acquainted virtually through team communication channels, such as chat rooms and web conferences. Schedule multiple online two-hour team conferences to complete the team development process with clear agendas for each session. It's more challenging to stay fully present for a full-day meeting when virtual, so break into smaller sessions. If you will be facilitating virtual team meetings, download this book's free how-to bonus chapter on virtual meeting management.[3]

Face-to-face interaction always helps teams form fast, and the team development process is ideal to launch in person. Include support functions and key stakeholders appropriately in sections of your virtual team development sessions in order to build relationships important to the team. Confirm project expectations and deliverables and establish stakeholder communication. Use this time to agree on how the team wants to be supported, managed, and evaluated. If the team isn't familiar with the project and task management system, educate the members about how to simplify their work and collaborate with the team. Structure communication, feedback, and follow-up in partnership with the tools. (Don't forget that paper, pencil, and scissors are viable tools, too.)

Team Charter and Parameters

Launch the team with a discussion about the underlying principles that will guide them as they prioritize and decide, engage and behave, work and produce. This leader discussion is more clarification than it is a negotiation. Review and confirm team member understanding and agreement about the following:

- Team purpose/project justification (problem or opportunity addressed)
- Reorganization and stakeholder expectations
- Team goals and deliverables
- Success criteria (including project metrics such as schedule, cost, quality, innovations, and improvements)
- Deadlines and milestones
- Scope and authority of team, roles, and team influence
- Metrics, team evaluation, compensation, and recognition
- Scope management issues (including ways that scope changes will be handled and contract change orders will be processed)

Work Flow and Coordination, Processes and Procedures

Technology is the enabler, so enterprise policies regarding collaboration tools will dictate much of how work is completed. The virtual team has choices about how to adapt the organization's processes to fit its needs. Develop as few or as many group guidelines as the team needs, but commit to using them.

Customized Collaboration

Define common language to simplify understanding and ensure shared meaning. When you can, use few methodologies and processes to keep it simple. For example, I'm on the Virtual Workplace University design team. We use only a few tools. We use Google+ for our team communication and home office. We decided against task management apps, such as Wunderlist and Asana, because our customer management tool, Insightly, includes a robust task management application for our team needs.

Decision-Making

Start by surfacing criteria for both project decisions and emerging team needs. Create and commit to the way the team will inform and involve one another and relevant stakeholders, especially if the project scope shifts and different decisions are required.

Communication

Decide team availability (work hours, time zone, emergency and off-hour availability). Set meeting requirements, attendance options (virtual or in-person), and schedule protocols. Think through what the group uses to verify shared understanding, formally and informally. Anticipate when and where the team needs to influence, and coordinate communication accordingly. Remember to incorporate multiple or shifting team members' needs into communication. This is discussed more fully in chapters 11 and 12, the communication and tools chapters.

Team Dynamics and Engagement

The virtual manager is not the only person who can support the team; everyone shares responsibility for keeping the team on track. Develop interpersonal relationships individually with team members. Encourage the team to do the same. Aim for fair division of team caretaking labor. Share responsibility for getting the team back on track if virtuality becomes a problem.

Acknowledge occupational and cultural differences, while developing the team's culture. Talk during team formation about what would create commitment. While together, take a team picture and encourage team members to upload it to their computer's wallpaper or screensaver. Listen for metaphors and team anchors that emerge during launch sessions. Use them so everyone can reference the metaphors and anchor the team's way of thinking of itself as a team. Basically, attend vigilantly to the team's need to be connected to one another during and after the team launch. The team may not think it matters, but you know better.

Team Agreements

Help team members agree on how they will work with one another. Set expectations while you facilitate team development. Individuals need to know they will be evaluated not only on their expertise and end product but also on their ability to meet the social contract of the team and the organization.

As you develop team agreements, you want team members who will perpetuate the team's well-being. The team's ability to weather storms helps solidify team power and influence in the larger organization, and political maneuverability. Team members who span boundaries as representatives of the team help seed functional integration and innovation for and beyond the team.

Team agreements serve an immediate purpose—to develop the team's influence and respect with and on behalf of each other. Determine the team's preferences and differences, and then negotiate shared agreements about team functioning, such as the following:

- Participation and availability to the team (as already mentioned)
- Loyalty and commitments
- Representation in the larger organization
- Team values (e.g., does your team value sharing over secrecy?)
- Accountability and peer management
- Slippage and scope adjustments
- Conflict and disagreement
- Tone and how team members talk to one another

Team Development Planning Agenda

Your team's launch and development should cover six factors. How detailed you get is up to you and what your team needs. A complete checklist detailing the six factors is available for download, including starter questions to consider when building your team's development plan. Use it as is, modify it, simplify it, and improve it.[4]

The six factors anticipate essential areas of team functioning that are impacted in a virtual environment. Negotiate each area with your virtual team, and review the agreements when a new member joins the team. By facilitating team development, you will have a team charter, a project plan, agreements, and communication protocols in place.

The Six Factors of Team Launch and Development

1. *Getting acquainted*: Getting to know the team members
2. *Team charter, vision, values*: Governance
3. *Team/project planning*: Project planning is the time to confirm project goals, identify resources, set milestones and deliverable deadlines, and delineate everyone's roles and responsibilities; also the time to decide how to share and embed learning, team norms, and team reflection time
4. *Team processes*: Determine how you will ensure the team functions effectively together as a collective
5. *Communication and collaboration tool infrastructure*: The subject of chapters 11 and 12
6. *Membership and maintenance*

Facilitating a team development process implies a promise to your team. You are promising to lead in certain ways based on shared agreements and an understanding of what you came together to do. The plan your team creates provides a basic structure for action that brings forth a new future together. Since the future is essentially unknowable, your team has taken its first big step in cocreating itself. The First Path of high-performance virtual teams has been laid. It's time to live up to the team promise by building the Second Path.

Notes

1. "Tuckman's Stages of Group Development," *Wikipedia*, last modified September 6, 2015, https://en.wikipedia.org/wiki/Tuckman%27s_stages_of_group_development

2. Another, less well-known team development model is the Drexler/Sibbet Team Performance Model. It illustrates team development as seven stages, four to create the team and three to describe increasing levels of sustained performance. It also works well as a development model for virtual teams. "Drexler/Sibbet Team Performance™ Model," The Grove, accessed August 14, 2015, www.grove.com/ourwk_gm_tp.html

3. Download free at www.WorkingVirtually.org

4. All downloads (management aids and assessments) are available at www.WorkingVirtually.org

THE SECOND PATH—
SUPPORT YOUR TEAM

*"I reject the Great Man theory. . . . We make each other better every time we operate together. . . .
It's most important to get the team to believe in a common effort and a common cause. It takes a
group of people who believe, moving in the right direction. You don't become committed to a task,
you become committed to each other."*

—General Stanley McChrystal, *Team of Teams*

"I'd have done anything for that man."

—General Bill Garrison, General McChrystal's teammate

"We all do better when we all do better."

—Paul Wellstone

ngaging and supporting people are the work of the Second Path.
Establish communication protocols that help teams relate well and
perform at their best. "Good communication" isn't enough to achieve
virtual team synergy. One reason virtual groups fail to become performing
teams is that we fail to remember that most work gets done through relationship, not task. Peter Drucker reminds us,

> We are not going to breed a new race of supermen. We will have to run our
> organizations with people as they are. . . . The essence of management is to
> make [people and their expertise] productive. *Management, in other words,
> is a social function.*[1]

Teamwork Is Fundamentally Social, Regardless of Whether the Team Is Virtual

The virtual leader is the lead pathfinder for her team's success on the threefold path. As you can see in Figure 11.1, the Second Path of high-performance virtual teams is one of team support.

Unless you are managing a henhouse, *you do not want to be your team's primary relationship at work*. All team leaders, virtual or not, support their team by unleashing talent, connecting to resources, and removing obstacles. *Good* virtual leaders also facilitate opportunities for team members to expand emotional bandwidth with one another, especially virtually. *Great* virtual leaders are servant leaders, facilitators who become the invisible glue that connects people to the organization until they develop their own relationships.

What if you could unleash the agility and cohesion of a high-performance team? It takes time to become a trusted, collaborative "value node" in the larger system. The virtual leader sets the standard and guides the team. Start by being an entrusted, collaborative team supporter. Then nudge the teams to continuous improvement and innovation. Reinforce team-balancing behaviors that produce exceptional flows, pathways, and rhythms. Support happens when everyone is doing the work of work.

The Virtual Manager as Facilitator and Servant Leader

Servant leadership[2] was first defined in 1970 and further developed by many leadership masters like Peter Block and Adam Grant, author of *Give and Take: Why Helping Others Drives Our Success*.[3] Servant leadership tenets reflect the qualities needed in a virtual team leader. They stand strong as guiding principles for all virtual leaders:

> Servant leaders are the beneficiaries of important contacts, information, and insights that make them more effective and productive in what they do even though they spend a great deal of their time sharing what they learn and helping others through such things as career counseling, suggesting contacts, and recommending new ways of doing things.[4]

Servant leadership is not an altruistic act. Servant leaders are value nodes, connectors for the team and organization. Valuable connectors think of their own careers and work commitments *while also* thinking of the organization and team's needs. They function as chief team advocate. Very little we accomplish is truly ours, but the result of a team. Team leaders, when the most powerful and effective, know this and are servants to the team's effectiveness.

Figure 11.1. The Threefold Path for high-performance teams.

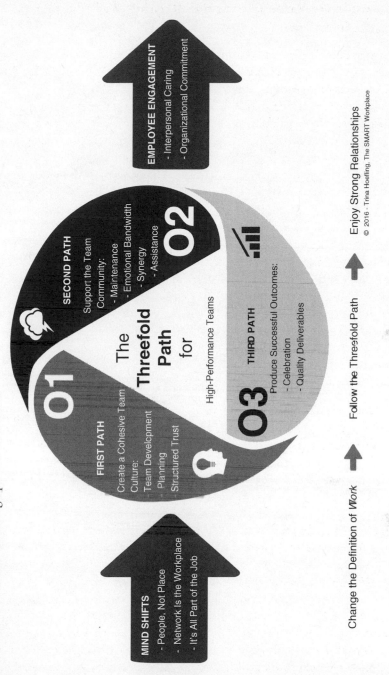

MIND SHIFTS
- People, Not Place
- Network Is the Workplace
- It's All Part of the Job

01 FIRST PATH
Create a Cohesive Team
Culture:
- Team Development
- Planning
- Structured Trust

02 SECOND PATH
Support the Team
Community:
- Maintenance
- Emotional Bandwidth
- Synergy
- Assistance

The Threefold Path for
High-Performance Teams

03 THIRD PATH
Produce Successful Outcomes:
- Celebration
- Quality Deliverables

EMPLOYEE ENGAGEMENT
- Interpersonal Caring
- Organizational Commitment

Change the Definition of *Work* Follow the Threefold Path Enjoy Strong Relationships

Team advocacy begins with member selection. You want to uncover candidates who demonstrate cooperation during the interview, as we discussed earlier. If you have a team member who isn't open with the team, coach him off quickly.

Noncollaborators do not thrive on healthy teams; being a service-oriented team works only when mutual. Being of service does not mean accepting poor performance or disrespect. Sometimes the team will see poor team play sooner than the manager. If the team is performing, the members will often manage the problem themselves. Aim for that kind of self-directed virtual team.

Teamwork First

Jeff Bewkes, chair and CEO of Time Warner, insists the most important workplace competency is teamwork. "You have to know how to work with others who want to work with you. It's probably the crucial skill and yet education is mostly about solo performances."[5] Best-selling leadership books perpetuate the myth of the lone hero. Even heroes rely on their teams for execution. An outlier in leadership literature, respected U.S. military leader General Stanley McChrystal wrote a book called *Team of Teams*.[6] He found the lone hero myth crumbled quickly to a more accurate truth—it takes a "team of teams." Since work gets done through others, we all benefit from continuously getting better at building and supporting teams.

Can a Virtual Team Have a Home Court Advantage?

Where does the team gather digitally? In a virtual environment, take extra time to give everyone a sense of "place," a sense of a home community. MIT professor and architect Kevin Lynch[7] asked community residents to draw a map of how their home city was laid out, from memory. Several elements helped people make sense of where they live—physical markers like a town square, for example. A virtual team doesn't have the familiar elements of an office to anchor its sense of place—no statue or flag in front, no hallways or break rooms, no departments sitting together, no executive suite. The team has to re-create a sense of place, on the network. Here are a few elements of community to re-create virtually:

- *Landmarks*: Provide context, reference points, logos and other items that support self-identification with the team and organization community.

- *Paths and edges*: Help your team walk the virtual hallways of the organization and learn where the less obvious boundaries and edges might be. Discuss politics and cultural norms that may not be obvious to a virtual worker. Map the connections of the organization for your team.
- *Districts*: We don't walk down the hall and around Legal to get to Accounting anymore. Departments are the metaphorical districts of a community. They still exist virtually, but the boundaries aren't as obvious. Again, map the virtual territory for your team members, and have them help improve the map as they foray into the districts and discover new paths.
- *Nodes*: Information has always been power. Today it's about sharing, not hoarding. Hoarders stop flow, are the opposite of connecting nodes, and eventually lose value to the organization.

However you integrate the team's way of working and coordination, prioritize one digital team hub that will host a dashboard, team directory, virtual watercooler—a team home place to gather and become a community.

Rhythms and Flows

Mihaly Csikszentmihalyi,[8] positive psychology master, defined *flow* as that timeless mental state of focused effort that brings the joy and power of *being in the zone*. Repeating that timeless flow state helps people create flow state habits, making it easier to jump-start flow on demand. Teams can be conditioned for flow as well. To get to flow states, teams establish rhythms and flows, repeatable habits and routines. They create the conditions for people to quickly and naturally jump into team flow.

Four Flow Starters to Guide the Virtual Manager

1. Give the team influence.
2. Make the work intrinsically rewarding by deploying to strength and passion.
3. Set up and use multiple sources of feedback, including project and task management tools.
4. Help team members protect their space for focus without interruption.

Rhythms

Rhythms are organic. They are the natural connecting and interdependent activities that bring teams together and apart in routines and habits that are easy and repeated. They keep people informed and flowing individually and as a team community.

Knowing and Caring Help Us Want to Stick Around!

People are more willing to help each other when they *know* one another. We *want* to help people we like. Facilitate relationships as well as meetings, projects, and performance; help the team develop bonds and be able to give direct feedback to one another.

If managers and teammates display confidence in each other, workers feel trusted and valued, and they are more likely to hold their own work to higher standards. If every team member has confidence in his or her work and knows it is valued, *the team will synergize*. When everyone can relate to one another, they are better able to collaborate virtually.

People also tend to attach to people with whom they share common ground. A team certainly qualifies as common work ground. Commitment is deepened when the team actually feels that it is a "community" with shared purpose, responsibilities, rituals and habits, successes and challenges, stories, symbols, brand, and history. It's easy to jump into teamwork without first taking precious time for team development. Don't skip developing your team (First Path) if you want your team to be supportive and supported (Second Path)!

A virtual team manager needs to help the team intentionally develop shared experience together. Out of shared experience, people come to know one another and, hopefully, respect each other enough to trust the team. Not everyone may like each other, but the goal is to grow enough team commitment so that everyone extends support to the whole.

Keep the Conversations Going

In virtual teams, we often ask team members to trust one another and become interdependent, sometimes sight unseen. Trust is tentatively given; *it's not guaranteed to continue*. We give it temporarily until experience proves the trust is deserved. Research shows that virtual teams maintain high trust through social communication interweaved with task-based conversations.

Virtual managers have to facilitate the team's talk, at least at first. Conversations are an irreplaceable way that relationships develop. Trust grows or declines, and collaboration happens. Small talk actually improves social intelligence, especially as people get to know each other. Chitchat gives everyone a chance to get familiar with each other's style. Some people are more naturally animated or reactive. To know that helps the team recognize when something is off, when behavior is out of the ordinary *for that person*.[9]

High-performance teams talk, a lot. Much informal learning occurs through conversation. Getting people talking about something they care about gives conversations passion and opens a path for easy sharing. A good conversation is a gestalt—it creates something bigger than the sum of its parts. "Talking" explores new territory and creates new understandings, especially if the team gets past the download and debate style of communication so common at work.

People hanging around and talking isn't a distraction. It's the work of collaboration.

If it isn't happening, the virtual leader's job is to stir things up and get tongues wagging and fingers smoking on the keyboards. Talk about the game last night (NBA play-offs are going on as I write this). Ask Mary how her minitriathlon went last week. Invite cooking aficionados to share recipes.

Pointers for a Conversation-Rich Team

- Remember that a team leader does not need to be aware of all conversations going on. You don't have the time.
- If you have team members working together on a project, ask about each other's perspective on it.
- Invite responses to a question or issue in an online team conversation.
- Get a discussion going simply for exploration, not decision.
- Remind people to speak directly to one another. Especially if there is tension among team members, encourage them to "send the mail to the right address."
- Assume the team is communicating. Expect people to be aware of each other's contributions when asking about the project. Verify with simple questions in your one-on-ones, such as, "When you spoke to Carol last, did she have any insight?"

Realize each meeting, e-mail, phone call, and IM becomes a stream of interrelated business conversations that impact team relationships. Conversation is part of the team's work—encourage it. People are shyer virtually. As one coaching client shared,

It's more difficult for me when I don't know the other members or don't know them very well. I often feel like I'm not participating enough for fear of being too pushy or overbearing. I sometimes don't contribute to the discussion because I often feel like an outsider.

Facilitate!

Create Stories Together

The team must come together in real time to maintain emotional band-width. It takes time for the team's culture to form, a curation of experiences and stories, norms, shared rituals, repeated interactions, and fun. That can't happen if the manager doesn't provide opportunities to meet—both face-to-face and digitally. Even henhouses benefit from together time once in a while. Shared experience creates shared stories. Shared stories deepen bonds.

How Do You Spell Relief?

Support is more than interpersonal connection. Practical helping hands are extended on a supportive virtual team. Ever had one of those days? The project is offtrack and behind schedule, the children are sick, the customer is cranky, and the network has gone down twice. These are the days when teammates become friends, when the delivered pizza is so appreciated.

In the team development session, discuss how to handle expected chal-lenges like technical access issues and dependent care surprises. One of the benefits of being on a team is being able to support one another. That doesn't change virtually.

Interpersonal support doesn't have to be driven by crisis. Knowing each other allows for team give-and-take. Some people like to be more fully informed; others prefer to have information on a need-to-know basis. It gets more complicated when one person's need-to-know looks different from another's desire for autonomy. Not getting clear with one another about interpersonal needs and preferences can push patience to the limit.

Most of us know that commitment on a team is desirable but not guar-anteed. If issues continue or crop up often, go back to the First Path, team development, to uncover what's derailing synergy. Even the best team will launch without anticipating every need, so continue to ask, "What does full support look like for this team?" The answer depends on organizational cul-ture to some degree, but also, more importantly, the interpersonal prefer-ences of the team members themselves and the work requirements, of course.

On challenging days when the strength of the team's emotional band-width holds up (or doesn't), look for ways to make ongoing support easier. It may be difficult for people to call a team member they barely know and ask for help. Facilitate it at first.

Of course, you want a team that doesn't need to structure kindness, but structure it anyway until genuine care is the team norm. Compassion at work is not automatic, or at least obvious. Approximately 66% of team members in a recent survey stated they would "extend more effort if my supervisor

TABLE 11.1
Compassionate Teams

Compassionate Team Guidelines
1. Take the other person's perspective.
2. Be available to listen.
3. Remember a time when . . .

listened to me and cared." The Saratoga Institute found that 80% of employees left their previous position because of an "undesirable relationship with someone at work."[10] Genuine compassion comes through, but some people need a little coaching in compassion.

Three Compassionate Behaviors

The following are three ways to practice compassion, as shown in Table 11.1

1. *Take the other person's perspective:* No one has to adopt anyone else's beliefs or values, but to work well on a team, people have to be able to put themselves in another's shoes. When we truly understand where another is coming from, we become less judgmental.
2. *Be available to listen:* Unless a team member is offline and checked out, the team should be available to help one another, as should the virtual leader. Often this simply means listening as a teammate thinks out loud.
3. *Remember a time when . . . :* When it's hard to appreciate someone else's struggle, remember a time when you were tired, confused, unhinged, or discouraged. I like this reminder from Brene Brown in *Daring Greatly*: "When I judge myself for asking for help, I can't offer help to others without judging them."[11]

Virtual Storming—Feel the Static in the Air?

Have you ever been on a conference call when something was obviously being said "between the lines"? Have you noticed sudden changes in the tone of e-mails from a colleague in the length and frequency of channel posts? These can be signs the team is moving into the storming stage. This is a challenging time. It takes effort and energy on everyone's part. Storming is particularly risky in new virtual teams.

"Well-facilitated conflictual conversations can open the team to rewriting its future together," shared one virtual team member I coached recently. She's right, but avoiding conflict at work has become an art form for many.

It seems noble to avoid conflict, but avoidance often fans flames, resulting in more strife and keeping teams functioning less than optimally. Often political or polite behavior stifles flow. *Teams need dynamic tension to be fully learning.*

Every group that develops into a team negotiates and renegotiates. Its work agreements are the foundation that recommits the team. As the team begins to live its agreements, important and meaningful feedback will hone and adjust the team members over days and weeks. The storming stage of team development can be a scary time, or it can be a curious discovery process. More conversations about the adjustment period ease the path through storming.

Invite team members to ask questions about the team's process. Note observations and bring them to the team as feedback. "What new understanding did we get about the role we play in the value chain? What information do we need that we don't have? What issues continue to take our attention? What did we try this week that has made work easier?"

Instead of focusing on what's wrong, help the team focus on improvement. An appreciative inquiry into how the team is doing, especially in the early weeks, helps members let go of old habits that just won't work with this team.

There's no need to keep circling the wagons. Don't drag it out: Discuss, agree—done. It's time to get real, see things and people as they are, adjust, and get on with it. I've seen too many virtual managers let the team indulge too many individual habits and workarounds. Too much flexibility slows down synergistic team rhythms and flows. Team members can flex themselves into ineffectiveness and sucking up precious meeting time addressing preference disagreements.

Your team won't be perfect. (Your job probably isn't perfect either.) Strong leaders, regardless of title or role, lead from the team agreements. The team will normalize itself. Facilitate healthy norms during the storming phase before bad habits settle in.

Psychological Distance

Risk is high if you want a problem-solving team in a culture of blame and shame. Storming can stir blaming and protective behaviors. A blaming culture creates psychological distance, triggering protection, a human survival instinct. Social and geographic distance can add to a sense of isolation, a real vulnerability of virtual teams. Nip the blame game in the beginning by reframing conflicts into solution-finding or improvement conversations.

Virtual team members can feel isolated and not an integral part of the team. This is especially true when some team members work together in an office while others work virtually. Until your team is high performing, *you* are the primary link between the team and the organization. Initially you help link the team members to each other. Without regular contact, the virtual worker loses peripheral vision of what is occurring on the team and in the organization.

We are social creatures. In the movie *Castaway*,[12] Tom Hanks's character formed a friendship with his only island companion, a ball named Wilson. The world was created for "we," not "me." When Hanks's character had exciting news, he needed to tell somebody. Wilson, the inanimate object, became his "other." To help your virtual team feel like they are not talking to a ball, close psychological distance across the miles. In one-on-ones, talk about personal and professional goals, not just the team's work. Demonstrate you care. Develop your own virtual team support rhythms by scheduling simple things, such as sending birthday e-cards and promoting team successes. Be sure the right people are aware.

Recognition and appreciation are two very powerful motivators to bring the team closer psychologically, *and it makes people want to stick around.*

Renorm to Perform

A good team development process will serve the team, but that is not enough. Regularly review the norms and agreements, systems and tools, processes, and the team's well-being. Team and work needs shift naturally and often. Adjust and negotiate to better fit the team's emerging needs. Ask them what is working and what is not, and what they think needs to happen next. Are there common technology challenges that need additional support or training? Make modifications or recommitments to keep the team energized, cohesive, and balanced.

Remember that in most teams, trust has to be structured first. Find vehicles to "speed up" the familiarity period. Include face time.

Holding (Virtual) Space

The team exists, even when it isn't electronically or personally connected. Virtual team effectiveness is directly linked to nonwork-related, informal interaction that keeps the team connected between meetings. Team leaders hold the space for the group between getting together, ensuring that the sacred space continues regardless of who is currently "in the virtual room."

The lack of access to the atmosphere in a shared office workplace changes dramatically in a virtual environment. It's why virtual team communication must go beyond traditional communication. The leader needs to informally re-create the organization's atmosphere virtually. When in a colocated work office, the team room or "space" holds the energy of the group, forming a sort of container, just as a glass holds water or a pocket holds personal effects. Usually, remnants of previous meetings linger on the whiteboard; people walk in with their favorite coffee mugs, gravitating to the same chair at the table; habits breed familiarity, comfort, and a sense of belonging.

Virtual Teams Experience Energy Leaks

Distance does impact team energy, especially soon after a high-energy team session. It's as if the glass is tipped over if sacred virtual space isn't created and nurtured. The team needs help occasionally to keep the fires burning. When two team members have their heads together and hit a "Eureka!" moment, they need to run virtually to the whole group and share the excitement. Then. Not later. When a team member receives a special award, feature her in a podcast or press release. Develop a habit of posting fun and exciting news to a team dashboard or shared stream (similar to your Facebook timeline). Celebrate accomplishments as a team, even when dispersed. Celebrate again when you are face-to-face.

No team can be too spirited, whether virtual or colocated. Do a virtual jig. Send e-cards. Have fun. It's a good thing. Meet face-to-face and take a team picture to post on the team's dashboard. Post a map with everyone's locations. Use the "like" button in conversation channels. Schedule lunch with team members. Encourage team members who live near one another to join the same gym. Schedule more social time when you are face-to-face and facilitate virtual icebreakers before starting virtual meetings. Facilitate conversation starters while waiting for everyone to join the web conference. Make it about work if that's the culture, but get people to converse informally.

At the same time, energy cannot be at full throttle all the time, or the team would burn out. If the energetic ebb and flow aren't managed, the team risks too much dissipation virtually, resulting in lagging commitment and difficulty keeping focus. Practical mechanisms can help develop rhythms and flows that balance out the workweek. Make sure your team has known ways to reach out—quick communication channels and virtual watercoolers, like IM (instant messaging); open and ongoing chat rooms, like Skype and electronic dashboards; as well as virtual and face-to-face team meetings.

Check-Ins and Check Outs

Frequent check-ins should be the norm. Most of us don't know to ask for help as soon as we should, so check-ins help us get our heads up to look around a bit and breathe. Sometimes we need to check out. Burnout is high in corporate America, and virtual workers experience it at higher levels. Whether it's the thin boundary between work and home or the extra pressure some virtual workers feel to prove they're really working, checking out and unplugging should be mandated for all team members regularly. Help people refresh.

So Why Did Mayer Ban Telecommuting? Synergy and Innovation

"Communication and collaboration will be important. . . . Some of the best decisions and insights come from hallway and cafeteria discussions, meeting new people, and impromptu team meetings. . . . We need to be one Yahoo! and that starts with physically being together."

—Melissa Mayer, CEO, Yahoo!

Mayer's argument holds water. Yes, studies have found that employees, particularly employees in process-intense jobs, are more efficient when working from home. But employees are most *innovative* when they know each other and work together often. It turns out Mayer's declaration that communication is needed for collaboration wasn't so much about working virtually or not as it was about *building synergy*. Her choice was to build that synergy during turnaround by gathering the troops together physically.

Innovation is critical in most companies today, so the impact of virtual work on a team's creativity is relevant. Most innovation happens because of teamwork—communication and collaboration—whether in the office or virtually. The interplay of thoughtful face-to-face conversation is more natural and helps innovation take off. It can happen virtually also, but not until the team has synergized. Innovation happens more naturally, regardless of work environment, when a team thinks together, combining efforts and resources. Facilitate that kind of synergy and spark virtually, and you are on the Second Path of high-performance virtual teams.

Communicate Results

Words are powerful tools. Add one or two more sentences to every e-mail to expand emotional bandwidth. For instance, if someone has done something outstanding, call out the performance, and continue by saying, "And this is

exactly the kind of behavior we all want to see in order to reach our goals"—
it takes five seconds and it works. Always be looking for ways to reinforce
teamwork, to help team members have a sense of themselves as a team.

The Rolling Present: Entry, Exit, Reentry

One of the benefits of virtual work is that you can bring in new members
from anywhere as required by the project, although the challenge remains to
form a team quickly or add new members fast. Virtual teams do have a distinct advantage when onboarding new team members who enter or reenter
the team along the way. Much work is done asynchronously; thus, much is
documented and provides a history to review. On the other hand, the sheer
volume can be overwhelming. The team manager needs to help new team
members sort through the history for fast assimilation of knowledge. Here
are questions to guide team members who are rolling onto the team:

- What reference documents, history, strategic-planning documents,
  progress plans, and deliverable requirements do joining team members need to review? Can you create a static infographic road map, or
  will a more dynamic orientation be needed?
- Whom do joining team members need to talk to, and about what?
  Structure their onboarding plan.
- Who will serve as an orientation coach? A work buddy? Make it easy
  for people to know where/who is the first point of contact for what
  kind of help.
- How will new team members learn the operating norms of this team?
  Don't leave people to watch and learn through trial and error.
- How will new team members be introduced to the existing team?
  Hopefully, it won't be just before the new team member's first report
  out.

The informal aspect of rolling entry is more social. Minimally, conference virtually to introduce the new team member. Have the team share
in onboarding new members to the group's culture, metaphors, rhythms,
norms, and etiquette. Structure scheduled interviews between the new member and the rest of the team. You cannot fully replace the juicy human energy
that gets created with live conversation, so have live conversations.

The last act of the virtual manager is to prepare the team member for
exit, the next deployment. This may be as simple as a LinkedIn recommendation, but often also includes introductions and advocacy onto another

team. This kind of team support builds people's commitment to you even after they are no longer working for you.

At the End of the Day . . .

Everyone is busy processing information and demands moment to moment. In the midst of the busy, be a role model. Show caring and support for your team. Take just a few moments daily to reflect on the team's well-being, taking at least one action that helps a team member (and thereby the whole team). Others will follow your lead. The team is on its way to healthy norming and soon to performing. The few rough spots will be remedied with little disturbance to the overall efficiency and functioning of the virtual team that consistently and easily produces results, the Third Path of virtual management.

Notes

1. Zachary First, "Technology Changes, Good Management Doesn't," *Harvard Business Review*, Managing People, April 7, 2016, https://hbr.org/2016/04/technology-changes-good-management-doesnt

2. Home page, Greenleaf Center for Servant Leadership, http://www.greenleaf.org

3. Adam Grant, *Give and Take: Why Helping Others Drives Our Success* (New York: Penguin, 2014), www.giveandtake.com

4. James Heskett, "Why Isn't Servant Leadership More Prevalent?" *Forbes*, May 1, 2013, www.forbes.com/sites/hbsworkingknowledge/2013/05/01/why-isnt-servant-leadership-more-prevalent/

5. Quote taken from CNN interview, Fareed Zakaria GPS. Aired November 30, 2014. Transcript available at www.cnn.com/TRANSCRIPTS/1411/30/fzgps.01.html

6. General Stanley McChrystal et al., *Team of Teams: New Rules of Engagement for a Complex World* (New York: Penguin Random House, 2015).

7. "Kevin Lynch," The MIT Press, accessed August 14, 2015, https://mitpress.mit.edu/authors/kevin-lynch

8. "Flow (Psychology)," *Wikipedia*, last modified September 8, 2015, https://en.wikipedia.org/wiki/Flow (psychology)

9. Yolanda Wikiel, "Get Smart, People," *Real Simple*, July 2015.

10. Tasha Eurich, *Bankable Leadership: Happy People, Bottom-Line Results and the Power to Deliver Both* (Austin: Greenleaf Book Group Press, 2013).

11. Brene Brown, *Daring Greatly: How the Courage to Be Vulnerable Transforms the Way We Live, Love, Parent, and Lead* (New York: Penguin Publishing, Gotham Press, New York, 2012).

12. *Castaway*, directed by Robert Zemeckis (2000; Los Angeles, CA: 20th Century Fox, 2001), DVD.

I2

THE THIRD PATH—
PRODUCE SUCCESSFUL
OUTCOMES

"Teamwork is the fuel that allows ordinary people to achieve extraordinary results."
—Dale Carnegie

"People who feel good about themselves produce good results."
—Ken Blanchard

"Culture drives great results."
—Jack Welch

While team support matters, mission accomplishment is still the goal. The trust developed within any team is fragile and even more so in a virtual team that isn't performing up to standard. The Third Path (see Figure 12.1) of producing successful outcomes actually begins with the First Path—clear and shared purpose, roles, goals, and expectations. All teams need clarity to achieve concrete, complete results—mission accomplishment.

More Structure

In order to accomplish team missions virtually, more structure and planning are required. Emergency gatherings and on-the-fly planning are exhilarating, and can be done virtually as the exception rather than the rule, but they cannot be the standard. Chaos and frustration result and virtual team members see through the exhilaration to the disorganization lying beneath the surface.

Figure 12.1. The Threefold Path for high-performance teams.

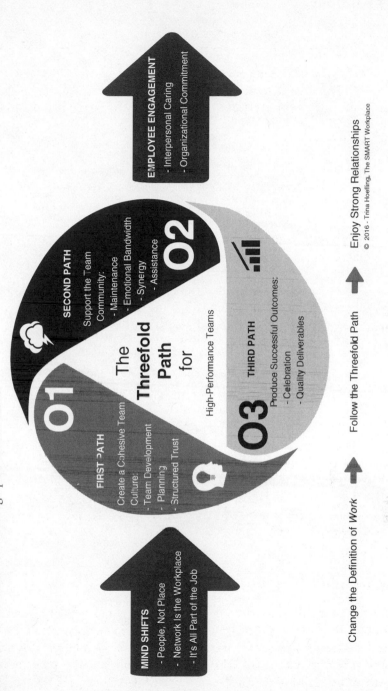

MIND SHIFTS
- People, Not Place
- Network Is the Workplace
- It's All Part of the Job

O1
FIRST PATH
Create a Cohesive Team Culture:
- Team Development
- Planning
- Structured Trust

O2
SECOND PATH
Support the Team Community:
- Maintenance
- Emotional Bandwidth
- Synergy
- Assistance

The **Threefold Path** for
High-Performance Teams

O3
THIRD PATH
Produce Successful Outcomes:
- Celebration
- Quality Deliverables

EMPLOYEE ENGAGEMENT
- Interpersonal Caring
- Organizational Commitment

Change the Definition of *Work*   Follow the Threefold Path   Enjoy Strong Relationships

© 2016 - Trina Hoefling, The SMART Workplace

If everybody starts with the same vision and knows what their role is in the agreed-upon plan, and if the team has a clear structure for communication and feedback in place, you're off on a good performance management path. The structure, using collaboration tools when possible, keeps everyone focused. It's easy for virtual members to work hard but get four degrees to the left of where they originally meant to go. Undetected, six or seven people are going in different directions without knowing it. Nothing is more frustrating than working hard only to discover rework is required because the focus was slightly off—and no one knew. Everyone needs to take an active role in making sure feedback loops keep everyone aligned.

Less Structure

Paradoxically, less structure is also required. Command-and-control management doesn't work in a virtual work environment. Relationship and communication hold the team together, not controlling oversight. The mission and goals are the North Star, and the team relationships are the best accountability mechanisms. Margaret Heffernan, an expert on competitive and collaborative work cultures, reminds wisely that

> genuine critical thinking and innovation require that the mind is allowed to wander, to try out answers that don't work, to test concepts, and, crucially, to make mistakes. All of this is directly discouraged when the focus of learning is on results.[1]

If performance management and measurement are structured too tightly, people will "perform to the test," rather than seek to excel.

Manage the team through personal relationships—team development and support, team agreements, organizational relationships, individual performance, coaching, decision-making, and advocacy—as well as through project management tools.

What Am I Really Managing?

Other than e-mail, do the team tools you use primarily function to capture information and control and monitor activity? This would be typical when the culture expects adherence to goals and metrics. Ask yourself the following questions unabashedly as team leader (or about your manager if you're not the leader):

- How much time do I give to managing performance (walking the Third Path)?
- How much time do I give to supporting my teams in the organization (walking the Second Path)?
- How much time do I have to develop my members (walking the First Path)?
- How much time do I protect for reflection and my own requirements (the Fourth Path of career leadership, which we cover in a later chapter of the book)?
- Do I need to adjust anything to have a better balance for the team?

There is only one wrong answer—and many right answers—to these questions. How you prioritize your time shifts based on many factors, such as the stage of members and team development, or mission and organization complexity. *If, however, you spend most of your time managing the Third Path, you've got the wrong answer.* This chapter helps you adapt performance management for virtual teams so more time is spent on the First and Second Paths of leading high-performance teams.

When Am I the Performance Boss?

Manage individual performance on such matters as the following:

- Technology competence
- Social intelligence and team play
- Stage of virtual team effectiveness
- Engagement and career goals
- Job skills and competencies
- Individual deliverables

Manage team performance on the following:

- Team play and virtual communication
- Customer service (internal or external)
- Engagement and commitment
- Quality standards
- Milestones and deliverables
- Team learning

Moving from colocated to remote management is like moving into management for the first time. The more you are a results-based leader of the team and its members, the easier the Third Path will be. You are coaching people *individually*, and you are managing *team* outcomes.

You aren't just managing virtual performance. *You're managing virtual employee engagement.* Virtual workers say the biggest drawback to telecommuting is feeling out of the loop. "I don't know what's going on," "I'm not included in the scope change conversations," and "I don't have enough information" were the most common complaints heard from virtual team members.

Overdo information sharing, announcement posting, and team feedback. Never back off the communication for long, as it guides effective performance and team alignment.

Let the Tools Facilitate Self-Management

You spend most of your time as a facilitator and connector. When your team partners with enabling technology, the team becomes increasingly self-managing. This is important because you want to spend more of your time

- nurturing relationships throughout the organization's network;
- seeking professional development and redeployment opportunities for the team, especially near the end of a team's charter;
- clearing obstacles and finding resources and commonalities across competing priorities and boundaries; and
- cross-pollinating—facilitating, connecting, and developing the organization networks. Even with great communication protocols, it can still be hard for virtual team members to keep up, so get out and connect.

Let technology free your time and keep the team focused on work, minimizing reporting. A relevant team dashboard is visual, quick to grasp, an indispensable task and project management aid, a team home page, and a conversation starter. It guides every team member's day and structures prioritization. Your team will use as many collaborative tools as it needs, aggregating much of the performance activity for you. Task management systems and other project management software help everyone stay on track. Virtual teams who embrace task management software will have an edge on productivity and work-life balance. It's a time-saver and a team-focusing agent.

A virtual leader also has a more objective set of information to consider in evaluating performance through the software. This frees everyone to spend more time working smarter and less time documenting work activity. You are aggregating activity and production information automatically that informs you about individual performance as well.

Your job isn't done yet, though.

The Rule of Three

Some performance management still falls to the virtual manager, of course. Whether focused on the team or individual performance level, apply the Rule of Three against all performance evaluation:

1. *Relevance:* Be sure the information you collect is relevant to the performance of the job or the effectiveness of the team.
2. *Fairness:* Ask periodically if you'd have monitored the same way if the team member were colocated with you. Are you managing fairly in terms of frequency, type of questions asked, and making judgments based on similar observations? These are especially important questions to ask if you manage some team members virtually and some in person.
3. *Completeness:* Note positive and negative events and observations over a period of time. We tend to remember the unusual and the recent, so keeping a record of objective observations helps control our natural bias.

Establish Baseline Performance

All of the results across the organization must align to achieve the strategic goals. The virtual leader aligns his team's work and outcomes to be accountable as well as to hold the team up as a winning success story to the organization. *It's one thing to manage a person's work, it's another to manage a team of smart people freed to work at their best.* You want to manage as little as possible while still having your finger on the pulse of performance.

As you lead your team to produce successful outcomes, use the collaboration tools so that results are ensured—in other words:

- What are your metrics, and what collaboration tools capture that information, or what could be adapted to do that?

- How will you know the team is on track? Does your project or task management tool set up production feedback loops, leaving as little "reporting" and activity documentation responsibility to virtual team members as possible?
- How can your team results leverage careers and deliver excellence? Is information captured in such a way as to be able to broadcast good news? For example, how easily can you note an accomplishment in the virtual employee's file?

RAMP Up Productivity

Of course, you can monitor only what you tell the technology, which means you and the teams have to know your own metrics first. The Third Path to outcomes actually begins during the First Path of team development. Hopefully, you and the team have determined the team's metrics during your team planning. Your organization may have a robust performance management process also, which is integrated into your team's results and management processes.

Whatever you have already in place, it should answer a few questions that help high-performance virtual teams stay productive. The Results and

TABLE 12.1
Results and Management Process

WHAT is effective performance?	HOW do I recognize and measure?	HOW do I communicate about performance? (Map to your team's communication commitments.)	WHEN do I communicate and how often? (Map to your team's communication commitments.)
What results are desired?	How much? How well? How many? How often?	When live (synchronous)? When pushed out and available (asynchronous)? Documents and collaboration tool reports?	Daily? Weekly? Monthly? Quarterly? About what?
What are minimum standards?	What are our collaborative management tools that track performance and activity?	One-on-one and team sessions?	Milestones?

Management Process (RAMP) in Table 12.1 is a very simple framework you can bring to your team. Use or adapt the framework as a team activity with the sole purpose of getting everyone's agreement and understanding about how they will be evaluated.

Before You Go Too Far Down the RAMP . . .

Command-and-controlled hierarchical structures are less effective than most managers believe, though 86% of people surveyed for a Future of Work study said that leaders believed wrongly, and needed to change to be more collaborative.[2]

Distrust Is Natural in Corporations, Especially Bureaucracies

So much so that risk management is a department. You don't want your virtual leadership style to breed distrust unintentionally. If management hovers, appearing to distrust people, team members will be suspicious, too. New virtual managers tend to hover.

The trust will not increase or decrease in a virtual environment if old habits get re-created virtually. You are simply finding different ways to perpetuate a climate of distrust. Instead, you can build trust (possibly change the culture to be more collaborative at the same time) through managing the Third Path of production with this or another team-negotiated RAMP.

Remember, more and less structure is required virtually. Structure your RAMP, but accept the limits of the structure. I've never known a documented performance agreement to motivate anyone to give 100%, but I have seen a lack of performance clarity wreak havoc. You need the structure and the involvement of your team.

Focus on Ends Before Means

One of the most common fears expressed by managers whose employees telework is, "How will I know they're working?"

The simple answer is: "You won't." Keep in mind that realistically you can't be sure they're working when you see them in the office, either. Your team tools will show if they hit milestones, match activity levels with other team members, and deliver results. Partner with the project management tools to know if they're working. Let the tools inform you first; then engage in conversation and give everyone feedback and coaching. A management habit that can suffer from virtual distance is forgetting to give ongoing feedback. The best feedback is offered informally, regularly, and intentionally in the virtual environment. When you notice good performance, say something. Make extra effort—a brief voice mail or e-mail works wonders. *Remember, virtual workers' biggest stated dissatisfaction is lack of feedback.*

Make yourself accessible to your employees.

One way to be available without breeding dependency is to set office hours—periods of time when you will be available. Some leaders set a fixed time each workday, and others block off time weekly. Decide, let your employees know, and then stick to the schedule. If your organization uses a team discussion tool (similar to Facebook for organizations), use it. If you have open chat rooms, post your chat availability for "office hours." Virtual workers need an echo—to know there is someone else out there. Ping people and encourage the team to ping back.

Just as you would for any other employee, schedule regular one-on-ones, as well as quarterly or semiannual performance reviews as a team, perhaps individually. Face-to-face meetings are always more effective, but chatting by phone or videoconference works, too.

Make every business conversation and every operational meeting count. Virtual work tends to bring out impatience when time isn't valued. You'll want to talk to your team often, about many things. Ensure your team comes to conversations or meetings prepared. You'll facilitate a better meeting, provide better guidance, and keep yourself organized and on point.[3]

Types of Conversations

Table 12.2 shows a way to help structure yourself for leading performance and project management conversations. (This is a sample. You or your organization may already have its own structure.)

Don't Confuse Activity With Achievement!

This final guideline for producing successful outcomes may be the most important. Virtually, busywork is less an issue since no one is watching. Nevertheless, keep yourself and your team focused on the horizon. At the end of the day, the results determine all.

TABLE 12.2
Types of Conversations

Conversation/meeting focus	Frequency	Conversation/meeting structure	Purpose or outcome sought
Business processes	Daily scheduled at same time	Live web conference Stand-up meeting	Check in on progress, course corrections, updates Celebrations Suggestions for improvement
Quality control checks	Weekly	Quality metrics/report Live web conference	Identify root cause and correct issues Assign actions (in task management system)
Stakeholder feedback (formal and anecdotal)	Monthly team meetings	Assessment and feedback results—report reviewed prior to session Live web conference	Encouragement Discover and correct problems Assign actions
Productivity and financial results	Quarterly executive webcast Team meeting follow-up	All-company webcast Follow-up web conference	Encourage positive behaviors Discover and correct problems Align team results and relevance Should be informational, inspirational, honest, strategic and holistic, and tells the story
Operational and planning sessions	Midyear and year end	Team sessions, ideally face-to-face Stakeholders are invited	Reenergize the team Resolve issues and improve process Celebrate successes Plan upcoming year
Employee engagement	At least annually as an organization At least monthly as a team	Surveys and quick polls Conversations Team meeting process debriefs	Gauge understanding and commitment Improvement plans to support team members

Notes

1. Margaret Heffernan, *A Bigger Prize: Why Competition Isn't Everything and How We Can Do Better* (New York: PublicAffairs, 2014).

2. Multiple citations support this. A few especially cogent sources include Dorie Clark, "Are Workplace Hierarchies Becoming Obsolete?" *Forbes*, August 8, 2012, www.forbes.com/sites/dorieclark/2012/08/08/is-workplace-hierarchy-becoming-obsolete; J. Strikwerda, "Organization Design in the 21st Century: From Structure Follows Strategy to Process Follows Proposition," *Social Science Research Network*, February 9, 2012, http://papers.ssrn.com/sol3/papers.cfm?abstract_id=2002236; Lowell Bryan and Claudia Joyce, "The McKinsey Quarterly: The 21st Century Organization," *CFO Journal*, August 16, 2005, http://ww2.cfo.com/human-capital-careers/2005/08/the-21st-century-organization/; and Brian Robertson, "What's Wrong With Your Organizational Structure?" Holacracy Blog, August 5, 2013, https://medium.com/about-holacracy/whats-wrong-with-your-organizational-structure-91dd71a76eb7

3. For step-by-step guidance in planning for, setting up, facilitating, and following up on effective virtual meetings, download a digital *Working Virtually* bonus chapter at www.WorkingVirtually.org

PART FIVE

FROM ME TO WE

"The network is the amplifier."

—Reid Hoffman, founder of LinkedIn

"The digital universe is a portal to connect people with people. . . . The technology is the clothing on the actor of this interactive space experience."

—Jaron Lanier, computer scientist, author, composer

"Build more nets than walls."

—President Bill Clinton, founder, The Global Initiative

13

COLLABORATIVE TOOLS
THAT WORK

The figure slowly climbed toward the summit of the mountain; hand over hand, pulling up toward the guru's cave. The climber reached the top, fingers raw and clothes tattered. He beheld the master: long white hair, wearing a flowing robe, indeterminate age. The master sat in the lotus position and seemed totally detached from worldly concerns.

The pilgrim knew he could ask only one question. A question for which there were no answers in the books, the journals, or from consultants. He approached the master and asked, "Master, what is the secret of staying connected across time and distance?"

The master was quiet for a long time, considering this question. At last she spoke. "You could just Skype."

—Adapted from *The Grenierian Chronicles*

Seventy-four percent of executives say collaborative tools increase how fast they access knowledge; 58% say they have reduced technology costs with the aid of integrated platforms and tools.[1] Global HR trends of 2016 suggest that organization leaders are redesigning systems and processes to build and support networks of teams, including setting up real-time information networks. Smart leaders are designing for organization connection, not performance control. They're adapting performance management processes to be more systemic (i.e., recruitment through retirement), automated, and team driven. HR is integrating big data and analytics into talent management. Most organizations have adopted the kinds of team-based tools discussed in this chapter.[2]

Teams and technology go hand in hand, jointly affecting each other. As you configure your team's tools, ask how the team wants and needs information to move around, where it needs to go, and when and how it comes back. In the next chapter you'll ask these questions more deliberately, since team communication and collaboration tools are inextricably linked.

This chapter reviews, from a nontechnical perspective, the types of tools most often used to configure virtual teamwork and when each is used best. Analyst David Coleman recently surveyed over 500 people working collaboratively in corporate and government enterprises. Eighty-seven percent collaborate virtually, but he discovered the vast majority of work teams are using tools ineffectively and practice methods that limit effective collaboration.[3]

Essentially, you and your team are customizing your virtual office from what is (or will be as organizations redesign) an orchestrated, integrated technology set that coordinates work and facilitates communication and collaboration.

Collaboration Tools Are "Sticky"

Unified communication is increasingly simple, thanks to fast evolution in technology. The team obviously needs to take advantage of collaboration technology in order to coordinate work. Less obvious is how much the tools facilitate team synergy when used well, helping the leader keep the team connected. Utilizing tools more effectively also helps virtual teams identify with their organizations. For virtual teams, the tools are the team's primary vehicle for connection. They represent the company's "hallways"—the places we go to find each other. This chapter explores the most helpful collaborative tools your virtual team will use.

Tools should support types of conversations that serve multiple goals. Virtual work is supported or derailed because of people's patterns of interaction or isolation, their habitual communication pathways. Teams need to talk, as we've discussed, but for what end? Conversations, like meetings, serve a purpose. It helps to have a sense of *why* communication needs to happen before determining *how* and through what technologies virtual teams will best communicate.

There is wisdom in the Chinese proverb "*Calling things by their right name is the beginning of understanding.*" Most conversations are both task and interpersonally focused in order to support the work *and* the relationships. Understanding the importance of both, of incorporating and adapting to the social needs of the team while being productive, is paramount when we communicate.

Every conversation or meeting should further the relationship, the work, or both. You want your virtual team to easily find pathways for free-flowing conversations, within reasonable structure. Some messages may be best delivered through an e-mail for one team member, while someone else needs an in-person call. Still another prefers a text message. The more you learn about your team, the easier it is to find habits and communication rhythms that flow for everyone.

What if your team could be in a chat session and seamlessly switch to voice with one click, like you can with Skype? Are your shared virtual work spaces organized with a clean and friendly interface? Can you add web links and files with full previews to a team discussion channel? Are you capturing tasks during team meetings directly into a tracking system without leaving the web conference?

Collaboration platforms already provide this robust set of capabilities. Your organization has some form of platform with integrated tools, perhaps invisible to the typical employee. For example, most American corporate employees already collaborate using a web application platform in the Microsoft server suite called SharePoint.[4] SharePoint combines various functions that used to be separate, like intranet, extranet, document and file management, enterprise social networking, intranet search, workflow management, e-mail, shared calendars, and so on.[5] SharePoint servers might be deployed alongside Microsoft Exchange, Skype for Business, and private company web servers, for example. Employees use the tools, unaware of the technology backbone making it all happen.

In 2015 Gartner named a relative newcomer, Redbooth, as a Cool Vendor in Unified Communications. Redbooth was founded in 2008, but is rapidly becoming the choice of agile, self-directed teams who want to gain competitive advantages by changing the way they work. Redbooth's user experience is engineered specifically to drive collaboration, while it also provides team managers with analytics to quickly and accurately track and measure the effectiveness of a team's work.[6] Things are evolving quickly, and companies have more and more choices for technology providers. I'm not recommending Redbooth; it's just one example of a steady performer in a fast-changing environment.

Remove the Mystery of Online Collaboration

For reticent virtual team members, insist that the technology and communication protocols be followed. In developing your team, some members may advocate against changing their habits. Respectfully but firmly expand the team's willingness (and provide training) to leverage the tools more fully. *Coach, provide training and support, and remind, but do not let the expectations or standards slip.*

Most of us, by nature, resist change we don't understand or didn't choose. Recently I provided instructional design support to a colleague. This person was unwilling to use a virtual office or shared storage because she was so conditioned to e-mail; phone; and, most important for her, face-to-face. I drove 200 miles multiple times to accommodate her, which was unsustainable for my schedule. Eventually, I completed my handoffs and left the project early, even though I co-design often with teammates virtually. The difference is virtual comfort, competence, and desire to work together cut through all virtual barriers.

That's the difference virtual team competence can make for your team. Reinforce increased and regular tool use to build competency and confidence. If a tool clearly is not performing well, or the tool choice seems inappropriate to the task, then—and only then—revisit your choices and make any adjustments or changes.

Ideally, collaborative tool training for a virtual environment is available organization-wide and will not fall to the virtual manager. However, be prepared to resource training yourself. If the members are competent with the tools, they will quickly develop as a team.[7]

Principles for Selecting Collaboration Tools

Communication is the most critical success factor for any team, virtual or not. Virtual leaders have a responsibility to model good communication using virtual media, as well as face-to-face. No one choice will always be the best choice, so be versed in multiple tools. Consider three additional factors before choosing your team's toolbox:

1. *Time.* How much of our communication will be live (synchronous)? Not (asynchronous)?
2. *Place.* Will a communication event be in a colocated or virtual environment? Both?
3. *Forum.* If colocated, the medium is face-to-face conversation in a conference room. A meeting may be partially colocated, with some team members web conferencing in. If that's the case, the team room needs to be media equipped for the remote connection.

Obviously, technology has evolved, providing many tools to achieve effective and timely communication with options. Types of tools that most of us are familiar with include instant messaging, a company social network (e.g., Jive), shared file management (e.g., Google Docs or Dropbox if your organization doesn't have an intranet), group calendar scheduling and alerts (SharePoint with Outlook), project plan software (like Microsoft Project), decision-making support systems (anonymous and named voting, polling, and other group decision-making tools), wikis (evolving shared knowledge databases), and web conferencing (Citrix and GoToMeeting being well-known options), to name a few.

Which do you use, for what end?

What Are You Trying to Accomplish?

Match the tool to the intention of the communication. How people interact virtually—how deeply, thoroughly, honestly, thoughtfully, quickly, slowly, patiently, individually, or collectively—is greatly influenced by the tool, setting, tone of the facilitator, and who else is in the "virtual room." For example, a telephone conference call with three or four people can be highly interactive, fast-paced, energizing, and as productive as a face-to-face meeting, assuming there is no need for visual focus and everyone has patience with unintended interruptions. Take those same three or four people and place them on a facilitated bridge call with 100 others, and the telephone conference takes on a whole different feel. The medium is still the same—the telephone. The forum, however, has changed from a team conversation moving at a fast clip to a facilitated bridge call with rules for participation, such as muted telephones.

Ask first, *What are we trying to accomplish?* Then find the options that will fit your purpose.

System Requirements

Any collaborative tool must meet your organization's system requirements. The IT department manages most of this, but for the nontechnical person, it helps to be aware of some typical functionality and requirements:

- *Security:* System security for intellectual property and sensitive information (customer data, financials, etc.).
- *Authentication/authorization:* Only allowed individuals get access
- *Workflow:* Adhere to basic workflow processes.
- *Backup:* Information and processes backed up for the team.
- *Availability and access:* The information and processes must be available when needed from anywhere.
- *Administration:* An authorized IT staff to manage assets, users, and related communications and permissions.

- *Forum:* A dynamic social communication application (e.g., Jive, Slack, or Trello, currently popular team discussion tools) that keeps an inventory of threaded and linked conversations.
- *Wiki:* A more static knowledge storage system for team resource sharing.
- *FAQ/trouble reporting:* A way to report and assign resources to problems, saving virtual team members from needing to be technical troubleshooters.
- *Document and file collaboration:* Contributions to a single file (or multiple documents) by multiple contributors, simultaneously or in parallel.
- *Project and task management:* Basic tasking, resource entry, status, adaptation, and reporting; assign actions required and follow-ups, and name project owners by using the tools during team meetings, or post soon after each meeting.

When you explore what is available you will see how many choices there are. By the time this book goes to press, some of the players will have changed, though the focus on functionality for the team remains. Have team needs match up to tools. The overriding goal is always to sustain a cohesive team.

Rely on this checklist when considering different tools.

Virtual Collaboration Tool Checklist

Rely on the following checklist when considering different tools.

- Time (Does the team need to connect live or not?)
- Place (Do we need to meet in a virtual conference room or face-to-face?)
- Forum (When does the team need a small interactive group, when an information-sharing forum, and so on?)

To help set the stage for effective communication, now ask:

- *"What is the intention of each major type of communication/meeting we will need?"* What are the primary and secondary objectives or outcomes expected? What is the timeline for our meeting and must-do goals (define milestones if possible)?
- *"Do we have any limitations to consider?"* Is there a time or cost factor that might limit choices? Do we need training? Are there user limitations we need to consider?

- "*Who is the target audience?*" Is the receiver of a communication going to be a team member? The manager? The whole team? A different department? A customer? A team of teams? The entire organization? Anyone who may be interested?
- "*What is the focus of this communication?*" Is it primarily information sharing? Relationship building and interaction? Will they be only listening, or engaged? This impacts not only the message but also how you deliver that message and in what forum.
- "*How critical is time?*" Is immediate communication required? Is an immediate response equally as critical?
- "*What tone does the communication set?*" Is it a formal or informal message? Personal? Coaching performance? Fast or slow? High or low interaction?

For years I was chair of a conference planning team that communicated through three media:

- Potluck dinners every quarter (we traveled some distance to be together)
- Individual side conversations (telephone and e-mail)
- Team channel (we used Yahoo Groups) for free-flowing conversation, document sharing, and planning logistics

Each team member initiated communication in the forum (dinners, side conversations, or team channel) appropriate to the communication. The caring and commitment of the team came through in all forums, yet each had its own "presence" and tone. My favorite was the potlucks; they included wine and laughter!

Being heard and seen virtually changes how we interact. Most home office networks can handle the bandwidth that video streaming requires. Consider using it frequently since seeing one another adds "space and presence" virtually. It is not just "more." Team members can scan their work space with their camera, giving others a "picture" of the environment they work in each day. Having facial expressions, a voice, and the visual to go with the sound warms up the conversation. Visual presence holds meaning long after the interaction is complete.

You may want to experiment with various forums for variety and to notice the differences in team dynamics. The more choice a team has, the more competence in multiple tools, the more flexible and powerful the team can become. Eventually the team will settle into its ways.

If your team is relatively new to virtual collaboration, you can use collaboration tools to check in on the team and gather individual input on how each is doing. For example, virtual polling is ideal to elicit divergent opinions. You can also poll to get a quick pulse check of members' energy at any given time. A simple poll function becomes a team support mechanism as well as a decision-making device.

As team members gain tool competence and trust in one another, even complex and conflict-ridden issues can be resolved virtually.

What About Informal Communication?

In colocated work environments, much "real work" gets done in casual places, like bathrooms and break rooms. The virtual watercooler doesn't happen by itself the way it does when people work in the same building. Set up and use enterprise social networks (a private Facebook-like interface) to have conversations that used to happen casually when walking by and wandering into conversations, and in "oh-by-the-way" catch-ups when passing one another in the halls. In other words, provide a virtual space for posting and participating informally in conversation and appropriate work gossip. Set up and add to company wikis where people can ask, "*What does XYZ acronym stand for? Who can help me with ABC?*"

Don't stop there. Conduct fun polls for the team and organization. "*What are you doing with your volunteer day off this year?*" "*Who's your team in the NHL playoffs?*" "*Can you spot the spellling error in this sentence?*" Jive, an intranet social network used by many enterprises, has a virtual praise feature where you can give someone a beer or flowers. *Use the fun functions and emojis.*

Choosing Well

The group's communication habits, norms, and culture (e.g., one of giving forth over holding back) influence the communication tools you choose. Other than your organization's enterprise requirements, there is no hard-and-fast rule for tool selection. It helps to consider your team's tool competency and the culture you want to create when deciding. Think through how your options integrate to create a fully functioning virtual office. If your enterprise has not made tool choices for you, progressing through the sets of questions and considerations as we are doing in this chapter will help you and your team choose well. Do you need a robust project management software like Microsoft Project, or will a team task management application suffice, such as Asana,[8] a popular tool with small teams? Do you also need to manage customers? Consider Insightly[9] because it includes a dandy task and project management tool.

You want the tools to talk to one another if they're not already integrated. For example, when a task management system assigns a document review to a team member, it should automatically include a link to the document to be reviewed, which is connected to the team member's calendar for task management reminders. The team member should not have to hunt down what he needs to complete the assigned task. Setting alerts keeps the right people informed about progress without the virtual leader needing to do the reminding. Use the tools to make your team's work easier.

Think of your virtual work tools as a configuration of activities and virtual places around a web-centric hub that is your virtual office. As Figure 13.1 shows, your collaboration tool configuration equips the team for project, workflow, calendar, document management, web conferencing and other message vehicles (like e-mail and IM), team learning, and shared task management. Your integrated tools also facilitate casual and ongoing conversation.

You have a fully functioning virtual office that integrates in the background, allowing your team members to focus on work, not tools. Technology is the enabler, and good enablers become nearly invisible.

Figure 13.1. The virtual team office.

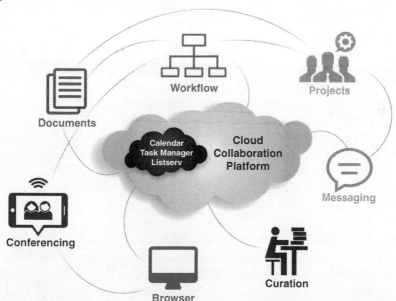

This sample virtual office configuration represents typical relationships among necessary technology functions needed to support virtual work teams. Functionality has moved into the Internet cloud and off team members' equipment. As organization tools move to the cloud, you will see more of this network of functions integrating. Of special note is the developing role of "curation." Curation is much more than a simple collection of datasets or a robust wiki. It involves additional analysis and evaluation that sort and synthesize on behalf of the team. It is becoming a central tool for distributed teams to curate and share the critical information, while archiving the rest.

You are structuring your team's community commons, a virtual office work space that organizes work-related conversations and activity. You want your team to be able to find what and whom they need. Does everyone in your team community know where to check current project status? Find policies and procedures? Do they know how to find a needed resource in real time?

This is a time of fast improvements in virtual collaboration tools, so do your own research. If, however, you are not part of a corporation that has its own intranet and platform, some of the more popular options you may want to try include:

- Dropbox: Personal and shared team storage and collaboration, file backup.
- Slack or Trello: Two virtual team office and communication hubs that integrate with complementary platforms. For example, Slack connects task management (Asana), file sharing (Dropbox), audiovisual conferencing (Skype), e-mail, and other tools.
- Asana: A virtual team task management tool.
- Insightly: An easy-to-use customer management system with task management.
- Various web-conferencing companies (Zoom, GreenLight Collaboration, and GoToMeeting are three I use frequently).
- Pocket or Evernote: Research and intelligence sharing.
- Skype, FaceTime, telephone: One-on-one and small-group live conversation.
- E-mail: Communication that doesn't happen elsewhere.
- FreeConferenceCall: Audio conference and bridge calls. It just launched videoconferencing in 2015.
- Yahoo Groups and LinkedIn: Learning communities and professional networking.
- Google+, Hangouts, Gmail: A fairly complete virtual office and cloud hub.

So Which Tools for What?

The rest of this chapter defines various collaboration mechanisms and suggested uses for each.

Dynamic Document Management

Most shared work involves collaborating dynamically. To stay effective, the team needs a robust file-sharing and management system that does the following:

- Supports version control
- Supports many file types (text documents, CAD drawings, etc.)
- Handles large files
- Provides simple viewing and markup capabilities for multiple users
- Has security to protect against unauthorized access or document changes
- Is intuitive and requires little or no training
- Performs archiving, backup, and recovery

E-mail

E-mail is great for quick, short messaging that keeps conversation and information moving. It is good for individual quick conversations, howdies, straightforward and noncontroversial communication, and logistical coordination if collaborative software isn't available. E-mail is best suited for one-on-one communication, and occasional group messaging and copying others. E-mail and telephone communication are probably the two most common one-on-one communication tools.

E-mail is not a good medium if the sender is expecting fast turnaround. E-mail obesity has become a real problem. I used to limit myself to 25 e-mails in my in-box, forcing me to act on them. At this moment I have over 900, 17 unread. If my in-box were my task management system, I would drop balls all the time. E-mail remains, however, an indispensable tool, being the destination where most team members will want to have their alerts sent.

E-mail and all communication tools have limits because they are one-way with no immediate feedback. Without added clues like voice, eye contact, and body language, a message can be "heard" much differently than intended. For example, one virtual manager found that communication challenges between two team members were magnified when the workers began to rely on e-mails. That manager insisted that for the time being, the first communication attempt for this duo had to be by telephone. This was not "normal protocol" for the team, but situational leadership saw the negative impact remote communication was having on this particular relationship. It eliminated the problem, and within two weeks the duo was able to return to team protocols, including e-mail.

Broadcast E-mail and Team Channels

The Listserv was developed in 1986. A Listserv is a group forum for conversations, the technical backbone of online discussion communities. When e-mail is addressed to a Listserv, it is automatically broadcast to everyone on the list. This is a better vehicle for group communication than e-mail alone. Yahoo Groups was early to offer Listservs for self-formed groups. As I mentioned previously, I've led online planning teams using Yahoo Groups for years. Listservs are great for any ongoing communication that impacts more than two people, with all the advantages of e-mail and the added feature of threading to track conversations. Look for a group channel communication tool that can be sorted by sender, topic, date, and what's new since the team member last participated. Most have taken on a Facebook-like interface so the learning curve is nil. It's more a matter of the team developing new habits.

The advantages are obvious. New or returning members can get up to speed by reviewing the discussion history, "lost" messages can be searched more easily than they can with e-mail, team channels keep in-boxes cleared without fear of losing important communications, and the platform does some organizing for the team. Each team member can choose messages to be delivered on a schedule, or held on the server until accessed, though the team may set protocols for everyone.

Live Voice

The telephone and VOIP (voice over Internet protocol) are indispensable for virtual team conversations. The gain in immediate, live conversation is a much richer, more accurate communication than text-only forums, like e-mail and Listservs. With wireless mobility, it also increases the chance of reaching someone now, not later. Obviously, it is great for highly interactive conversation. Many VOIP options also provide a recording function for reference later. Highly interactive teams use Skype, Google Hangouts, GoToMeeting, or the enterprise's equivalent, sometimes for no reason except to check in.

Voice Mail

Occasionally people are still not available, and voice mail becomes the tool for relaying a complicated or sensitive message. Sometimes you don't want to disturb the receiver, such as late at night, but want to describe something that is easier than when writing. It is another one-way medium, however, so it isn't ideal for resolving conflict.

Audio Conferencing and Bridge Calls

Conference calls are a great forum for meetings if a visual focus, like a shared document, isn't required (in which case, use web conferencing). It's also helpful when bandwidth is limited for some participants, eliminating the need for video broadcast. Conference calling is good for high interaction with small groups. Bridge calls are better for larger groups when a presenter or speaker is the primary focus, with question-and-answer periods built in at specific intervals using chat or opening phone lines.

Chat Rooms

People seem to love or hate chat rooms. Some insist that the artificial environment interferes with full conversation, while others love it as a medium for work, online community, and other quick uses. Some teams like having chat open at all times for easy reach-out, while others see the chat room as an open door to disruptions. Keep chats to a relatively small group, and remember that unless in a private chat, any team member can lurk (watch without participating). Instant messaging is a better choice for dyadic, private conversation.

Instant Messaging

Instant messaging (IM) is just like a chat room except it is between two people and private. Through IM, a team member can seek another team member to see if he is online at the time. Status can show a person is available, in a meeting, away from his or her desk, or set to "do not disturb." Through IM you can also quickly share a document on your screen, or make a video call. The IM chat box pops on the screen, and you're live.

Home Pages and Team Dashboard

Team home pages and dashboards serve as places to post progress and updates, as well as create a bridge to the larger networked organization. In addition to progress updates, post upcoming events, hot links, strategic company wins, and whatever seems relevant.

When a team member wants to get a quick overview of where the team or project is, this will be the first stop. When a new team member joins the group, this is a vital forum for orientation.

Task Management System

A good task management system keeps everyone clear. Less slips through the cracks. A vital collaboration solution, it connects the worker to the task assigned. For example, a project task could be the following: "Review design document and user requirements." When the responsible team member sees this in her task list, she has linked access to the work flow and document associated with it. Notification settings are set so the team can control reminder frequency. As manager, you can check on an individual's progress and better prepare for your next one-on-one coaching session.

Project Management Software

Planning, coordination, and tracking are standard tasks handled by all task and project management tools. Collaborative project management software can be lightweight and super easy to use, or robust like Microsoft Project, the lodestone of project management software. Project management software is more robust than task management systems because it is dynamic, linking sets of behaviors and adjusting schedules automatically. As things in a project change, participants' tasks and deliverables will also change, pushing notification to all participants about these "big picture" changes and the team's sense of ongoing progress.

These tools also help team members know where they fit in the big picture. Individual team members don't know how their work "belongs" to the bigger picture, possibly interfering with their sense of meaning and purpose. As we know about today's workforce, most are motivated by having a sense of work purpose. Choose a project or task management solution that is transparent so that it helps everyone see impact.

Video Web Conferencing and Web Casting

Video is no longer a high-end solution. It does not mean, however, that every team meeting should use video. If video can add something to the meeting or conference, then use it. Most web-conferencing software is designed for training and group meetings, and includes decision-making support systems using group techniques, like polling, surveys, shared screens, and video-recording capabilities. A chat room runs in the corner. For working meetings, the facilitator can turn over the "reins" and let others "drive" the meeting and share screens with others.

With web casting, some limited interactivity is usually possible, such as polling and chat. It is a perfect forum for large "keynote" meetings, like CEO state-of-the-enterprise talks, guest presenters who will have wide appeal, or anytime a team needs to send a consistent message to a large audience.

For many virtual workers, data are still being moved through home networks, however. With streaming technologies, video streaming can slow down the transmission. With asynchronous playback, that may not be an issue; the document, animation, or presenter's image can be buffered and stored in temporary memory. If the conference is live, however, bandwidth still matters. I live in the mountains, where I get "up-to" speeds but no guarantees. I participate in video conferences often, but on days when my upload speed is slow, I turn off my video upload feed, saving bandwidth. And I don't have to fix my hair!

Many still find web conferencing cumbersome in a team meeting format because there are built-in limits to simultaneous input. Sometimes organized "chaos" is necessary to get juices going for synergy. When people talk over each other in meetings, that can be a good thing; in a web conference, *it's just noise*.

People rely on visual cues to know when to "jump into" a conversation. Like me, some people prefer to be visually unavailable or are calling in by phone, so it's easy to accidentally jump in and "step on toes." Until a team gets its own cadence, patience and a good facilitator help.

Facilitation of a web conference is similar to face-to-face or audio conference facilitation, but there are virtual facilitation competencies worth noting. In-person facilitators often rely heavily on their observations of the group and their own personal presence. These elements—especially if video is unavailable—are missing in a web environment. Feedback features like hand raising are intended to provide the facilitator feedback, but they are limited.

The facilitator gains tool comfort with practice. For newcomers to web conferencing, pick a low-stress meeting topic to start so that you can focus on increasing tool and virtual facilitation competence, not the content of the meeting per se.

People participate slightly differently when in an online conference. People tend to be more aware of what they say or hesitate to speak up for fear of interrupting. This can stifle spontaneity, so remind people that some awkwardness is okay, especially with a new team. It is important, just like any team meeting, to facilitate a good summary of each session. What were the key learnings? What decisions were made? What are the next steps?

Synchronous Web Conferencing

Synchronous, or live, web conferencing captures energy and enthusiasm that feeds on itself. Everyone is present, and this supports fast movement. An advantage of synchronous web conferencing is that meetings are generally shorter, forcing the team to focus. Sideline conversations (e.g., sidebar chats) can occur without disrupting the meeting flow. Decisions are recorded and captured, making next steps easier. Shared screens keep the team focused; everyone is walking away with the same visuals.

One disadvantage of synchronous web conferencing is that extroverts may overrun the meeting. It's also easier for quiet members to remain quiet. Facilitators need to be aware of this and pull out all relevant voices.

Asynchronous Web Conferencing

Asynchronous web conferences occur over a designated period of time where people participate on their own schedule. They are underutilized as a team learning forum. An asynchronous conference can have one subject or entire "learning tracks" with different events scheduled at different times, similar to attending an in-person conference. Synchronous web presentations can be recorded for later, asynchronous listening. Team members can participate in the whole conference or only those sections relevant to their responsibilities or interest. *Time becomes a range rather than an event.*

People have a chance to prepare a response, and then post during the asynchronous session, moving the conference objective forward over time along with everyone else. Side conversations cannot interrupt the meeting. People can participate when convenient. Teammates can leave and re-enter, quickly catching up.

If facilitated and focused well, web conferencing, synchronous or not, can serve to unite a team around specific work, just as effectively as a team celebration.

Mix It Up Until Synergy Strikes

Team communication needs to be robust and full, which is hard to accomplish using just e-mail, the most common communication tool despite the better options that are available. Try different solutions and combinations. You may not always be happy with the results, especially in the beginning. Through trial and error you may find the task management system is redundant to the project management platform and can be eliminated. When technology creates unnecessary complexity, it doesn't mean the virtual tool has failed. It could be just a bad meeting, lack of familiarity, the facilitation, *or* the tool itself. Examine all possibilities before changing course.

As you browse your options, know what you want your team to be able to do together and learn together. Use both virtual and face-to-face communication to facilitate conversation and connection, especially relying on virtual communication when you want to harness the group's collective intelligence.[10] With your team's input, choose purpose-defined, integrated tools that allow for easy collaboration, provide true anytime/anywhere mobility, and enable the team to access information and each other.

Now that you're familiar with the tool options, you're ready to facilitate your team's communication habits.

Notes

1. Forbes Corporate Communications, "Increasing Complexity Is Driving Value of Collaboration and the Right Collaboration Tools, Says New Report by Forbes Insights and join.me," *Forbes*, December 16, 2014, www.forbes.com/sites/forbespr/2014/12/16/increasing-complexity-is-driving-value-of-collaboration-and-the-right-collaboration-tools-says-new-report-by-forbes-insights-and-join-me/

2. Josh Bersin, "Predictions for 2016: A Bold New World of Talent, Learning, Leadership, and HR Technology Ahead," Bersin by Deloitte, 2016, http://joshbersin.com/2016/01/the-bold-new-world-of-talent-predictions-for-2016/

3. David Coleman, "Top 10 Collaboration Trends for 2015," *CMS Wire*, February 20, 2015, www.cmswire.com/cms/social-business/10-collaboration-trends-for-2015-028173.php

4. Joel Oleson, "7 Years of SharePoint—A History Lesson," Joel Oleson's Blog—SharePoint Land (Microsoft Corporation), MSDN Blogs, December 28, 2007, http://www.collabshow.com

5. Mark R. Gilbert, Karen M. Shegda, Gene Phifer, and Jeffrey Mann, "SharePoint 2010 Is Poised for Broader Enterprise Adoption," *Gartner*, October 19, 2009, www.gartner.com/doc/1209350/sharepoint--poised-broader-enterprise; "What Is SharePoint?" Microsoft Offi ce 2010 Answers, Microsoft, http://ww25.microsoft-offi ce-2010.com/answer/q/What-is-sharepoint

6. Home page, Redbooth, August 22, 2015, https://redbooth.com

7. Luckily good online and classroom training is available, synchronously and just-in-time. The site www.Lynda.com is another popular resource. A new online university for today's workplace is www.virtualworkplaceuniversity.com (In full disclosure, I'm a founder and course developer/facilitator.)

8. Home page, Asana, https://asana.com

9. Home page, Insightly, www.insightly.com

10. David Engel, Anita W. Woolley, Lisa X. Jing, Christopher F. Chabris, and Thomas W. Malone, "Reading the Mind in the Eyes or Reading Between the Lines? Theory of Mind Predicts Collective Intelligence Equally Well Online and Face-to-Face," *PLoS ONE* 9, no. 12 (2014): e115212. doi:10.1371/journal.pone.0115212; Chloe Medosch, "I Know What You Think: Collective Intelligence in Online Communication," PLoS Blogs, June 22, 2015, http://blogs.plos.org/everyone/2015/06/22/i-know-what-you-think-collective-intelligence-in-online-communication/

14

PRACTICAL GUIDELINES FOR VIRTUAL COMMUNICATION

"Precision of communication is important, more important than ever, in our era of hair-trigger balances, when a false or misunderstood word may create as much disaster as a sudden thoughtless act."

—James Thurber

"You can have brilliant ideas, but if you can't get them across, your ideas won't get you anywhere."

—Lee Iacocca

"Keep things informal. Talking is the natural way to do business. Writing is great for keeping records and putting down details, but talk generates ideas. Great things come from our luncheon meetings, which consist of a sandwich, a cup of soup, and a good idea or two. No martinis."

—T. Boone Pickens

Now that you have a sense of the tools and technology your team has available, this chapter provides considerations to structure your team's communication processes. Team communication focuses on work (task) and interpersonal relationships (social). Both deserve attention if your team is to become high performance faster. Teams that communicate mostly about task can reach the third stage of team development and normalize quickly, but seldom reach high performance. There's so much competing for attention that it's easy for the team to stay task focused, reactive, and impersonal.

Don't let them. Formal communication protocols provide valuable structure for new teams to learn to trust one another. Haphazard communication is the enemy of team effectiveness, so begin with more structure than might be needed when a team is colocated.

This chapter integrates the principles of communication for the larger organization as well. You'll collect a series of communication guidelines and principles to weave into your team. We'll look at how to do the following:

- Use (and improve) systems and processes already available.
- Leverage tools for cohesive, robust team communication, structured and informal.
- Structure communication to support trustworthy behavior while managing performance.

Can Communication Serve?

All communication impacts the team's relationships, and every communication has a purpose.

Web conferencing isn't just for meetings or sales presentations. *Actually, it never was; the collaborative capabilities of virtual conferencing have been significantly underutilized.* Does your team need to make presentations? Use web conferencing to form a mini Toastmasters group, for example. You want your team to get in the habit of being in touch, to develop rhythms and flows of information sharing and check-ins, and to think about how to use tools to collaborate and communicate.

The previous chapter focused on the technology, while this chapter focuses on the structure of team communication itself—*the purpose, tone, and message*—all the choices that elevate the quality of communication happening on multiple levels.

Communication is both structured and spontaneous, of course. In developing the team while on the First Path to high performance, focus on structured communication that ensures the work of the team gets done. While communication is usually task focused on the surface, all communication is about relationship—the team's process of being open, transparent, reliable, and clear about its commitments. The tone of all communication channels, conversations, and meetings underpins the emotional ground of team communication. Develop team communication habits that support healthy and productive relationships among team members.

In general, teams communicate for one of at least five reasons (the five Cs), all necessary for the team to be fully engaged. The five Cs of team communication inform how your team develops its communication infrastructure. Everyone communicates across the five Cs for full effectiveness. Use the five Cs or a similar structure with your team to decide why and how you will communicate. You should *expect* your team to have a general sense of where everyone else is in their work at any time. The more virtual employees communicate virtually, the more assurance that work stays coordinated.

The Five Cs of Purposeful Team Communication

Table 14.1 shows the five Cs, one way to thoughtfully organize and plan team communication based on knowing the reason for the message. This kind of purposeful communication builds and strengthens the team's relationships.

A busy virtual leader may want to create a personal plan for purposeful communication. I set personal task reminders for myself to follow up with key people so that if I get too busy and forget to reach out, a task ping reminds me. Adapt the five Cs to reflect your leadership style. For each team member ask yourself the following:

- Have I checked the team member's understanding of task, authority, responsibility?
- Is the team member connected to me, the team, the organization? *How do I know?*
- When talking, are we communicating candidly and authentically?
- Are we moving the team's work forward (not being perfunctory or on autopilot, shutting down innovation and creative potential)?

TABLE 14.1

The Five Cs of Team Communication: What Communication Should Accomplish

Purpose of communication	Communication actions
Clarity: Gain or confirm under- standing	Facilitate on-the-fly conversations virtually if people don't know one another in order to gain understanding of each other. Confirm working agreements and reaffirm with the team. Clarify understanding and verify decisions and task agreements—big and small.
Connection to purpose: Link to the work, each other, and the stakeholders	Have regular connecting conversations that focus on the why as a way to keep teams focused. Keep in mind that connections let isolated virtual workers know their place in the bigger mission. Create emotional proximity and give virtual team members a sense of belonging. Ensure a shared team understanding of why the interde- pendent work of the team matters. Note that reliable technology is critical to feel connected.

(Continues)

TABLE 14.1 (*Continued*)

Purpose of communication	Communication actions
Candor: Willingness to be honest and bring all relevant information	Willingness to trust takes time, but less time when the virtual leader creates a safe work environment. Safety begins when the leader is candid and responds openly when others are candid. Systems and structures for sharing knowledge are usually built into global enterprises, but their use depends on team members' willingness to share. Build it into your team's communication rhythms. Lack of proximity—emotional or physical—creates a safety that enables people to tell their truth. Use this tendency to your advantage. Lack of social cues makes for easily misunderstood communication, so virtual members must take care in messaging and be willing to speak up when confused or upset.
Cocreation: Collectively create and innovate together	Virtuality limits the easy build of team synergy, so match, accommodate, and structure time for thinking together. If not intentionally facilitated, cocreation and innovation don't happen often. Feeling heard and valued is less clear virtually, so be sure contributions are acknowledged to keep contributors actively engaged. Seek "net neutrality" in how we value everyone as contributors, assessing the ideas, not from whom or where the ideas originate. Be inclusive. Ask for input from everyone. Some participants will be reluctant to jump into the conversation (especially in a large virtual group) and may need prompting.
Commitment check: Verify to help everyone stay on point	Follow up on commitments. Doing what we say is a communication in itself. Local demands may take short-term precedence—the cry of the urgent—so keep distant team members informed of any priorities that will impact them. Focus on the whole person. People are more than their job descriptions. Care enough to exert effort to understand what's being said, inquire deeply, and advocate assertively for your own point of view. The goal is a better outcome, so commit to striving for it. Show interpersonal support. Teams don't stay strong without feeling support.

Note. Adapted from *The Handbook of High-Performance Virtual Teams* (San Francisco: Wiley, 2008).

- Have I confirmed the team member's commitment to the team and the mission?
- You also want your communication to show you care. When communicating, consider asking about their lives outside work. "Did I ask how little Maria's T-ball game went last weekend?"

Team Communication

One outcome of your team's development is an agreed-upon formal communication infrastructure. It informs everyone about how the team works. You can count on team members having different preferences. *Navigate differences with the team's needs in mind first, not individual's.* If it's going to work for everyone on the team, everyone needs to speak up and make sure they can commit to the team's decisions.

The millennial generation, for example, embraces text messaging, social media, and being hyperconnected, while boomers tend to prefer more personal connection like phone calls and coffee dates. Boomers may resist what millennials simply expect. People rely on familiar communication habits, and I still find most virtual leaders hold themselves and their teams back unintentionally by defaulting to personal preferences, not team needs.

A few years ago I was part of a corporate conference team led by a millennial. She asked everyone to communicate logistics by text during the conference. I was a boomer team member who had a "Eureka!" moment. I realized how limited my thinking had been. I'd never before thought to use text at work, a ridiculously late awareness for me. This was 12 years after I wrote the first edition of this book!

Communicate with people the way they like as much as possible, but facilitate differences until you get the team to agree. Team members who have strong preferences but don't speak up lose their right to complain. Virtual team members may occasionally feel out of the loop, but leaders should remind the team to reach out whenever these feelings begin.

The team gets to practice swift trust and openness, and the leader gets to practice candor and create a safe environment and a container for trust. As the team learns about each other, adapt the team's communication pathways to ensure that team trust doesn't break down due to unintentional misunderstanding.

Four Team Communication Criteria

Basically you are getting your team to agree on a strategy to manage and coordinate your work. *A warning*: This can become too cumbersome to be useful, so simplify as much as possible how the team shares critical information. The goal of structured communication is communicating the right information to the right people about what's needed at a time and in a way that people can take it in. Begin with four simple guidelines. The team's formal communication should be:

1. Standardized
2. Organized
3. Timely
4. Easy

In any organization larger than one, we need to communicate. There are myriad choices about how to do it. Structured communication isn't everyday, people-to-people discourse that happens spontaneously. It is structuring communication *to make sure it happens.* This may be a revelation of the obvious, but the number one stated reason for big and small organization issues is poor, inconsistent, or haphazard communication. The effective virtual leader will *not* leave communication to chance, especially task-related communication.

I teach University of Denver graduate students who are full-time professionals. Across several courses and topics, when students conduct root cause analysis of organization challenges, *the leading organization failure (and ultimate solution) involves communication.* Communication is vulnerable to breakdown at the organization and relationship level, impacting trust and commitment. The better the communication, the higher the commitment and trust on a team.

We all listen but not well—we filter what we hear and process the information based on our experience, education, and background. Even the best communicators aren't always clear, and messages aren't always complete. The best listeners don't listen without bias, or always understand what they're hearing. To complicate things, people's preconceived notions about what is "good communication" vary greatly. Add to this dangerous brew the reality that most people draw judgments about others based on often unexamined assumptions.

For example, when I moved to Colorado I was highly offended when business colleagues would take days to return calls. In the Midwest, one day was an unspoken but clearly shared protocol in my business circles; not so in Denver. First, I had to realize that I made an assumption about business etiquette being the same everywhere. Second, I acknowledged that I was correlating my ability to trust "these Denverites" with timely callbacks, even though I had not shared my expectations clearly. I needed to take responsibility to be clear in my message if I needed a faster call return.

That simple change worked. In virtual teams especially, it is easy (and smart) to set agreed-upon and articulated protocols and team agreements, preferably developed collaboratively during the team development process, adjusting as needed. Prevent unnecessary confusion and conflict, and quickly establish the virtual ground under the team that builds a sense of safety and confidence; it makes everything easier.

The Four Ps of Structuring Communication Flow

The four Ps are a simple way to map communication flow. They are an easy way to think through how best for the team to communicate habitually (also with the organization). The four Ps also help prevent overcommunication and flooding people with so much information that all meaning gets lost in the volume.

The four Ps of communication flow (summarized in Table 14.2) are as follows:

1. *Pushed communication* is important enough to intrude into people's days to get through. Individuals or groups can *push* information out to people. For example, CEO web casts, project change orders, and company newsletters are examples of communications that can be *pushed* through e-mail and other one-way communication methods. The team dashboard is a push destination, for example. *As a communicator, is your message important, timely, and necessary enough for you to push it out?*
2. *Pulled information* is available to find when needed. When someone *pulls* information, that person is going to a resource, such as a database, and *pulling* the data out of a database, an analysis, a person, or another resource. Asking to pick a mentor's brain about a report due by end of week is an example of pulling information. Doing a web search pulls information immediately. Putting out a request for assistance through your professional network pulls information.
3. *Posted information* is just what it sounds like; information that is *posted* for viewing as needed. The age-old cork bulletin board is a post methodology, as is the more current electronic bulletin board. The shared network, or intranet, is the destination where the team most commonly posts.
4. *Positioned communication* informs people about what is coming so they can be prepared. The virtual leader is a change manager, and change doesn't happen without early and ongoing communication. Change-related communication is more a campaign, multiple waves of information sharing,

rather than a communication event. Position communication messages early enough to set the stage for what's next. More communication will follow when it's time. Table 14.2 summarizes it briefly.

TABLE 14.2
Four Ps of Structured Communication Flow

Communication action	Purpose of information	Timing
Push	Inform	Now
Pull	Ask for input	Immediate or by requested deadline
Post	Make readily available	24/7
Position	Prepare for what's coming and provide relevant information	Before the "event" and over time

Teach your team about the four Ps before developing your communication infrastructure so together you can ask, "*Should we push, pull, post, or position this communication?*" Communication flow is a shared responsibility of everyone, so build it together. Use the four Ps to ease the communication labyrinth and keep everyone informed without being overloaded.

Organization Impact

Get everyone collaborating by building the team's bigger social network. Consider who and what parts of the organization will impact and are impacted by the team. You want to clearly articulate key interdependencies, as well as identify where the team may want to build social capital. Encourage your team to develop key relationships and seek opportunities to expand emotional bandwidth in the organization.

Style Differences

Extroverts want to think ideas through with someone before writing a strawman proposal. Structured types like to document processes. Millennials are more comfortable digitally, rarely using voice mail.[1] Our personality types and generational preferences affect our communication choices. Some appreciate a warm greeting and some small talk before getting to the task request. Others want to cut to the chase. I find in my own communication I convey more warmth by voice than I do written words, so I am aware of that tendency and adjust my messages. Find *this* team's way.

Cultural Considerations

Especially if you manage a global team, you also must navigate cultural considerations. One young U.S.-based millennial virtual manager had a database analyst on her team from India. He was culturally respectful of hierarchy despite the manager's collaborative style. He was not comfortable asking questions on a conference call. He would IM his question to his manager, and then she would ask the larger group. Rather than expecting him to deny a lifetime of culture, this millennial manager wisely factored the cultural norms into her team's communication protocols and adjusted her personal management practices with this team member. (Many experts have written about the impact of diversity on the team, so while I've considered diversity in writing this book, I've not focused on it. Others have written brilliantly about managing diversity, so I focus on my expertise—managing relationships across the miles.)

Supply Chain Considerations

If your team is part of a nonlinear, complex supply chain (or supply web), the team is a node of great importance. Node teams have a responsibility to consider communication throughout the network in addition to internal team communication. It's too critical to be left to chance. Determine, given the additional communication responsibilities, what additional protocols might be needed:

- Who can or should participate in what kinds of conversations?
- What roles do other parts of the organization need to play?
- How must others interact with the team?
- How will disputes and competing priorities get resolved?

The complexity and lack of linearity in a global supply web create signals and communication flows among network nodes. The flow of information is as important as the physical flow of materials. Establish a communication infrastructure that facilitates information flow to all involved individuals. The virtual leader has to know how to lead and coordinate a vast and decentralized communication web, or risk being caught in it.

Communication Standards, Limits, and Easy Flow

Teamwork is inherently cooperative, so mapping communication flows enables cooperation among multiple individuals and groups, but it's still people talking to people that brings teams to life. As you negotiate and decide your team's communication, function from the premise that the structure facilitates work getting done while still relying on conversations.

Your organization may have set communication protocols. Structurally, the collaboration platform contains much of what the team needs—file-sharing notifications, messaging and team communication channels, and project and task management deadlines, for example. You have all the tools to structure what works best, simply, easily, and well for your team.

It's time for the team to make some team structure decisions, completing the First Path of team development and setting yourselves up for success. Set the following according to the team's standards of participation and team play:

- Availability to one another (hours of availability, time zone, emergency availability)
- Shared file protocols
- Required meetings, attendance options (virtual, in person), group scheduling, and notifications
- Standard team response times (e.g., e-mail and voice mail responded to within 24 hours)

Next, clarify the team's boundaries, key relationships, and how far the team's communication needs to reach and to whom. Ask the following:

- Who needs to communicate to whom about what, and through what medium?
- How often does this communication occur, and who else needs to be informed or involved?
- What issues command full team attention, and what forums do we use to come together?
- How will knowledge and scope changes be managed and shared?
    o How much information is enough? Too much?
    o What's the preferred format? Pushed? Pulled? Posted?
    o What upcoming information needs positioning?
- Who is the first point of contact for what kinds of issues or questions?
- What does help look like for this team? What is appropriate to ask for, offer, and leave alone? By whom?

Team Communication Infrastructure

Use or adapt this structured set of questions suggested in the team communication infrastructure shown in Table 14.3 to facilitate these communication decisions and help capture your team's agreements.

TABLE 14.3
Team Communication Infrastructure

Who	Needs to talk to/ respond to whom	About what	For what purpose	How (through what medium)	Push, pull, post, or position	In what time frame	How often	Who else needs to be informed
	Manager							
	Team							
	Individuals							
	Strategic partners							
	Customers/users							
	Support functions							
	Other supply chain partners							
	Other stakeholders							

Make sure the team commits to honor agreements and give feedback to you about what's working, what's not, and what needs adjustment. Especially in the early weeks, modify agreements and protocols as needed based on emerging team hits and misses.

Additional Considerations

- If any team member has technical limitations, remove the limits or build the communication infrastructure to the lowest common denominator.
- Some personal preferences can be accommodated. If so, document team members' primary and secondary ways to connect spontaneously. For example, I prefer digital communication, but I am also available by phone.
- Respect others' work-life balance regarding time zones, work hours, and off-hour availability.

Simple Matters That Matter

I conducted a simple survey of virtual team members, asking for one suggestion that makes team communication better (and that most people wouldn't think of). The advice was powerful in its simplicity:

- Think about who should have information pushed to them—for example, does the team push out to impacted people in copies of e-mails (cc) or can it be posted for anytime retrieval? It's tempting to overcommunicate, but balance informing with overloading.
- Easy descriptors help e-mails stand out. Change subject lines or start new channels if a topic expands. For example, lead with "Action Required" (e.g., the CFO needs a signature on a supplier letter).
- Decide how often the team needs to check in (e.g., check e-mail four times daily during core work hours, one time daily during weekends) and acceptable response times (e.g., respond to all nonurgent e-mail within 48 hours).
- People define *urgency* differently, usually based on their own needs. Decide what is urgent *for the team*. How will the team prioritize messages marked as high importance?
- Decide appropriate and inappropriate uses for nontask communication (e.g., Internet jokes and other humor is/is not acceptable).

A Word About Words

The language we use when writing is infinitely more important than the language we use when we are speaking. With voice and visual, people have multiple cues to interpret meaning. Digital words are flat. They do relay emotion and attitudes, though often inaccurately or in a way that is distorted through the lens of the reader. For example, these six words convey six different meanings, depending on which word is emphasized:

I didn't say she loved me.
I **DIDN'T** say she loved me.
I didn't **SAY** she loved me.
I didn't say **SHE** loved me.
I didn't say she **LOVED** me.
I didn't say she loved **ME**.

Read this aloud—you will clearly hear the differences in *meaning*.

Our tone obviously impacts how our words are heard, similarly to the way meaning changes in the example based on emphasis. Be aware of your mood when you make requests, declarations, observations, or assessments. Give the communication your full attention out of respect for your audience.

Let's say you want everyone to update their tasks in the project management tool before the stand-up meeting. You send out a reminder message. *Did you proof your message?*

I often write quickly, thinking I'm being efficient and keeping everyone informed. I've learned to read before sending, as my writing style can sound authoritative and even demanding. A simple copyedit greatly enhances my clarity and intended tone, which I want to be collaborative though fast-moving.

Unintentional distancing in written communication is common, unfortunately. Without meaning to, managers limit open sharing and response with their tone. A task-driven, efficient manager is invaluable for team performance. At the same time, efficient communication can close down conversation. Many resent taking orders, especially if the manager says, "We respect all employees," or "We value your feedback and opinion," but doesn't slow down long enough to listen or ask how someone is.

Enlivening the Team's Written Conversations

Here are a few suggestions to enliven your team's written communication:

- Lighten up on the formality. Use emoticons and font changes to communicate tone of message. Emojis are increasingly popular not just because they are fun; they contextualize meaning by implying mood and emotion. Use humorous expressions that everyone can understand, and that are culturally and media sensitive. Work doesn't have to be serious all the time.

- *Show excitement with punctuation and font emphasis, too!*
- Personalize your e-signature with a quote or inspirational message. Add a tagline that reflects the team's "brand."
- Unless the communication is a written report, it's meaning that matters, not grammar. Online communication is less formal, so forgive little things as long as the message comes through.
- Become skillful at understanding the meaning of an entire idea from a few words. When in doubt, ask. In other words, clarify meaning as a habit.
- Verify understanding and agreements as a precaution.
- Use simple words and metaphors. People think and integrate with pictures, so use them freely. Build an infographic to communicate concepts and present positions.
- Obtain local translator assistance if crossing cultural language boundaries.

Despite your best efforts, miscommunication happens, no matter how hard you or your team tries. Be patient and "check in" more frequently and actively about the quality of communication until the team feels confident in the team's ability to track group dynamics. Do this formally at the end of every meeting or milestone, as well as informally as a managerial practice. Adjust and adapt, all while remaining fully committed to the team finding rhythms and flows that work.

Rolling Present

Unless clear protocols are set for checking in, there may be disparity among team members about what is considered "current." What is current is usually driven by how much time has passed since a team member last logged in. One team member may be logged in up to 14 hours a day, checking his team dashboard and e-mail numerous times. For him, the current is literally backlogged only by hours. Another team member may be committed to multiple teams and this team's project isn't her only priority. She may check in only once weekly. For her, what is current covers a week. You may need to set and adjust protocols to slow down or speed up the team's rolling present.

Shared Work Space Management

Without clear protocols for how to organize the team's virtual work space, channels of communication and tools, and shared drives, things can get confusing, especially when team members are sharing documents and using different naming and file folder protocols. Agree to some basics. Information can be organized many ways, as needed by the team, customer, or organization. Minimally, items should be searchable by time, subject and tags, version, and person responsible.

Documentation and Storage Guidelines

A few team-defined protocols will eliminate much confusion. Here's what my interviewed virtual workers defined as most important:

- Create and work from predefined templates for plans, reports, status updates, project requirements, change orders, and cost estimates. As everyone gets used to the templates, they are easier to work with, read, scan, and complete quickly.
- Store all team documents on the shared drive. Team documents saved to local computer drives won't work for collaborative teamwork and increase the risk of multiple versions being active, risking much confusion.
- Put page numbers, version numbers, and dates on all documents if your document storage application isn't doing it for you automatically.
- Decide archiving and file storage protocols (that aren't decided for you by the technology). What's current and what's archived, for example?
- Adhere to security protocols.

A healthy caution is necessary here. Databases and shared folders can be cumbersome if not managed. Information obesity is a real danger for virtual teams because people tend to overreport and oversave files as a strategy to feel connected and noticed, or to CYA, or "cover your [behind]." This is especially true if trust is mediocre or there isn't much interaction among team members. Overreporting can be a way to make sure that everyone "knows how hard I'm working." Watch for spikes, seek more information, and archive files that are no longer useful and needed.

Information obesity can also occur if the document storage protocols have no mechanism for sorting and weeding information that has served its purpose. Just because we *can* store lots of information doesn't mean we *should.* Individual members may have different preferences, and some personality types will want to store more information than others. One team member may want to be a pack rat and save every version of every document (and he *can*, but not on the team's space). Another fast-moving teammate may be a minimalist record keeper, driving the pack rat to distraction if their work is interdependent.

Team protocols set the standard, and team members adapt to meet the team's norms. The fast-moving teammate will need to document more than she would otherwise. The pack rat will need to document less (at least on the team site). The negotiated protocol is for everyone.

What Happens to Paper?

The prognosticators used to say we were fast moving to a paperless society. It hasn't happened yet. It probably won't. Paper is comfortable and easier on the eyes. What is important to virtual teams, however, is that work is *moved* electronically, leaving the tactile choice about printing up to the team member.

Push Team Learning

Gestalt psychology discovered that the whole is greater than the sum of its parts. A team should be more "intelligent" collectively than any individual is alone. This is the power of teams and one significant source of innovation. If the communication infrastructure doesn't support cooperative discovery, learning, and communication, the team cannot function at its full capacity. Therefore, any communication infrastructure should include intentional dialogue, deeper conversation, and informal chatting so that people can think together better. Get in the habit of doing so.

When new learnings, insights, or information is valuable to the whole, the communication infrastructure should already have a strategy to "push" the information out. If it is relevant but not critical, have a method to "post" the information for access or "position" an exploratory dialogue, rather than forcing data into inboxes. Again, ask yourself the questions that inform how to best structure *your* team's communication.

This chapter has focused on the infrastructure of communication that facilitates structured and unstructured conversations. The team can structure its intentional communication, but it cannot—and does not want to—control or stifle free-flowing conversations.

Conversations develop relationships as people get to know each other better. Moving people from individualistic to collaborative behavior is nudged through communication structure, but unleashed through multiple conversations. That's what super teams do: They reach out, listen, make connections, and share more than average teams.

Communication is the backbone of all collaborative work, virtual or not. Synchronous or not. Technologically enabled or not. Attend to it. Get better at it. Enjoy the synergy that results. Communication is wonderfully messy and open—open to misinterpretation, open to potential. It builds trust or breaks faith. It's pervasive, an organization's lifeblood and the primary way we connect with each other. In developing the virtual team's formal and informal communication habits, you are ensuring communication flows *and* encouraging deeper relationships to develop.

I heard Tom Hanks summarize beautifully the choice people make about their connection to others and their willingness to communicate openly:

> Truth is, I'll never know all there is to know about you just as you will never know all there is to know about me. Humans are, by nature, too complicated to be understood fully. So, we can choose either to approach our fellow human beings with suspicion or to approach them with an open mind, a dash of optimism, and a great deal of candor.[2]

Notes

1. Steve Raabe, "The Multigenerational Workplace: Today's Employers Must Manage a Workforce That Is a Mixture of Young and Old," *Denver Post*, April 11, 2012, www.denverpost.com/topworkplaces2012/ci_20358187/todays-managers-must-manipulate-workforce-that-is-mixture

2. www.tomhanks-online.com/tomHanks/quotes/

15

VIRTUAL TEAM RISKS AND HACKS

"All married couples should learn the art of battle as they should learn the art of making love. Good battle is objective and honest—never vicious or cruel. Good battle is healthy and constructive and brings to a marriage the principles of equal partnership."

—Ann Landers

"Is anyone so wise as to learn by the experience of others?"

—Voltaire

"What I like about experience is that it is such an honest thing. You may take any number of wrong turnings, but keep your eyes open and you will not be allowed to go very far before the warning signs appear. You may have deceived yourself, but experience is not trying to deceive you. The universe rings true wherever you fairly test it."

—C. S. Lewis, *Surprised by Joy*

The Best Laid Plans of Mice and Men . . .

Even the best, most experienced virtual leader has challenges. This chapter provides targeted advice to be able to do the following:

- Quickly see early warning signs of team struggle.
- Know when to step in and when to let the team work it out.
- Act fast before struggle becomes dysfunction.
- Use team challenges to help the team become a team.

Some issues are more stubborn, and predictable, in a virtual team. Bad habits can get exacerbated in virtual environments, and new risks are introduced. Disengaged employees are more difficult to motivate virtually. Conflict can more easily go underground and be ignored, risking a trust rift.

Distance Creates Distance

Distance exacerbates how much time and energy we spend interpreting others' actions based on limited information and wondering what others interpret about us.

> "She didn't answer the part of my e-mail where I shared my concerns, but she did decline my invitation to lunch next week. What do I make of that?"
>
> "Margaret hasn't given me comments on that marketing brief, and I need to deliver the final to Steve by Thursday. Is she blowing me off, or is the writing that bad? Did she even get it? I know she's busy, but. . . ."

Virtual work makes relationships less easy to read. Everyone is functioning with more data and information, but less knowledge about each other. Having face time and breaking bread together speed up relationships.

Plan to be together in the same place regularly.

Virtual teams experience risk because it takes longer to learn people's nuances, things that are easily misunderstood. At the same time, team members must trust one another quickly. To manage risk, team leaders move teams from structured to genuine trust by removing barriers to connection. This chapter identifies risks likely to occur and how to identify and prevent issues, and shares ways to hack fast remedies when things go wrong anyway.

The Impact of Virtuality on Feedback Loops

Cause and effect are seldom closely related in time or space, yet we act as though they are. If there is a problem with sales renewals, managers provide incentives for salespeople to find new customers rather than research the problem. If call center wait times are too long, we incentivize representatives to improve average speed of answer and reduce call length. It's easier to address the immediate issue than look for the root cause.

In a complex system, the cause leading to the effect is seldom linear. Renewals may be down because technical support is slow, or call reps rush the call. (That may be too simple, but it's a real client example.) When the organization doesn't look for the larger feedback loops that link root causes with true effects, it can exacerbate the problem.

Add time and space, and feedback is often delayed more. Slow feedback loops contribute to organizations over- and underreacting. Knowing this happens helps the organization (and you) prevent breakdowns when working virtually. Consciously link causes and time or geographically distant effects on your virtual team. Be conscious of the impact time and distance have on relationships.

In a virtual team, when things go awry, they can do so for a longer period of time before they're noticed, so the virtual team leader—or any team member—must be vigilant to catch early warning signs. The problem is not usually intentional. It's usually some communication or feedback breakdown.

Eliminating or reducing delays shouldn't involve Big Brother monitoring. Instead, practice the tenets of this book, use the collaboration tools, and build a professional team that maintains strong ties.

You Need to Know When It's Not Working—Fast

When problems erupt in a virtual team, the problem is not usually differences or inability to handle conflict. Rather, the problem is usually mutual trust erosion stemming from hidden conflict gone unaddressed or unrecognized. Miscommunication and misunderstanding also erode trust, or at least confidence. When you've got people colocated, red flags are more obvious. Virtually, problems can go on too long.

Symptomatic Warning Signs

Let's examine the symptoms of a problem, probable causes, and fast hacks and solutions.

Direction Is Lacking, Focus Is Confused

Symptoms
Miscommunication. Lack of feedback. Holding different assumptions about what matters. Pieces aren't coordinating smoothly. The team experiences frequent direction switches. Frequent disagreements erupt about what the team should do next.

What's Happening
The team charter is no longer clear. Virtuality has allowed misalignment to go undetected or without response, increasing virtual distance. The workflow process or communication infrastructure is failing, not being utilized, or wasn't clearly understood in the first place.

Hacks

- Have everyone conduct stakeholder interviews with each other and key organization members. Help them see their role from others' points of view. This helps them practice empathic listening and appreciative inquiry[1] and provides information to get back on track.

- Collectively review stakeholder interview results, and then clarify the team charter and expectations, and make adjustments to the project plan. *Do this together as a team.*
- Acknowledge the confusion, get past the racket, tell the truth, and minimize risk by clarifying or adjusting team agreements. If the conflict is between team members, hold coaching conversations individually and together.
- Consider a blank canvas and rebuild interpersonal agreements consensually.
- Bring an expert in to realign and broaden perspectives.
- Celebrate small victories, and acknowledge great work.[2]

Excessive Caution

Symptoms

Team dynamics change. Team members who used to be transparent and engaged can hesitate or exercise excessive caution and political posturing. Normally outspoken team members become withdrawn. Work products are timidly introduced. People say "okay" too much. People overinform, as though they need to prove they are working.

Aggression may also grow. People may make out-of-the blue critical comments. Harsh words slip out. Rushed statements are tossed into cyberspace without much thought to how they might be received. These may be unintentional, but words have impact.

What's Happening

Usually, trust is broken or at risk. One team member can negatively impact whole teams. Unfortunately, people can be cruel in a faceless environment, or they forget that written words are easily misunderstood. E-mail bullying is rare on teams, but fast-paced teams are breeding grounds for getting straight to the point and forgetting a real person is at the other end of the missive. Unintentional disrespect happens. Attention to the interpersonal impact of language and tone cannot be stressed enough virtually.

Hacks

- Privately let the team member know his or her missives were not productive. Some people just need a reminder.
- Ask the team members how they like to receive feedback.

- Suggest team members reach out directly to each other, especially if a behavior is causing them to withdraw or react. Help sort out what is his, hers, and theirs.
- Coach the team about timing and intensity. The pace of business and forceful communication can shut people down, even if not meant to. If a team member is accidentally closing people down, coach to the behavior. Growing professionals appreciate coaching, as we often don't see our blind spots.

Information Anorexia or Obesity

Symptoms

Team members aren't sharing quickly or fully. Information is hoarded. Or the reverse, information obesity, is another clue to virtual team problems. The database doesn't hold all the latest information, holds skimpy documentation, or has conflicting versions of documents. Too many people are copied into correspondence. The team isn't using the same filing system, causing confusion when looking for documents. When information obesity comes primarily from one person, it also indicates that a team member needs a simple organization training, or that person may be feeling isolated and looking for some forced acknowledgment, recognition, or reassurance.

What's Happening

Sometimes it isn't a people problem. "Accidental" discovery is less likely to occur virtually. Informal sharing hasn't been re-created virtually. Team agreements may not be fully functioning yet, or there may be inadequate information-processing protocols or team disagreement about them. Or maybe the organization rewards information as power.

"Information as power" still lingers in many company cultures. One of your team members may believe hoarding knowledge creates job security, but it creates slowdowns, bottlenecks, and frustration for the team, inevitably interfering with productivity. Eventually, trust issues develop between information hoarders and others, which interferes with team learning and severely limits the team's potential.

Hacks

Utilize your tools! Project and task management systems resolve much when people realize how a good document management system works. The tools should help drive the team's effectiveness. Change the reward system to support protocols. Coach them if they're changing tools or habits, but hold the performance standard as team habits adjust. Hold the team accountable to protocols and agreements; revisit; revise; reinforce; and, again, coach as needed.

Conflict Goes Underground

Symptoms
Sometimes people are *too* nice, and there isn't enough healthy difference of opinion. Most people don't seek conflict, and the virtual environment makes it easier to let the conflict go underground, remaining hidden. When it erupts suddenly, it has been boiling. Similar to excessive caution, this is usually an interpersonal issue within the team. When conflict goes underground, communication is interrupted or diverted. The low-touch communication exacerbates any team alignment challenge as well as any interpersonal issues rumbling. Team members may be following the team protocols literally, but not following their spirit. A team whose heart isn't in it is communicating perfunctorily, and it is in danger.

What's Happening
Low-touch communication leads to miscommunication and misunderstandings. The risk of misconstrued messages increases in virtual communication, and trust can be broken unintentionally as a result. If trust is low, a conflict *will* go underground. When the team is forming, consider ground rules for surfacing issues, *and then follow them.* It prevents a lot of problems.

Hacks
Get back to the basics. Reestablish trust. Consider a team outing (jam session, volunteer day, happy hour). Remind people of good experiences (when they felt appreciated, why the project matters, the vision of the future). Expand emotional bandwidth so relationships are more resilient.

Have one-on-ones with team members. Give everyone a chance to vent frustrations, share concerns, and make suggestions without disrespecting others. Revisit team member preferences for support. Do they need to ease into things with casual conversations about sports and the weather before getting down to work, or the opposite, jumping straight to the agenda? Stories are powerful, so tell one to unite the team again, reminding them about why the team matters.

Four Individual Barriers to Honest Communication

Four internal barriers prevent us from moving beyond minimally engaged conversation that is task focused.[3] They may be intentional or not, conscious or not, but they are common. We see evidence of barriers in others more easily than we see our own, so ask yourself what you might not be seeing or saying as you read about the barriers. Internal barriers risk reverting teams into storming or worse—disengagement. The four barriers are as follows.

Barrier 1: Not Recognizing What We See

We all have blind spots, at our own risk. A team that doesn't see reality is vulnerable. Teams and individuals "go blind" at work sometimes. If you want to be an adaptive team, see what is, even if it's not what you expected.

Barrier 2: Not Saying What We Think

People feel pressure to be politically correct and polite. Some fear speaking up, bringing negative experiences with them when they join new teams. Fear limits our brain's functioning, which limits our ability to do our best or even to know how to speak up. Excessive peer pressure, bullies, and cynical corporate cultures keep people quiet who *need* to be heard, especially when it affects the team's work.

A virtual manager knows that team consensus means that while the decision made may not be everyone's first choice, everyone agrees it's the best decision at the time. Everyone commits to not only live with but also support the decision. If people acquiesce more than discuss, people aren't saying what they think or they aren't engaged. They're going along, but not in consensus. *This is a risk and a warning.*

Barrier 3: Not Doing What We Say

Integrity matters. Very simply defined, *integrity* is meaning what we say and doing what we say we will. If something interferes, people with integrity communicate with enough notice to adjust and correct in order to maintain team trust.

Barrier 4: Not Seeing Our Impact

Self-awareness is a team competency. If needed, coach teams to see themselves accurately. This includes bolstering the team when they underestimate themselves, providing formative feedback, and compassionately uncovering blind spots that interfere with performance.

What About Other Team Issues?

What if a team member's travel schedule requires videoconferencing, which is difficult because there is seldom privacy when on the road during business hours? Simple realities not anticipated are the best opportunities to address team issues before they're a problem. As teams gain synergy, they facilitate their own effectiveness.

Virtual Hacks That Help

- *Accept some loss of operational efficiency, at first.* This doesn't always happen, but it's less frustrating when a certain "acceptable slippage" is allowed as the team forms. It will be regained. As Sheryl Sandberg reminds us, "Done is better than perfect."[4]
- *Fuel the fires of synergy.* For team members used to colocated collaboration, going virtual is jolting. Synergy happens with virtual teams, but there isn't always that extroverted high. Help them develop energizing team habits. As early twentieth-century minister Frank Crane reminds us, "Habits are safer than rules; you don't have to watch them. *And you don't have to keep them either. They keep you.*"[5]
- *Find the space between the notes.* Asynchronous communication dissipates group energy. The team can drift apart without regular, live contact. Team leaders *must* help the group feel that it creates music together. The lyrics are written metaphorically by structuring the team's systems, processes, and working agreements. The melody, however, is in combining notes (together time) with silence between the notes (working independently). Good songs have breaks, musical bridges, crescendos, and quiet tones; a virtuoso virtual leader helps the team experience its song when together *and* apart.
- *Remember that structure serves.* Too much focus on rules and procedures provides an illusion of control. Structure is a servant, not a master. Treat it as such. The collaboration tools help structure work and connect people, not become a way to virtually look over people's shoulders.
- *Embrace "I" and "us."* Acknowledge the differences among the team members, while developing "*this* team's culture."
- *Be scrupulously fair.* Avoid any temptation to rely on the closest person. Have the *entire team in mind*, not just the team members you see regularly. Attend to all team members' needs, opinions, and contributions.
- *Confront all nonperformance.* Management responsibilities do not lessen in a virtual environment.
- *Don't be tempted to wait it out.* Make a special effort to catch conflicts early and deal with them fairly.

A Bit More About Conflict

If team members' miscommunication doesn't get acknowledged and remedied, it can lead to bigger trust issues. This can happen with colocated teams, too, but virtual miscommunication goes unrecognized, unaddressed, and unresolved far too long, too often.

It seems easier to sweep conflict under the rug (at least until it can't be ignored). *Don't be tempted.* Employee commitment decreases when conflict goes unresolved. Luckily, issues are opportunities for team development. A well-managed conflict increases team commitment.

It's the work environment and your job. It's the virtual leader's most important charge to create a team environment to produce results. Most virtual risks can be prevented or managed by coming back to two things: knowing people's habits so anomalies show up early as symptoms; and following the First Path of team development, which clarifies purpose, commitment, communication, and agreements.

Notes

1. *Appreciative inquiry* is a model that seeks to engage stakeholders in self-determined change. Wikipedia defines it at https://en.wikipedia.org/wiki/Appreciative_inquiry

2. Thanks to global virtual team leader and millennial rising star Allison Kessler for hack suggestions that cross generations and distance.

3. Otto Scharmer, *Theory U: Leading From the Future as It Emerges* (San Francisco: Berret-Koehler, 2009).

4. Sheryl Sandberg, *Lean In: Women, Work, and the Will to Lead* (New York: Alfred Knopf, 2013).

5. Frank Crane, BraneyQuote, https://www.brainyquote.com/quotes/quotes/f/frankcrane101522.html

PART SIX

EXPAND EMOTIONAL
BANDWIDTH

The Far Mosque
The place that Solomon made to worship in,
Called the Far Mosque, is not built of earth
And water and stone, but of intention and wisdom
And mystical conversation and compassionate action.

Every part of it is intelligence and responsive
To every other. The carpet bows to the broom.
The door knocker and the door swing together
Like musicians. This heart sanctuary does
Exist, but it can't be described. Why try!

Solomon goes there every morning and gives guidance
With words, with musical harmonies, and in actions,
Which are the deepest teaching. A prince is just
A conceit until he does something with generosity.

—Rumi

16

VIRTUAL TEAM TRUST

"We shall never be able to remove suspicion and fear as potential causes of war until communication is permitted to flow, free and open, across international boundaries."

—Harry S. Truman

"Trust is knowing that when a team member does push you, they're doing it because they care about the team."

—Patrick Lencioni, *The Five Dysfunctions of a Team*

In its original meaning, *intimacy* did not mean emotional closeness, but "the willingness to pass on honest information."[1] *This is the essence of trusting relationships.* Emotional bandwidth is the personal and sustainable connection created among virtual team members who are working together for a common purpose toward a goal.[2] The more emotional bandwidth, the more resilient the virtual team.

Technically, bandwidth measures the available capacity for information flow. The more bandwidth, the faster data can travel. In this light, think of bandwidth as how open or limited our capacity is to build strong relationships. We work through issues more easily and productively when we trust one another, believing one another to be well meaning. We manage conflict better when we like the people involved and trust them. Taking time to get to know and understand teammates expands emotional bandwidth, just as much as a five-bar cell phone signal yields better call quality. Expanding emotional bandwidth opens the collaborative capacity of virtual teams.

Research, surveys, and management gurus keep saying the best leader is authentic, has excellent emotional intelligence (EQ) and relationship management skills, listens, and is trustworthy. *Leaders who can broaden their own emotional bandwidth build better virtual teams.*

This chapter reexamines what we think we know about trust in teams. This is one area of virtual work that is nearly entirely people dependent. In collaborative work environments, trust *is* important—and more fragile.

We have almost unlimited digital bandwidth, but what about emotional bandwidth? During team formation, work agreements are made, and collaboration platforms and tools are deployed to build communication pathways and fulfill structured agreements.

Is it enough?

The Organization's Role in Trust

The medium is the message, or at least part of the communication package that gives the message meaning. If the organization is designed well and provides network tools, teams can trust the company cares enough to help them work smarter together. If, however, the organization's infrastructure is dated with clunky tools or processes, people will experience the opposite.

If organizations want employee commitment, they must be trustworthy. Unfortunately, many virtual teams are undersupported. In fact, telecommuting gets abysmal "official" company support,[3] which puts the burden on the virtual leader. Team trust doesn't build faster with better technology, but trust will decline faster when adequate tools aren't available. Technology connects us and facilitates communication, but it cannot drive commitment or trust. It's a hygiene factor, like adequate pay. When it's there, workers can focus on contributing; when it's not, workers are distracted by trying to get their needs met.

Surveys report that employee commitment and trust in their employer rate low in corporate America. Many workers not only believe they are undersupported organizationally but also have resigned themselves to a mediocre career. According to Deloitte's 2014 survey on worker engagement, people accept mistreatment by their employer as normal.[4]

Leaders who ignore the deflated mood of today's workforce do so at the organization's risk. Whether it's outmoded organization design, systems, or processes, insufficient resources or tools, or poor leadership, the organization sets the tone for mutual trust by how well it supports its people.

When leaders prioritize system and process redesign to provide more control and performance monitoring, instead of collaboration, this demonstrates lack of trust in people. Investments in tracking behavior, money, and "stuff" are necessary; however, the collaborative organization invests also in HR and team collaboration tools that help unleash talent, encourage innovation, and help virtual workers stay connected to the company. Adopting collaboration tools system-wide is practical. Teams form faster when the way they collaborate doesn't change from team to team.

To set a digital course for the organization with an analogue workplace is like asking employees to walk in quicksand. Their work lives get complicated, frustrating, and stressful. Without an organization-wide approach to the digital workplace, teams and business units tend on their own to acquire readily available cloud-based tools, add personal technologies, and start to work in ways that satisfy personal needs. So rather than reducing the complexity around technology, we add to it. To manage the complexity of the digital world, we need to step away from analogue workplaces and lead an organization-wide approach to making work easier.[5]

Is your organization's IT budget balancing management and control with open collaboration?

This chapter reinforces communication principles and collaboration technologies already discussed, blending task-related and social communication to lead virtual teams in a way that keeps the team on target while providing individual support.

For example, couple up questions to support your team member (the Second Path to high performance) while also ensuring alignment with the team and being on track for results (the Third Path).

The simple question *"What progress did you make today?"* can be coupled with *"Do you have everything you need to meet the milestone deliverable tomorrow?"* Or combine *"What did you get done today?"* with *"What do you see coming up that we all need to be aware of and position for the team?"* Coupling questions demonstrates care while ensuring progress, as well as invites deeper conversation when warranted.

Most Leaders Fail to Engage

Fifty percent of workers don't feel valued or that their work matters much. Only about 25% of workers believes his or her contribution matters at all. Even worse, 72% of millennial workers and 68% of baby boomers admit to having disengaged from work, no longer committed to their current employers.[6]

These are staggering statistics. *This is broken trust.*

The digital bandwidth is here for fast collaboration, and workers can quite easily communicate broadly and fully with anyone. Tools facilitate communication that is task driven and interpersonal, face-to-face and digital, human to human and human to technology.

It's easy to connect, yet we don't. Worker *disconnection* stands at 50%.

Retired Army General Stanley McChrystal is one of the most trusted military leaders in U.S. history. In *Team of Teams: New Rules of Engagement for a Complex World*[7] he concludes that *trust comes as leaders develop relation-ships on their teams, and as they do what they say they will.*

McChrystal summarizes that we trust our leaders—or don't—based primarily on three factors:

1. *Benevolence* (we care about and promote our team)
2. *Integrity* (our actions are consistent with our stated values and commitments)
3. *Competence* (we are competent to lead)

Benevolence is the Second Path of team support. The general reminds us that authentic support includes advocacy. The social office environment vanishes virtually. The team is a major vehicle for members' organization exposure. The virtual manager is an important connecting "node." Virtual team members want to know their virtual leader is concerned for and will advocate on their behalf. General McChrystal reminds us that the leader's job is quite simple. The virtual leaders help people gain confidence in their relationships and skills so they can function effectively and trust each other.

Trust and the Threefold Path

To build team confidence, the first development path for virtual teams cannot be skipped!

Most virtual team members begin with enthusiasm for virtual work. They want to work with a highly competent group of trustworthy, reliable folks who gel as a team. Trust is a precursor to virtual team performance, and begins while walking the First Path, developing the team's ways of working together. The team develops stronger trust as it drops into its rhythms, flows, and ways that work for everyone. The team's process will emerge as they work out agreements that are a reflection of their values and stated commitments, building team integrity.

Expand Emotional Bandwidth to Unlock Team Potential

Trust is found within a range of a relationship's experience. That range defines the emotional bandwidth available to the relationship. I discovered this while watching virtual leaders over time and after virtual management training. I noticed high-trust virtual teams were led by leaders who knew their people, enabling them to trust their teams and confidently build the team's exposure in the organization.

Motivating engaged team members takes expanded emotional bandwidth. The broader the team's emotional bandwidth with each other and the team leader, the more team potential is unlocked. Facilitate strong, honest relationships; it's a trusted leader's fastest path to high-performance teams. The quality of any work relationship often comes down to trust, knowing that you, as a team member, can say what you think with confidence and without fear, and everyone listens respectfully and attentively. Support people who expand emotional bandwidth, and coach those who don't. Develop relationships as a primary part of your job. Be an active contributor to team insights and creative thinking. Get to know people's strengths, preferences, styles, and peccadillos. Virtual teams expand emotional bandwidth through relationship, not geography. It's the opening where abiding trust begins. *Are your team relationships strong enough to discuss, disagree, challenge, suggest, and consider opposing opinions?*

Virtual Hallway Conversations

Maintaining work relationships when remote requires extra effort. People don't bump into colleagues in the kitchen for small talk. Mundane as they may seem, those moments are important for building rapport with people. Virtual workers have to build rapport with casual conversation, too, but it's not as natural. It's easy to dive into Monday and fire off an e-mail asking about a deliverable. I'm guilty. I've forgotten to ask, "How was your weekend?" when it had been a teammate daughter's wedding. As a manager, it's understandable to get task focused, but remember the power of simple care.

Start phone calls off with some personal conversation—the kind you might have with a coworker in the office kitchen while warming lunch in the microwave. If time doesn't allow, say so with sincere regret. Schedule personal celebration reminders and send notes or gifts for team birthdays and anniversaries.

Trust: The Simple Way

Without trust, team commitment is conditional and seldom full hearted. To overcome this all-too-common reality, virtual leaders generate trust in everyday interactions that inspire commitment and lower the threshold to connection.

In other words, talk to everyone. A lot. It is *the* foundational action needed to have a chance to engage today's virtual worker. Strong leaders have "the ability to engage in conversations that allow for clarity . . . and elicit mutual commitment to a shared future."[8]

Let's face it, team members' trust is partly based on our clarity. Poorly structured or confusing conversations between virtual leaders and their teams can cause concern about a leader's ability to lead clearly in the larger organization. If this is coupled with organizational trust issues, team members don't have a solid future they can trust. Team members buy in to the organization's proposed future partly based on a matter of trust in their manager as representative to the organization.

Trust isn't mysterious or difficult; it's simply a belief others hold that we are reliable, truthful, able, and predictable. Trust is given when people see consistent honesty. When people also see a future for the organization they trust, engagement, the subject of the next chapter, follows.

Frequent and ongoing communication also lets remote team members know you value them. Remote workers are especially vulnerable to being overlooked and feeling unappreciated for the work that they are doing. Conversations help virtual team members feel supported and appreciated, and conditional trust develops into genuine trust over time.

What Really Happens With Trust on Virtual Teams?

Many believe trust grows only over time spent together. Trust will continue to develop or erode based on experience. It is true that we're more inclined to be trustworthy when we have to see people again. In other words, we follow through on commitments when we have to "face" each other later.

Evidence also suggests that first impressions really do count, and that distance can create distorted impressions. Communication among team members drops quickly even when separated by only one floor in an office building. Physical distance remains very real and affects interpersonal relationships in a mobile work environment. On the surface, this seems to challenge trust potential in virtual teams.

Virtual Trust Challenge—Cynicism

Today's virtual manager has to get past cynicism that comes from people's past and current societal culture, as shown in the disengagement statistics of today's workforce. If current workplace research is accurately reporting workplace unfairness, cynicism is an appropriate emotional response. If management consistently fails to keep promises, people stop believing what they hear. Inspiring leaders encourage teams to put themselves wholly into an initiative, but if the inspiration isn't backed by resources and support, cynicism is sane.

Yet we want to be optimists. Most people want to believe their next team will be a good one—hence new teams' initial excitement. Some team members are less optimistic and don't trust easily, if ever. This isn't completely within the virtual manager's control. When hiring your team, avoid hiring cynical people.

Reversing Cynicism

We don't fully control organization or team fails. In fact, innovative teams that are working near their competency edges *should* fail sometimes. Failure is not a broken agreement. Innovation doesn't happen without missing the mark. The virtual leader creates space for mistakes, encouraging learning and renegotiation. This keeps the team from judgment, excessive worry, or discouragement. These are distractions that hijack team attention. Trusting teams function with a spirit of learning, course correcting instead of placing blame or pretending mistakes aren't made.

A Solid Road Map to Virtual Trust

With decades of virtual experience and documented best practices, the virtual leader has a solid road map for building trusting virtual teams. The most important tenets, when followed as described, work. Most of us want to be trustworthy. The team reflects individual reputations; we are invested together, committed to mutual success.

The Māori culture has a word for commitment: *utu*, which means "balanced exchange." The virtual leader pursues team *utu*, actively seeking input about what's working, what's not, and why. She helps to produce results. This helps the team develop genuine trust.

Very simply, *utu*, or balanced exchange, supports everyone, including the organization it serves. How a team finds its balance determines whether true trust develops, or whether it will remain a structured trust. It's facilitated by spending "real time" together, finding common ground, fixing problems together, sharing excitement, and celebrating progress and milestones together.

What Helps Virtual Teams Trust

Band-Aids Are Okay, at First

The team's rhythms and flows get established early and become deeply embedded habits, regardless of whether they are effective. Even when given better options, most teams stick with habits once created, so establish trust-building habits early, beginning on the team development path. Structure is an essential Band-Aid until the team gels.

Structure Swift Trust

Software developers have taught us a lot about team trust. Swift trust has proven to be a key indicator of team success. It is the practice of assuming our teammates are competent and trustworthy. The trust cup starts full, and it is depleted or replenished based on experience. Team research findings have corroborated the developer experience. Virtual teams that can begin with swift trust are more likely to thrive.

The development path is a Band-Aid, in a sense, to give the team a structure from which to begin. It's normal for onboarding members to be uncertain and initially preoccupied with inclusion. The faster the virtual manager can help people overcome discomfort that comes with not knowing, the faster the team can move through its team development stages.

Use Band-Aids until team bonds are strong. Collaboration requires trust, but we don't start with it. If individuals' reputations are impacted by team performance, high trust is high stakes. Settle fears by developing team structure. Team trust is supported initially by the professional reputation of fellow members, but trust isn't guaranteed to continue. In other words, trust is granted based on assumed competence, temporary until experience proves it is deserved. As a result, trust may be at its height at the beginning of team formation.

Establish That Foundation

Organize and structure communication to get work done during the development path, as covered in chapter 10. Unintentional trust busting results from misunderstandings, so clear confusion before it happens with team agreements and active communication.

Create Safety

How a team handles early conflicts drives a team's long-term trust. The more interpersonal conflict, the more team members want to quit a team, usually. If a team isn't talking outside formal communication, conflict has gone underground. Left undetected or unresolved too long, conflict can break a team. When trust erodes, a member's disappointment impacts team commitment *and* individual productivity. Voluntary communication typically declines. Team trust will never evolve beyond structured trust when conflict is not managed because people naturally self-protect. When people feel unsafe or disconnected, they are less committed, so help work things through. *The leader should get involved.*

If the team is communicating, it can use inevitable conflicts to deepen trust. A study from MIT's Human Dynamics Laboratory confirms that *the leading indicator of team success is how well the team communicates informally*: "With remarkable consistency, the data confirmed that communication plays a critical role in building successful teams. In fact, we've found patterns of communication to be the most important predictor of a team's success."[9]

Even in the best teams members get on each other's nerves. Just like neighborhoods, team members tolerate little irritations because they share common ground and experiences, and develop genuine community. *How can you help your team see itself as a community?*

Reinforce Predictable Communication

High-performance virtual teams communicate many ways, sometimes intensely. How often is less important than the regularity. Task communication and social communication weave throughout the week. Teams that begin and end with high trust take time to know one another informally, *and* they follow structured agreements, *and* they give rich feedback to one another. Also, no high-performing teams rely on their manager to intervene but deal directly with each other. The opposite happens in virtual teams that never reach the performing stage of team development, never getting to sustainable synergy.

The bottom line is when communication falters, the team is at risk. When communication flows, team members are more able to trust the process, not to mention each other.

Sonar Is Reassuring

Virtual team members seem to share one universal trait—a need for a response. "*Are you out there?*" Echoes are unnerving when feeling isolated. People want to be reassured they're not lost in cyberspace. It's hard to trust people we don't see, especially when we depend on them.

A simple response is all we need. When we hear only our own echo, we don't know if we've been heard, or heard accurately. Acknowledge the callout, and commit to follow up. On virtual teams, responding is as critical as reaching out. Distance constantly needs to be "closed."

Colocated teams interact naturally because of shared space; we "learn" our team simply by being around. Virtual teams don't.

It may seem redundant to say again, but trust is eroded when people don't talk on virtual teams. The most underrated virtual trust-building strategy is simple interaction—lots of it—the full team and subsets. People are more likely to trust people they know and talk to regularly. Feedback happens when people talk, too, enhancing team performance. *Find ways to make it happen.*

Find Common (Virtual) Ground

Common ground is "a basis for mutual interest or agreement."[10] A team certainly qualifies as common work ground, with shared purpose and responsibilities, rituals and habits, successes and challenges, and history. Use the First Path of team development to help the team intentionally design opportunities to develop common ground.

Virtual teams have a more difficult time seeing themselves as a whole that holds common ground. Team structure helps, but it's also important to help each member see how they and the others contribute to collective team movement.

Imagine a mobile. Each team member dangles from a wire, and the wires connect together into a flowing creation. The mobile pieces seldom touch, but they "flow" together without effort and based on each other's movements. The team leader "wires" the team with shared purpose so that they are not isolated pieces but an integrated whole. This synergy, this "wiring" of individuals together through finding commonalities, helps everyone feel like an individual *and* part of a team.

Is there a metaphor or analogy that symbolically wires your team together powerfully enough to remind everyone why you are together? Find ways to build common ground, such as team training or other shared experiences.

Provide Context

Contextualize people. Take extra time to give everyone a sense of team cohesion. Team culture is a product of shared stories, norms, rituals, repeated interactions, and experiences. Provide opportunities to create "*us*-ness." Provide context about each other personally, too. Share fun personal news before starting virtual meetings, for example.

Contextualize tasks. When groups move too fast and act without seeing the bigger goal, they develop more slowly as teams and more frequently miss their marks. If speed to productivity is what the virtual team needs, "speed up" the familiarity period and create shortcuts the team understands to contextual information enough to keep teams on point.

Sacred (Virtual) Space

Remember the last time you were in a meeting that was synergistic, with creativity flowing? You could feel the energy bouncing off the walls. One question led to an insight, which led to an improvement, which led to a breakthrough. The room, the space itself, held the energy of the group, forming a sort of container, just as a glass holds water or a pocket holds personal effects. An ordinary conference room was transformed into an energy vortex, a sacred team space.

Virtual teams experience energy leaks, as though the glass has been tipped over. Team leaders *need* to create a virtual container for the energy. Energy cannot be at full throttle all the time; the team will burn out. If the ebb and flow, however, aren't naturally energizing the group, the risk is too much virtual dissipation, lagging commitment, and wandering focus.

Each type of collaboration tool can be its own container and help manage the energy of the group. Just as a kitchen feels cozier than a dining room, or a meditation space is different from a family room, the communication tool you choose creates a different ambience. It gives a sense of the "room" one is entering. One-on-one conversation tools, such as Skype or IM, have more immediacy than e-mail. Chat rooms are casual, offering conversational freedom that team discussion forums do not. Well-facilitated web conferences can corral team energy much as a physical room when live and mics are open. Web conferences are flexible, amenable to different types of communication—brainstorming strategies, weekly stand-ups, or client presentations, for example. Each is a web conference, but the meeting's virtual work space changes to reflect the meeting purpose and formality.

The combined communication tools are the team's virtual office, the sacred work space everyone knows is the team's ways of coming together. *The team exists, even when it isn't digitally connected.* The virtual office, the collection of team tools, holds the space for the group between connections, ensuring the team is available even when no one is in the virtual room. The "sacred space" of the team becomes its commitment to each other, not a work space. As the team connects formally and informally, it develops habits that help the team know it is always a team, even when not together.

A few guidelines:

- Minimize discussion of organizational hierarchy and other "power" variables unless they are highly relevant. It sets up a tendency to defer to the most powerful influencer. Power suppresses people's free flow.
- All teams hold private conversations that are not relevant to the whole. This is essential and appropriate, and helps bond team members. Help them find virtually private conversation spaces. Just watch for cliques.

- Honor team members' personal values about their work space. A fast way to splinter a virtual team is to offend someone's beliefs with a careless remark or raunchy joke.
- Keep private conversation private unless it is relevant to the group. Private jokes hinted at in team meetings will isolate those on the outside.

Stoke Virtual Team Fires

The energy is built, the space is set, but virtual teams need to keep fires burning. When two team members hit a "Eureka!" moment, encourage them to run virtually to the whole team and share the excitement—then, not later. Broadcast in ALL CAPS. Let your enthusiasm show; embrace exclamation points! Deliver pizza and beer to everyone's virtual office. When a team member is recognized, feature her in a podcast sent to key stakeholders. Develop a habit of pushing team news to targeted influencers. Celebrate accomplishments as a team together, even when dispersed. Celebrate again when face-to-face. Virtual teams simply can't be too spirited, especially when it's bubbling up from the team. Do virtual jigs. Send e-cards and song links. *Have fun. It's a good thing.*

Create Team Bonds

Shared experiences keep teams connected and feeling part of each other. In the office environment, happy hours, team sports leagues, and learning lunches are opportunities to bond. If your team is virtual, create nonphysical ways to bond. What are people interested in? Video-desk yoga class together? Virtual book discussions? Start a Fitbit support team with goal achievement incentives that everyone can win. Essentially, structure the team's connection *enough* to keep the team members communicating and engaged with each other about more than work.

Contract for Trust

Contractually, workers agree to adopt organization rules and values, to represent the organization appropriately and ethically. We receive compensation in exchange for our agreement. Virtual team agreements are soft contracts, transactional agreements that guide team behavior. Ideally they balance the team's needs with individual preferences and organization priorities. They structure agreed-upon operating principles that keep everyone clear. Every team should have open discussions about expectations, making sure everyone commits.

Clearly stated agreements also help onboarding team members. Team agreements are trust builders simply through their clarity. Ideally, team values and agreements will be similar across teams. It's comforting to recognize similar agreements across teams and over time. This layers organizational trust through systemic predictability.

Expand Organization Connection

Rather than getting lost in a large enterprise, most virtual workers limit their world. They "understand" the larger organization through who they know, usually colleagues, customers, and other stakeholders. Virtual workers rely heavily on the people they interact with to navigate the organization. Team member alliances and friendships strengthen the team's network. Be a facilitator of teams getting to know their organizational neighbors.

After the team is performing well together, virtual team members still want feedback and to see the impact of their work. Build links between team members and the organization so that feedback loops extend beyond the borders of your team.

Let Team Values Emerge

When the team is working well and meeting its commitments, trust more naturally develops. Core team values begin to emerge because everyone is behaving in ways consistent with their commitments.

Limits of Structure

When structuring trust during the First Path of team development, you are also aligning the team to the organization vision and mission. If your team fails to develop into a fully performing virtual team, you will always need the team communication infrastructure, working agreements, and accountability measures. You may or may not have deeply shared commitment, trust, or a sense of safety. Use organization policies, project requirements, and team agreements to structure trust until genuine trust develops on the team, and to help the team function well enough if it never does.

Push structure too far, and you will create a greater trust barrier between you and your virtual team. The team may begin building its own alliances that you know nothing about. Structure is a good thing, and serves important ends, starting with establishing healthy boundaries, clarifying roles and responsibilities, jump-starting team communication, verifying quality standards and production goals, and so on. In essence, you are defining what behaviors are trust building and what outcomes are needed. Agreements do nothing to create trusting relationships, but they clarify behavioral standards that everyone understands—because they helped create them. People trust more easily when they feel they have choices, so share decisions with the team when you can.[11] Shared agreements and a safe work space enable teams to bring full strength, personality, heart, and mind to the job, and open the door to fast team trust.

Strong Relationships

Strong relationships are resilient. At the team level, simple conversation is the most powerful strategy for expanding emotional bandwidth to strengthen relationships. Face-to-face conversations, juicy e-mails, long telephone calls, online conferences—all add value by simply spending time together, as a team. Frequent "check-ins," perhaps even daily, should be the norm when virtual. As a committed team leader, keep the conversations going.

Courtesy Matters

With the busy work pace, basic courtesy often gets left behind virtually, and it risks virtual teams. I witness global team members fire off communications and assigned tasks as their day ends, leaving colleagues on other continents to greet their morning with a full in-box of demands. Is this rude? Leveraging? Efficient?

It depends. . . . *Your* team decides what serves, and what impedes. What is authentic for *this* team? *This* culture? *These* people? Treat global colleagues as you would those sitting next to you, with courtesy as defined by your team. Your virtual colleagues are just as real as your cubicle mate. When you talk work, maybe ask something about them, and listen to the answer before jumping to the task. It doesn't take long.

Communicate, Converse, Connect

Teams have to talk about the work to maintain trust. Social, informal communication that complements task communication strengthens trust faster but isn't enough. An exclusively task-focused team runs the risk of dry communication revolving around logistics, coordination, and reports. Teams have learned to trust the structure, but may never learn to trust each other. *Facilitate your team's balance.*

Have many kinds of conversations. Convene to discuss strategy, prepare team reports, and debate the merits of different approaches. Encourage open-ended dialogue at team meetings that goes where it will. The broader the communication, the greater the opportunity for the team to get to know how to work together better. This is invaluable.

Some worry that too much talking interferes with our individual production responsibilities, believing (wrongly) that getting to know people better takes too much time and is unnecessary virtually. Distance can make faceless abstractions of us all. Virtual team members are people with hopes, fears, and needs. We have to know people to know their needs, and we have to know their hopes to unleash their full talent.

If you're a busy virtual manager reading this, you may be wondering how to possibly get all these virtual tongues wagging and still get your work done. *Find a way.* Leverage your time however you need, but neglect team connection at your team's risk.

Leaders who fail to effectively engage teams do more than slow down a team's development. A weak relationship with a manager typically leads to polite unwillingness to challenge, itself a risk. Generate trust in everyday interactions and talk about team progress. *Everyday interactions.* Steve Dorn, director of client strategy for Pivotal Resources, states it bluntly: "Today a necessary leadership competence is the ability to engage people in conversations that allow for clarity and elicit mutual commitment to a shared future."[12]

Trust Is the Bottom Line

Trust precedes willingness to collaborate with another person whose behavior cannot be controlled. Unless we strongly believe that others will not abuse our trust, we don't *really* trust them. We structure implicit and explicit agreements in the meantime.

If agreements are met, trust is built. If they're not, trust has failed (or a poor hiring decision was made). It's almost that simple. When asked, virtual team members say lack of trust and poor communication are the most common reasons teams underperform.

When Can I Relax? You Know You Have a Trusting Team When . . .

All team members freely do the following:

- Admit mistakes.
- Ask for help.
- Accept input.

- Give one another the benefit of the doubt.
- Offer feedback and assistance.
- Speak freely but without controlling the conversation.
- Appreciate (and show appreciation for) one another's skills and experiences.
- Focus time and energy on important issues.
- Offer and accept apologies as necessary.
- Look forward to opportunities for collaboration.
- Support one another in ordinary—and extraordinary—ways.

Teams begin with swift, structured trust and hope to end with genuine trust. They show initiative and adjust to one another as team roles emerge and change, becoming a truly interdependent team that takes pride in delivering on its promise. Performing teams are, to summarize McChrystal, benevolent, behaving with integrity, and competent. Team conflict bonds them as they work through issues.

To simplify what it takes to be a trusting and trustworthy virtual leader, and to wrap up the essential learning of this chapter, ask yourself one question regularly: *"Does what I'm about to do create trust, or does it risk it?"* Make it a habit and your mantra.

Notes

1. The word *intimacy* stems from the Latin *intimatus*, to make something known to someone else. Another derivation is the verb *intimate*, which originally meant to notify.

2. Trina Hoefling, "The Three-Fold Path of Expanding Emotional Bandwidth in Virtual Teams," in *The Handbook of High-Performance Virtual Teams: A Toolkit for Collaborating Across Boundaries*, ed. Jill Nemiro, Michael Beyerlein, Lori Bradley, and Susan Beyerlein (San Francisco: Jossey-Bass, 2008), ch. 3, p. 91.

3. This is my conclusion from well over 30 years of consulting, training, and coaching experience, validated through several interviews with long-standing and continuing experts who implement flexwork solutions for corporations. All our experience is supported by workplace studies.

4. Deloitte Consulting, "Big Demands and High Expectations: The Deloitte Millennial Survey," White Paper, 2014, http://www2.deloitte.com/al/en/pages/about-deloitte/articles/2014-millennial-survey-positive-impact.html

5. "Digital World: Analogue Workplace," Sloan MIT Center for Information Systems Research, 2015, http://cisr.mit.edu

6. Deloitte Consulting, "Big Demands."

7. General Stanley McChrystal et al., *Team of Teams: New Rules of Engagement for a Complex World* (New York: Penguin Random House, 2015).

8. Interview quote from Steve Dorn, director of client strategy, Pivotal Resources, 2015.

9. Jeff Haden, "10 Ways Great Bosses Use Science to Lead Great Teams," *Inc. Magazine*, June 2015, www.linkedin.com/pulse/10-ways-great-bosses-use-science-lead-teams-jeff-haden

10. "Common Ground," Merriam-Webster.com, www.merriam-webster.com/dictionary/common%20ground

11. Steve Dorn, "Improving Radical Organizational Change Implementation by Focusing Leadership Efforts on Building Commitment and Trust," Capstone Project, University of Denver, 2015.

12. Quoted from telephone interview Hoefling conducted with Dorn, October 2015.

17

VIRTUAL EMPLOYEE ENGAGEMENT IN CYNICAL CULTURES

"Manners are a sensitive awareness of the feelings of others. If you have that awareness, you have good manners, no matter what fork you use."

—Emily Post

"When you hear the corporate motto, 'We value the individual,' get ready for the layoffs."

—Dr. Charles Grantham

A re you encouraged or disappointed when you read this?

I work remotely; we are scattered all over the United States. Our department has a primary purpose of serving the company and doesn't really consider the aspirations of the employees who make up the company. That makes it a challenge for employees to stay connected and engaged with the company. Our department has tracking software in place to keep employees on task, but this is obviously not the same as having a good manager who holds it—and us—all together, who makes it work. Our department is lacking in building commitment to team purpose.

Directors just don't appear to be interested in connecting with the employee as an individual. All of my coworkers and myself (although I'm just becoming aware of this now) operate from a "what can I get" mentality. We are currently working on our new computer system that will eventually (hopefully) help us keep better track of our project files, deadlines, meetings, and so forth. This new product is helpful in bringing us together as a team because it's putting us all on the same page as we work to develop it while building it. We're also getting to know each other. With some

214

leadership, we could continue to grow into a team as we learn how to use the tool to help us coordinate. (Virtual team member, a millennial, who still believes and hopes, 2015)

This young, smart, virtual team member recognizes team potential, but she also sees lack of leadership. Some readers will see the irony in how much budget, time, and corporate attention are given to collaborative technology, obviously without attending to the lever that most impacts how well a virtual team engages—*the virtual manager.*

Engagement is measured by how much workers are motivated to contribute to organizational success *by applying discretionary effort.* People in today's workforce tell us they want to be—but aren't—engaged; their leaders aren't getting across that the effort is worth it.

All-Time High for Low Trust

Smart organizations are redesigning with better technology, as this young professional's company is doing. They know the network is the workplace. Still, workers report alarmingly high levels of employee disengagement, costing money and productivity. Seven in 10 employees self-report disengagement from their jobs. Actively disengaged workers cost business $550 billion annually, according to Gallup in 2014.[1]

SMART Organization Guidelines for Virtual Engagement

Organization leaders must change to reverse this disengagement trend, starting with guiding principles that create a workplace environment for engagement. The following principles also remind managers how to engage their people:

- Structure teams as interlinking nodes in a network of teams and alliances, rather than as a hierarchical chain of access and reporting.
- Make conversations happen, rather than "cascading" information down and out.
- Activate robust (push, post, and pull) communication systems.
- Reach learners and develop leaders many ways (face-to-face and online, live and self-paced, individual and team learning).
- Tap people as knowledge-rich nodes in the network.

Cardinal Signs of Disengagement

A culture of fault-finding, finger-pointing, and self-protective behavior develops in organizations, even among members who usually take responsibility for their own behavior. Because company cultures are part of a bigger business culture that lacks perceived fairness and integrity, many people don't trust organizations easily. When workers see evidence of leaders who don't care, they are cautious, deflecting responsibility and disidentifying with their jobs, just as our anonymous millennial admits doing, *to her own surprise.*

You know your organization has an employee engagement challenge when the following is happening:

- People are afraid or unwilling to speak up for an idea or defend themselves.
- Corporate communication finesses the truth and sells positions to the workforce, perhaps providing specific talking points to managers to help perpetuate the "packaged truth." (*This is different when explaining a new initiative or strategic goal when information needs to be shared accurately.*)
- Workers have to compete with each other to get redeployed, or they are evaluated in a forced rank system. (*The old GE Jack Welch philosophy where everyone is ranked for performance and promotion in competition with their fellow employees.*)

The main indicator of disengagement, though, is a poor relationship between employees and the manager who is responsible for their performance evaluation.[2]

The Manager Is the Critical Variable

Every manager is arguably a critical variable for team engagement or disengagement. A *virtual* manager is *the* critical variable. Engaged managers are critical to virtual teams because they are the primary connective tissue to the organization. The engaged team with an involved virtual leader builds bridges to the bigger vision and organization mission, key to engagement.

As a virtual leader, you are key in each team member's choice to engage. The key competency correlating to employee engagement is *your communication skill.* Studies by such wide-ranging sponsors as Microsoft and the Future Work Forum show that today's managers *must have* better relationship competencies, beginning with self-awareness about how they come across to others. If you don't like interacting with people, you may not be a strong candidate for virtual leadership. Inauthentic interaction feels perfunctory to both the manager and the team member. Regular communication helps the virtual leader to do the following:

- Communicate face-to-face *and* virtually in a way that inspires and clarifies.
- Build and maintain trusting relationships.
- Manage collaboratively for results.

This chapter examines what we know about today's (demotivated) workforce and what to do about it, particularly with virtual professionals. We'll look at leading today's increasingly diverse, multigenerational, mobile, virtual, flexible workforce that *needs* to be engaged in order to feel connected, let alone motivated.

We'll look at how the virtual leader unleashes talent virtually to develop committed virtual teams that want to stick together. First, let's look at the organizational cultures within which many virtual teams function.

Silence That Kills

Workers are not getting what they want. Across American companies, workers don't trust their organizations to be fair or have integrity. We're chronically cynical, which saps potential and profit, if not the team's life force.[3]

When people see behavior they believe is unethical, most admit *they say and do nothing*. Research into organizational silence finds that most working professionals, especially executives, frequently have information they don't share and concerns they never voice. Two reasons are given:

1. People fear retribution for going against the system.
2. They feel hopeless that what they say will matter.

In other words, it's not worth it.

In recent years, I've seen unapologetic bullying by leaders. Virtual employees complain that their virtual manager hides behind the digital network, providing minimal genuine support. Communication is task driven. My graduate students report a preponderance of cynical cultures in their past and current employers. After investigating further, it seems workers justify bad managerial behaviors and adapt to demeaning cultures, letting go of initial hope and expectations.

Even involved managers become calloused, devolving to the managerial norm of the company culture. We want our employers to live up to our ideals, but more often see leaders who don't. At all levels of the organization, the workforce has come to expect little. It's no wonder people lapse into acquiescent disengagement, whether out of cynicism, fear, or disappointment.

Social capital is a psychological term used to describe the mutual trust and reciprocity practiced by groups that make society resilient in times of stress. Teams with high levels of social capital are genuinely more fair and cooperative. Social capital diminishes when competitive pressure takes precedence over sharing. Competitive corporate cultures are, in the long term, stifling companies' social capital and team relationship capital.

Threats to Integrity

Integrity is more than ethics. Integrity means the organization is structurally sound, like a well-engineered bridge. A competent bridge builder fixes structural flaws at the root cause to ensure a safe and durable construction. Organizational integrity means long-lasting companies.

Leaders who seek the truth are acting with integrity, as a bridge engineer would. Those who can't or won't hear bad news put the system at risk. A bridge's integrity *is* its structural soundness, its safety. If *executives* are choosing to remain silent, what kind of structural integrity does the organization have? What can a leader, in good conscience, promise her team that is bankable on behalf of a low-trust, quiet organization?

An organization's integrity is a reflection of its ability to see and hear what is really going on, continuously improve and innovate, and deliver on its promise. People who share what they experience are nodes in the feedback loops of a healthy system. When it's safe to speak up, when what we say is considered, we are more inclined to trust our effort is worth it. The virtual team needs its team leader to be a listener.

Whether out of fear or because they feel their comments will fall on deaf ears, people who don't speak up are surrounded by others who won't either, meaning mistakes are being perpetuated throughout the system. Those who choose silence over engagement will eventually lose faith in a system they see as flawed or at risk.

And they're right.

Fear-based silence is a symptom of ethical collapse in organizations.[4] Hypercompetitive company cultures are especially prone to poor ethics because winning is critical. The end becomes such a focus that the means become amoral. In other words, "winners" in competitive environments don't think about behavior as good or bad; rather, behavior is good if it moves the worker closer to a win.

People who are working in systems they see as structurally unsound or highly competitive (or both) feel unsafe. They learn that fixing the game is safer than playing fairly. Winning is more important than playing by or challenging the rules. Organization values and ethics get little, if any, consideration in strategic conversations. Any ethical pondering remains internal, often creating cognitive dissonance for the individual who sees but doesn't say. People act from basic survival first, understandably.

What happens in a void? People fill it with stories and theories, sometimes accurate, often distorted through the lens of cynicism, judgment, and fear. The virtual worker in such circumstances works in an echo chamber, loosening yet one more tether to the organization.

Myopia Is Disengaging

Most readers aren't surprised that we're cynical as a collective workforce, or that surveys report low levels of trust. Cynicism isn't the only problem organizations face when it comes to engaging people, however.

Small-picture thinking is also disengaging and confusing.

One of the best ways to build trust is connecting "the work" to the mission and strategic vision. Minimize any alignment issues by facilitating an emerging vision of how *this* team will manifest the strategic vision. Unfortunately, only 25% of today's workers feel connected to their company's mission, and an unsettling 50% feel disengaged. The rest don't know or couldn't state the mission.[5] This introduces another organizational integrity risk because fewer eyes are quality assessing the whole, seeing systemically. Myopia in the end-to-end organization processes and production puts the system at risk and certainly isn't motivating.

No strategy is sustainable if it has little energy or hope. Hope is the greatest motivation we have to attract people. When people have hope, their work matters and they emotionally connect to the organization and the team, which is energizing. A virtual leader harnesses this desire to connect to the vision. Hope may be the single commonality underlying all motivation. Even cynics are often tired optimists, so the more a virtual leader can uncover reason and meaning in the work, the better the chance to harness motivation and unleash energy.

We Bring Our Past With Us

Trust is not just the responsibility of the organization or manager. That is unfair. Not everyone comes into a team ready to trust. Many workers come with low trust based on previous experience, setting up a potentially self-fulfilling prophecy. Expect some people to trust slowly. Lead in a way so that people can safely lower their barriers.

Leaders come to teams with their own history, too. It's important that virtual leaders can trust their people. A fast way to erode someone else's trust in you is to not trust *them*. The more the virtual manager trusts his team, the easier it is to *be* a trusted manager. Continuously evolve your understanding of team strengths, talents, and shortcomings so you have no doubt about people's ability to do their job. You need to know you can trust them to perform to expectations. To trust and be trustworthy is the single most important commitment anyone can make to break down trust barriers.

Poor Communication Makes Everything Worse

It turns out that people judge others as untrustworthy when they are poor or sporadic communicators. Much of this book is about communication, so I'll simply remind the reader about the data. Interpersonal and relationship intelligence is essential in the virtual work environment. It's foundational because communication is what enlivens work groups to develop into teams.

Two Structural, Sticky, Fast-Acting, Tie-Tightening Organization Behaviors

Employee engagement has gone through name changes over the years and may be undergoing another with a resurgence in empowerment. In 1975, a "worker participation" initiative originated a shift to include labor's input about improving the workday and manufacturing efficiencies. Involving labor in the conversation changed how jobs were organized without disrupting line efficiencies and increasing job satisfaction. Job enlargement and job enrichment were early examples of work process changes that improved employee satisfaction with repetitive work.[6]

This collaboration between management and labor evolved, and a pattern emerged that identified four practices that historically catapult people's commitment in organizations. The first two practices are organizational options getting attention again today. The second two practices fall to the team leader.

1. Shared Ownership

Employee stock ownership plans (ESOPs) are becoming popular again as private companies look at talent retention. For example, Left Hand Brewing, a Colorado microbrew, is sharing its future with its workforce, building strong employee ties. The craft brewery deployed investor shares into an ESOP that gives its workers a majority share in the business. No company sale can happen without the vote of the employee owners.

That's a strong commitment to people, and a strong stand by cofounder and CEO Eric Wallace. He embraces that his company's future is interconnected with its people.[7] Chobani has shared stock with every employee prior to going public. Most business leaders say that people are a company's most precious asset; employee ownership is a potent way to prove it.[8]

2. Monetary Fairness

According to a survey sponsored by the Freelancers Union, as many as one in three U.S. workers identifies as a freelancer—roughly 53 million Americans in all. What that means for recruiting and retaining talent is a large pool of potential independent contractors. These independent workers also have other opportunities. The best workers, therefore, get to pick and choose the companies with which they work.

If you want to hire and retain the best people, set your organization apart by offering interesting assignments and good working terms, train team leaders, and pay well. The Container Store, for example, recently committed to paying retail associates a $50,000 base salary as their commitment to a living wage, sending the message that workers' time has intrinsic value, regardless of their job duties.[9] California and New York recently raised their minimum wage. Employers that want to retain a quality workforce are looking at fair pay.

Organizations can also provide incentives. Flexwork options work for employees and contractors alike. Consider team incentives by offering rewards tied to team metrics and milestones. This directly connects earning potential to the team's success. You have more commitment without increased financial cost unless results are achieved. Motivating incentives include nonfinancial opportunities as well. Today's professionals want learning and development opportunities they can't easily provide themselves, formal and informal. Send your department to an international expo to talk to thought leaders and test-drive tools, and then have attendees offer a virtual brown-bag lunch show-and-tell of what they learned. Start a team wiki for sharing tools and resources and acknowledge contributors publicly. Find fun, simple, and inexpensive ways to ensure people feel they are being compensated fairly for their contribution—financially and nonfinancially.

Two Collaborative, Commitment-Building, Employee-Engaging Virtual Leader Behaviors

The second two high-result motivation practices fall to the team leader. Collaborative teams thrive when teammates show up fully, work fiercely, and share willingly. Engaging team leaders create an environment for motivated team members by *developing the team*, which is, in fact, the development path of the Threefold Path to high-performance virtual teams.

1. Cogovernance and Collaborative Team Agreements

Shift people away from protective positions to open possibility by launching (or refocusing) your virtual team the right way. Navigate and negotiate until the team has a shared understanding of the mission, vision, values, outcomes and deliverables, work processes, and communication agreements—the team development path. Lead your teams progressively forward, learning from the past, seeing the present, and creating a successful future.[10] Nothing builds commitment like cocreated success.

2. Empowering Leaders

Technology enables collaboration in a way that we've stripped out of many business practices. The virtual manager's job is to bring *humanity* to the value chain processes. Let technology do the tracking.

If it isn't your management style already, learn to lead collaboratively in order to cocreate a better future with your team. People aren't just human resources or FTEs (full-time equivalents), but real people who bring competency, qualities, and ideas to work. Unleash people during the Second Path of team support, and expect honest and full participation from everyone. Let the tools provide appropriate controls, while you focus on being the collaborative manager.

For example, help your team switch from personal habits to team rhythms. This seems to be particularly tough for people not prone to collaborating. The benefits of using collaborative tools with shared protocols often require changing personal habits to a more transparent and precise way of communicating through team channels. Visibility can produce fear as often as motivation in cynical cultures or with low-trust personalities. The team's comfort with transparent communication channels may be an indicator of how much safety your team feels, or it could be simply individual habits that are hard to change. Habits, once in place as a team, keep your team together. Hold the team, kindly but firmly, to the communication commitments.

Motivation—Theory to Practice

Virtual leaders are often middle managers who did not create the company culture or its values. At the same time, they are the most important factor in determining employee satisfaction. The manager, even in cynical or fear-based cultures, can directly, positively impact trust. In fact, *virtual* managers may have an advantage over their colocated peers. The virtual environment gives the virtual leader a bit of room to insulate the team from the influence of a toxic culture.

If you find yourself building a team in a toxic culture, don't ignore or discount that problems exist. Teams shouldn't ignore what's happening that is outside their control; it will exacerbate fear. Control the controllable, influence the amenable, and be pragmatic about the rest.

Connect People's Hearts and Minds

The virtual manager creates an environment where people motivate themselves. Today's workers want to work for managers who connect emotionally.[11] Your best leadership advantage is fully in your control—*how well you connect with people's hearts and minds*. When people are motivated and engaged, they think about work when they don't have to, wanting to get back to it and anxious to hear how things turn out.

Psychologist David McClelland's achievement motivation theory was the basis upon which modern management theory was built. His mid-twentieth-century management model showed that most people were motivated by the need for *achievement*, followed by those most motivated by accumulating *power*, trailed by a group with a high need for *affiliation*.[12]

Achievement is no longer most workers' driving motivator. Particularly with the influx of millennials into the workforce, driving motivators have reversed. People *most* seek *affiliation* with an organization that is *doing meaningful work*.

When 12,000 workers (and their managers) were asked what they believed motivated them most, almost all managers ranked *recognition for achievement* as the top motivator. *Ninety-five percent of the managers were wrong*. By a vast majority, employees most valued *meaningful progress in their work*. Employee motivation is less about *being seen* and more about *seeing the meaning* in the work.[13]

Come Together Purposefully

In order for workers to apply themselves fully on the job and for teams to achieve their best results, they want to know how their work fits into the big picture. According to McClelland's motivation theory, our primary need, or motivator, *is not inherent*; we develop it through our culture and life experiences. The old management model underpinned managerial behaviors by determining that for most people achievement drove them. Therefore, competition gave people opportunities to be recognized for their achievements. That was true then.

Enter millennials and more contract workers who work easily with others, even on temporary assignments. Our life experiences give rise to a primary motivation of affiliation. A vast majority of today's workers report being motivated when they are contributing "meaningful work" with others. It has certainly been true for me. People want to be part of something bigger than them; they want to affiliate with groups and organizations they are proud to be part of.

Develop Authentic, Collaborative Relationships

People care about being cared about, and most of us smell empty flattery. It's almost biological. We can't fake caring (at least for long). It takes too much energy to keep up the charade. If you're reading this book and think people leadership may be too much work, you may want to get out of management. Virtual management is *all* about strong relationships. The foundation for healthy, long-lasting team cultures lies with our relationships—in other words, engaging people on more levels than a transactional job description and paycheck. Companies are missing out when they fail to help team leaders link organizational vision to teamwork.

Much corporate communication is so corporate centered that it fails to grab many workers' attention, let alone motivate them. Often it places too much emphasis on benefits to the company, not the people they're addressing.[14] As the virtual leader, be more than a messenger of cascading corporate communication. Bring meaning to the story.

Who Authentic Collaborators Are

Authenticity may not be teachable. I won't say much more except to describe what authentic leaders do that builds strong team relationships:

- They have integrity.
- They are honest.
- They tell the full story—what people need to do, and under what conditions. They don't sugarcoat.
- They tell their truth.
- They hear others' truth.
- They take the time to learn about others and what makes them tick.

Six Engaging Leadership Practices

1. Provide Positive, Honest Feedback

Build team confidence with feedback, good news, and constructive advice. Especially until milestones are reached, praise effort. Recognize and share progress. Coach to hit closer to the mark next time. This will call out excellence so the team can continuously learn and embed best practices. Help create an environment where people learn without fear and take reasonable risks without fear.

2. Provide Optimal Challenges With Just Enough Stress

To build a team's competency "muscle," you want to challenge its members. Unless people are stretching, they tend to fall short of potential. Teams are no different and do their best work when under some pressure (but not overly stressed). Virtual leaders focus conversations, meetings, and activities on team challenges.[15]

3. Ensure People Are Safe From Demeaning Treatment and Unfair Evaluation

Safety first. Bullies are inconsiderate, even when making valid points. People need honest feedback, but *how* they hear the feedback is just as important. Performance evaluations and coaching sessions can be formative without demeaning or shutting people down. Make coaching sessions and evaluations interactive, listen and respond openly to their perspective, and cocreate an improvement plan.

4. Ensure Empowerment

> In contrast to routine, coerced, or instinct-driven cooperation, genuine collaboration not only requires but creates and supports individual empowerment. A hallmark indicator of real collaboration is that it is empowering! Collaboration nurtures and brings out strong personal power, which, in turn, nurtures collaboration.[16]

Every leadership action is, in some sense, a moral challenge to see that everyone comes out fairly. You can buy a person's time, but not his heart or mind.

A motto I learned from a spiritual teacher guides my life: "*Is it fair, and does it serve the interest of all concerned?*" Reframed for the empowering leader: "*Does it empower my team to serve the interests of stakeholders?*"

5. Flex Your Style

Results will exceed expectations surprisingly often when we listen and adapt to our team. We are helping them work out how they work best. Work is more fun, people are more comfortable, and synergy comes more easily. Are you an adaptable enough virtual leader? Can you manage an effective response to any stage of a virtual worker or team development? I thought I was until an assessment showed me how predominantly I rely on only two management styles, limiting my ability to lead everyone on my teams. I couldn't flex until I knew I wasn't as adaptable as I thought.[17]

A 2010 Blanchard study found that 69% of leaders use one style exclusively. Only 14% are fully flexible.[18] Develop versatility.

6. Expand Emotional Bandwidth

Trust, engaged leaders and teams, effective communication, and collaborative tools—a great formula that expands the emotional bandwidth available to sustain resilient relationships.

Workers With Friends Are Happier

Great news! The virtual leader doesn't have to do all the motivating! There's one thing to do that trumps almost everything else to engage people and boost performance.

Make a close friend at the office.

People with a "best work friend" are seven times more likely to be engaged in their work. Those with three or more work friends register a higher overall satisfaction in life. Gallup confirmed strong work friendships increase job satisfaction, collaboration, and team commitment. It further found that people with trusted work friends are more truthful and resilient. People were less willing to seek help from acquaintances. Friends are built-in support, the Second Path to high-performance teams.[19]

Today's workplace often has trust challenges, but that doesn't mean you can't be a high-trust virtual team. Connect to your team members by watching, listening, and learning from them. Adapt your style to deepen the relationship, authentically, and encourage the team members to get to know and like each other.

Notes

1. Amy Adkins, "Majority of U.S. Employees Not Engaged Despite Gains in 2014," Gallup, 2014, www.gallup.com/poll/181289/majority-employees-not-engaged-despite-gains-2014.aspx

2. Deloitte Consulting, "Big Demands and High Expectations: The Deloitte Millennial Survey," White Paper, 2014, http://www2.deloitte.com/al/en/pages/about-deloitte/articles/2014-millennial-survey-positive-impact.html

3. I integrated, cross-referenced, and compared employee surveys and worker satisfaction research. I began with Stephen Covey's research published in 1991 in *Principle-Centered Leadership* and continued to integrate updated research through March 2016. Some major references will be cited separately, but to include all citations is unwieldy. The longitudinal comparative analysis and conclusions are summarized in this chapter.

4. Marianne Jennings, *The Seven Signs of Ethical Collapse: How to Spot Moral Meltdowns in Companies Before It's Too Late* (New York: St. Martin's Press, 2006).

5. Deloitte Consulting, "Big Demands."

6. Worker participation brought labor into the conversation about how to modernize factory technology. Carol Haddad was a primary leader because she documented and tracked results, summarized in this chapter that have held up over time. Haddad teaches at Eastern Michigan University's College of Technology and is the North American associate editor for the journal *New Technology, Work, and Employment*. (www.emich.edu/cot/faculty/faculty_profiles/carol_haddad.php).

7. Ed Sealover, "Left Hand Brewing Employees Take Ownership, Bucking Industry Trend," *Denver Business Journal*, July 1, 2015, www.bizjournals.com/denver/news/2015/07/01/left-hand-brewing-employees-take-ownership-bucking.html

8. Margaret Heffernan, *A Bigger Prize: Why Competition Isn't Everything and How We Do Better* (London: Simon & Schuster, 2014).

9. Deloitte Consulting, "Big Demands."

10. Teresa Amabiel and Steven Kramer, *The Progress Principle: Using Small Wins to Ignite Joy, Engagement, and Creativity at Work* (Boston: Harvard Business Review, 2011).

11. Bernard Burnes and Rune Todnem, "Leadership and Change: The Case for Greater Ethical Clarity," *Journal of Business Ethics* 108 (2011): 239–252.

12. "Need Theory," *Wikipedia*, last modified July 26, 2015, https://en.wikipedia.org/wiki/Need_theory

13. Amabiel and Kramer, *Progress Principle*.

14. Bill Jensen et al., "The Future of Work: Making the Future Work 2015–2020 and Decades to Come," Search for a Simpler Way Study, *Simpler Work: Compiled Research Results*, 2014.

15. Stephen Willis, *Power Through Collaboration: The Formula for Success in Challenging Situations* (n.p.: Willis Consulting, 2013).

16. Ibid.

17. The Hersey-Blanchard situational leadership theory was created by Dr. Paul Hersey, a professor and author of *The Situational Leader*, and Ken Blanchard, author of the best-selling *The One-Minute Manager*, among others.

18. Ken Blanchard, Situation Leadership II, www.kenblanchard.com

19. Tom Rath, interview by Jennifer Robison, in discussion with author of *Vital Friends: The People You Can't Afford to Live Without*, October 12, 2006,

"What Are Workplace Buddies Worth? A Lot, Which Is Why Managers Should Be Fostering Friendships in the Office," Gallup, October 2006, www.gallup .com/businessjournal/24883/What-Workplace-Buddies-Worth.aspx?utm_ source=position3&utm_medium=related&utm_campaign=tiles; and Jamie Hodari, "Is Working Remotely Sapping Your Creativity?," *Harvard Business Review*, April 27, 2015, https://hbr.org/2015/04/is-working-remotely-sapping-your-creativity

18

THE FOURTH PATH—LEAD
YOUR CAREER

"Above all, don't lie to yourself. The man who lies to himself and listens to his own lie comes to a point that he cannot distinguish the truth within him, or around him, and so loses all respect for himself and for others. And having no respect he ceases to love."

—Fyodor Dostoyevsky

"The only difference between the saint and the sinner is that every saint has a past, and every sinner has a future."

—Oscar Wilde

"Confidence . . . thrives on honesty, on honor, on the sacredness of obligations, on faithful protection and on unselfish performance. Without them it cannot live."

—Franklin D. Roosevelt

"Run from what's comfortable. Forget safety. Live where you fear to live. Be notorious."

—Rumi

Lead Yourself—a Networked Fourth Path to Career Success

Be the leader of your own professional life. This book shows how to be a valued team contributor by walking the Threefold Path, whether virtual leader or team member—key competencies today. A fourth professional path is fast becoming critical—the path of self-aware career acumen and relationship management. As Figure 18.1 shows, we are our own career developers and network managers. We aren't always navigating an employer organization; we're navigating multiple contracts, colleagues, and managers. As a Fourth Path professional, you negotiate on your own behalf, bringing attention to your value to the market. You manage a business back room, whether employee or contractor. You are your own human resources, finance,

Figure 18.1. The Fourth Path.

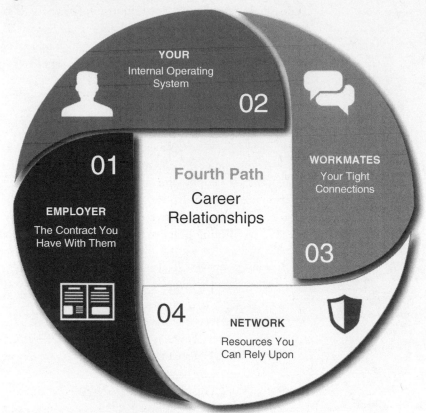

Note. © 2016—Trina Hoefling. The SMART Workspace.

operations, marketing, and strategist. You may also be sales. To be the leader of your career, you are the chief advocate for you.

When we consider the history of labor, working *for* employers wasn't common until the early twentieth century. We're returning to a time when work doesn't mean going somewhere to do it. But we're not tied to home, either. Many of us work for multiple organizations. One forecast estimates that over 60 million Americans will be "contingent" workers by 2020.[1] The rules of work are changing.[2] What defines employment is being tested in court with California cases against Uber and Lyft. As of this printing, Uber had agreed to pay a significant sum to drivers for previous worker misclassification. They also agreed to significant policy changes in favor of driver rights that hadn't been as clearly defined as they would have been if a traditional labor-management agreement were in place.[3]

Companies are recruiting differently as a result. On-demand contracts are common and include scientists, project consultants, faculty, marketing experts, programmers, process experts, trainers, change managers. HR recruiters use crowdsourcing platforms like Freelancer and Upwork to source talent, as needed, for projects and employment.[4] Companies utilize internships and host innovation hackathons to cull talent and assess whom to hire.[5] LinkedIn hires employees for up to five years without intending most to become career hires.

We have become a workforce that doesn't expect a long relationship with one employer. While companies still have employees to keep the engine running, often contract specialists do much of the engine building and specialist work. Virtual managers are leading people who may not be employees. In fact, the virtual manager may be a contractor.

For career professionals, this requires active Fourth Path navigation. Commit to develop these five continuing practices needed by today's smart career professional:

Self-leadership. This means taking personal responsibility for your own development. It begins with discovering your own purpose and passion. Align with the people you work with *and* your profession. Self-leadership also includes putting people and systems in place to get real performance feedback when your leader doesn't give it. Fewer human resources or learning and development departments offer fully developed programs to help you get better as a team member and leader. *It's up to you now.*

Mind shift from "me" to "we." This mind shift is the essence of truly collaborative teamwork and integrated organizations. Valued contributors suit up and show up, whether the job lasts a week or a career. Temporary teams require full commitment from team members. "Enlightened self-interest" has to evolve into a focus on the total ecology of the workplace, work teams, your community, and the entire social system that surrounds you, including yourself.

Adaptation to emerging realities. We're all change managers, adapting to disruptive changes faster than at any time in recorded history. Professionals move among organizations and cultures, changing teams and alliances. Adaptability is key. The mantra is "Learn and evolve to keep pace." We're expected to adjust quickly to different teams' rhythms and flows. Much is emerging that has no precedent, requiring innovative thinking—individually and with teams. Teams face challenges not solved by past learning. They need collaborative, forward-focused innovators. And so do you. Your focus is on the present and the emerging future, and how that fits your career plan. Regularly innovate your skill set, professional network, and career priorities. Reflect about what to hold on to, adjust, learn, try, and let go.

Relationship management. You are now responsible for managing your professional social network. It is *the* most common source of compensated work, professional resources, mentoring, and social support from trusted colleagues. You need to consciously build it, maintain it, and change it as conditions demand. Develop your personal "board of directors." Choose advisers based on their competencies, integrity, and dedication to your success. Develop a passionate network that opens doors for you (and trusts you to open doors for them).

Technology literacy. Collaboration tools are really about communication in the largest sense. Marshall McLuhan said it best: "The medium is the message."[6] Today's medium is digital—social media; mobile platforms; and knowledge-embedded, integrated networks. Everyone knows how to use the technology at a basic level for team coordination, such as calendars. That's not enough to be a strong virtual team member, a primary role of the Fourth Path professional. You have to master enough collaborative technology and social media to broadcast your competency and work with your colleagues.

Fourth Path professionals are on the leading edge of a bigger trend. Walking the Fourth Path is smart for the career employee (whether you've worked for one or many employers) *and* the professional consultant. If you follow these SMART career principles, you will be ahead of the trend before it directly impacts you. *You are in charge of your work life.*

Implied Promises in a Changing Landscape

You may be like many professionals who perceive the workplace to be unfair at times. Many contract workers (perhaps you) were previously career employees who got downsized, golden parachuted,[7] or blindsided in another way. Perhaps your team was sent home or abruptly redeployed midproject because of strategic shifts and with little explanation and no apology. Managers are unfair when they present to decision makers and forget to share credit with the team. Many people have been negatively impacted by economic realities that were unfair in the last decade, though no less real. Baby boomers were not expecting their last work years to be so unpredictable.

Today's world is different. Some professionals need to reinvent themselves, learning to play by new rules they never thought they'd need.

Trust is fundamental to effective relationships but can be easily broken. A promise is often interpreted as a guaranteed outcome, even though the future isn't guaranteed. Initial commitments change as relationships (or situations or organization priorities) evolve. An implied promise is usually locked in our minds, however unintentionally, risking trust if not fulfilled.

Has corporate America[8] broken its implied promise to a generation of the workforce? Minimally, we're more cynical and less trusting. Transactional work relationships are initially built on implied promises and contracted agreements. They can evolve into loyal alliances, but most won't—at least they won't without time and attention given to the relationship. Nurture relationships with people and organizations you want to work with again. Hang out to strengthen bonds, virtually. Team chat about last night's game or *Dancing With the Stars*. Get to know one another so trust survives changing landscapes.

Fourth Path Competencies

Today's career professionals aren't just good team players. They are virtual relationship managers, with or without a formal title. That requires a few additional Fourth Path skills.

Negotiate Terms

Compensation specialists know more about market pay rates than most contractors. Recruiting firms help organizations negotiate to their advantage. For example, one recruiter site posted this in 2014: "If the candidate has been unemployed, particularly for a long time, that could bring the pay rate down."[9] Research employee-to-contract pay rate conversion tables so you can become a good negotiator, account for tax consequences of your employee status, and know your skill-based market value.

Lead Through Influence

You negotiate the leadership value you bring because you are, well, *you*. As this book has reiterated, today's leaders are strong influencers. Influential leadership isn't something you can fake. Your leadership and influence skills should be obvious during the interviewing process.

Master Change

Change masters create a narrative for change that people understand. People aren't afraid or unwilling to change. They *are* resistant to what they don't control or understand. Contract professionals adapt every time they join a new team or organization, so control your own story.

Navigate Co-opetition

We tend to apply for positions as individuals, competing against people who may have been teammates last week. This forces people to carve out individual accomplishments to show their unique value, implicitly at the team's expense. Like political opponents who later become allies for their party's nominated candidate, opponents are expected to forget the past in favor of a shared vision once on the team. Understand that when teams form and end quickly, professionals walk a tightrope of cooperation while deployed, but competition to get deployed, if they share similar expertise. It's a paradox we all have to manage.

Make Your Net-Work

You need a good digital portfolio, starting with a LinkedIn profile, but that's just the beginning. A closed network of known, trusted colleagues is easier to manage. It takes time to nurture relationships, but a small network limits your capacity to learn and find opportunity—a professional risk. Keep strong ties with your most trusted network friends—those people you know will come through for you. *But don't stop there.* You need strong bonds with these trusted few, but you also need loose ties with a broad network. LinkedIn offers many ways to engage. It is my digital Central Station to stay current with my network. Use LinkedIn and other social media to maintain loose ties with professional and industry communities, promote your work and thought leadership, support your professional friends, and manage your contacts. And not just when you're looking for the next opportunity.

Relationships Are Personal

Who we are shows up. If we hide who we are behind a role we play, we show up as inauthentic and closed. Guarded team members aren't trusted as quickly. Work relationships affect us personally. We've been taught to leave our emotions at home. *But we don't. We shouldn't try.* If we want to have a career that makes a difference, if we want to feel proud professionally, we must find organizations, teams, and colleagues with whom we *can* work collaboratively and deliver good results.

Liking each other is nice, but respect is nonnegotiable. I've yet to find high-performance teams, virtual or not, that become effective without personal respect—granted and given. It's impossible to put our full focus on work when we have to navigate distrust, disrespect, politics, and internal barriers. The best way to help a team trust is to *be* authentic, open, and trustworthy. Understanding people is a process, not an accomplishment. We are lifelong learners when it comes to relationships. Teams are our greatest learning ground, and our professional network is our circle of influence and impact.

A Network of Relationships

The biggest responsibility of the Fourth Path is to manage a variety of relationships. Minimally, break your network into four types of relationships, shown in Table 18.1.

Each type of relationship has different requirements. They weave together on the Fourth Path, as shown in Figure 18.1, with many people coming and going in an active professional's network.

1. Yourself—You Matter, Too!

"We" begins with "me." In leading ourselves professionally, we figure out what we believe. Our beliefs influence what we expect and how we respond, especially when expectations aren't met. Be aware of what you believe about the worker relationship with the organization, what a successful career looks like, and what you believe about yourself. How do your beliefs open you to opportunity, and when do they limit your effectiveness? Know when and why *you* are difficult. Smart professionals work on themselves to manage relationship challenges, not expecting others to change. We take responsibility for contract and relationship quality. We know what makes us tick, our internal

TABLE 18.1
Four Types of Relationships

Relationship with	The impact of the relationship
Yourself	You live and work with yourself. If you don't advocate for you, who will?
Employers, clients, and stakeholders	Whether you navigate a career as an employee or contractor, you are still in a worker-employer contract that defines the terms of the relationship. (Stakeholders are key representatives of the organization or its customers.)
Colleagues	These are the people you spend the most time with to produce successful outcomes. What's your reputation with them?
Networks	These are your go-to people for help, intelligence, and support—loose and tight ties. Most career opportunities come through our network, not job boards.

operating system, what we're good at and enjoy. We're honest with ourselves about our weaknesses and deficiencies. We plan for managing them.

Blind Spots

Everyone has blind spots, things about ourselves that others see more readily than we do. Our blind spots *can* hurt us because we're vulnerable. We can be manipulated. Nudge your blind spot into the known, and see yourself honestly. When we see clearly, we can find opportunities to shine and claim strengths without apology. We are less vulnerable to fear or cynicism, know our value, and worry less about others' judgments. We simply show up and contribute as team players. We have real conversations, instead of trying to anticipate what others expect, posturing and protecting our myths about ourselves.

You will uncover blind spots that reveal your contribution to relationship issues, maybe a relationship that matters. If the air is cleared with more self-awareness, trust is strengthened in the relationship. Forgive others when they are unfair, ask for forgiveness when you've erred, remedy the issue if you can, structure trust more carefully next time, and learn.

Reality Checks

Self-assessments and coaches are two powerful ways to reveal blind spots.[10] Team assessments, well facilitated, also help teams clarify roles and expectations. Assessments help us understand our deepest motivations—what drives us, what we value, how we thrive. Style assessments inform us about how we get what we want, handle stress and conflict, and so on. Competency assessments help identify natural talents and strengths.

Here's my unscientific but quick self-assessment that, when honestly answered, can keep you focused on your career goals. Feel free to ask yourself these questions again and again until you feel complete:

- Who and what do I want to be?
- What is my unique value? What do I bring that is uniquely me? (*Hint: It's more than skill sets and professional certifications.*)
- What's my likely future if things continue as they are likely to, unless I make changes?
- Do I see myself living the life I want, and what can I do today to get closer to my vision?

2. Employers, Clients, and Stakeholders

The Hiring Relationship

Hiring managers are usually more experienced at negotiating than you will be, yet you carry the responsibility to reach fair terms. Learn to negotiate, and know your requirements professionally and personally. Just as a computer operating system can work only with compatible software and applications, so do you have an internal operating system (IOS) with its own requirements for optimal performance. Seek opportunities and cultures that fit you. Choose from the clear, conscious frame of reference that is *your* IOS. Look for organizations with a culture that brings out your best. Do you see a fit when you ask about management and reward practices (including compensation packages), career opportunity, coaching support and professional development, and so on? By doing this you shift your center of power. You are choosing your professional opportunities as much as you are being selected for hire. Realize how, where, and with what kind of people and circumstances you do best. Not every contract will be perfect, but you need sufficient fit. They need you, you need them, and customers need this contractual alignment to deliver.

Stakeholders

Stakeholder relationships include the people and teams to whom you are currently committed and accountable, and who impact or are impacted by your work. These are often tight relationships during a team engagement, and then become loose ties that move into your broader professional network as members roll on and off the team, or the team completes its mission. Some coworker relationships may remain tight, moving into your professional friendship network.

3. Colleagues—Does Your Reputation Precede You?

Independent contractors stay in touch with their best teammates. They depend on their tight network for professional companionship since team memberships are temporary ties. When you're able to develop true friendships in your network, you're building strong ties that may last a lifetime and, as we learned in the previous chapter, contribute to your work satisfaction.

Leaving a team ends a temporarily tight relationship. When you "exit" team relationships, do you stay in touch? Do you respond promptly to colleagues' e-mails when it's not about the project? What does that tell your previous teammates about you? I've watched professionals treat each other well while deployed on teams, and then have little use for teammates when the project is over. Most of us aren't anxious to stay in touch with people who are so distant and transactional. Many people engage their network only when they are looking for the next opportunity, lacking much real commitment to professional friends. They fail to develop trusted colleagues by being too utilitarian and communicating only when people help them in the moment. They go to networking events and speak only to those with the right title on their name tags. This utilitarianism translates. It doesn't take long for people to see a distinct lack of mutuality. Most colleagues silently withdraw support. Use discernment. Observe others. If someone acts in ways that are questionable to your values, choose to adjust the relationship and move the person to the periphery or out of your network.

Your previous teammates can share a lot about you professionally, about what it's like to work with you. Your reputation precedes you. Of course, your resume and portfolio are stellar, but what endorsements do you have that reflect your professionalism and team play? Do you deliver on time and with full documentation? Do you share credit for team accomplishments? Are you honest? Do people trust you with their worries and concerns, or do they tell you what they think you want to hear? Do your references speak of your generosity? Do people say you are top notch? Loyal? Fun? Are you easy to work with? *What do colleagues say about you?*

4. Networks

Connections with people can be fleeting, which is understandable because of the pace at which we move and the fluid nature of temporary teams. It becomes an excuse not to extend effort. The faster we go, though, and the more contractually independent many of us become, the more important it is to have a strong network that survives time, distance, and the ups and downs of a career.

I seek to work with those who are team oriented, smart, competent contributors who naturally follow the Threefold Path. Minimally, I want colleagues I can trust to be generous, honest, and *reliable*—people who work hard for the team but without sacrificing themselves. They have healthy boundaries *and* come through. Competent, self-directed *individualists* tend to move out of my network pretty quickly, and I am unlikely to recommend or advocate for them. They don't know how little they helped themselves by thinking only of themselves. *What are your criteria to move from your outer network closer to your inner circle?*

Extended Reach

Your social media network has extended reach. It includes those you know well, and people who are in the best position to open your career path, even if you haven't met them yet. It includes LinkedIn members you've met through a LinkedIn interest group, virtual and quite loose. It includes individuals you don't want to be closely affiliated with, such as "frenemies" or professional competitors. It reaches to colleagues you worked with previously but no longer do. It includes people you meet in professional circles. It extends to schoolmates, neighbors, and friends. Follow people you admire on Twitter—your "wise ones." Gather competitive market intelligence by following rivals and adversaries. Scan LinkedIn and Google+ communities aligned with your interests.

Online Forums and Communities of Practice

It turns out that Internet discussion forums are good for our well-being. The more active we are online, the more likely we are to be engaged locally in our geographic communities, and vice versa. Social networking sites like Facebook, LinkedIn, and Google or Yahoo groups have become destinations for discussion forums and virtual communities of practice, and dramatically increase our digital social engagement.[11] Find some forums and join if you haven't already. This isn't to sell yourself into a network. These are places to learn and connect professionally with like-minded folks for dialogue and peer learning.

Your Professional Tribe

Commit to a number of close relationships from within your network of allies and professional friends. Your personal network has only tight, trusting relationships. These are people you know, like, and trust. It's sustained on mutual integrity, quality conversations, and time. Your professional tribe grows out of loose relationships with employees, customers, online connections, mentors, colleagues—your bigger professional world. Build and nurture them.

Your professional tribe should be strong, the first place you go to find your allies and supporters, invested people who believe in you. Tribal members can be customers; managers; coworkers with whom you've developed good relationships; and your trusted advisers, such as your accountant and attorneys, too. Cultivate your own board of advisers if you're self-employed. Seek network members who bolster you.

Reach Out

Have proactive conversations. Schedule meet-ups. Conversations can be simple:

- "I need more of this kind of project. I bring. . . . Who might you know who needs me?"
- "I'm going to be at. . . . Is there anything you need that I can watch for?"
- "Before we finish coffee, how can I help you in the next week or so? We talked about that article earlier. Would you like me to send you the link later today?"
- "Our conversations energize me. Can I take you to lunch again next month?"

Ask for Stuff

Research suggests that a good method for deepening a friendship (and building trust) may be to ask for help. It turns out we feel good about helping others, so let others feel good by helping you. When we ask for something, we worry about seeming weak or that people won't want to help. Most of us actually enjoy being helpful. Help others in their careers, and ask for help with yours.[12]

Commit!

This has been a theme throughout the book, but commit to people, especially those you genuinely like and respect. It's okay not to care for someone; that doesn't mean we aren't reliable, respectful, and considerate. Our professional future is built on the Fourth Path of relationship and network management. It shows others we invest in our professional relationships. We need people to know and trust us, and not just when we're being paid to perform. Don't be someone who reaches out only when in need. Talented professionals severely limit their ability to collaborate effectively when they lead for themselves and forget it took a team to make them the professionals they have become.

The *Leading Indicator* of Career Success

Jeff Bewkes, chair and CEO of Time Warner, insists the most useful skill in business today is *teamwork*. You want people to want to work with you. He points out the irony of how we're taught to build our careers: "Teamwork is probably the crucial skill, and yet education is mostly about solo performances."[13] *Most of us have some unlearning to do.*

Give It Up, Girl [Boy]!

Be generous with your wisdom, resources, and connections. According to *The Go-Giver* author and relationship master Bob Burg, the most successful professionals are go-givers, not go-getters.[14] Go-givers are people who bring value to every relationship, understanding that their value, financial and nonfinancial, is defined by how much more they give than take. Go-givers know what really determines their value—how many people they serve and how well they serve them. Go-givers are authentic because they know the best they have to offer is themselves. Go-givers understand reciprocity and mutuality, and they are open to receiving as well. Most important, go-givers place others first. We become influencers because people know we are considerate and concerned for their needs. They are safe with us, and often better for having known us. We've added value to them. When we are generous, we don't deplete others. We abundantly increase our influence.

Do pay attention, though. Over time, if you're not experiencing mutuality in a relationship, no interest in *you*, begin to set different boundaries. Don't give with the expectation of getting, but neither cast your pearls before swine. Some will take without thought. You decide the minimum quality of your relationships, both loose and tight.

Over time, who we are is undeniably clear. Even if your reputation does not precede you, *it will follow you.* Care enough to be thoughtful, and if that's a bigger commitment than you can make, care enough to give colleagues no cause to question your integrity. Practice being a go-giver, a generous spirit. This shows you have the relationship intelligence to thrive and lead yourself down a successful career path.

Set yourself apart as a collaborator who delivers, shares credit, and cares about the team. In a networked world of loose relationships, certain realities are truer:

- We can thrive together or struggle alone, which means giving up some control when we depend on others.
- We resist losing control and tend to want to be self-reliant.
- It's harder to be self-reliant *and* successful for any length of time.
- Trust has broken at many levels of business and society.
- Trust still matters.

We have to come together quickly with people we don't know well enough to trust, in a work world that shifts on a dime and hasn't done much to earn our trust, and *we trust anyway.* I find that when a team is true to its agreements, team members who aren't generous fall away (or are moved out) and trusted collaborators are rewarded, getting many opportunities. *Collaborate as if your success depends on it. Maybe it does!*

Trina's Five Commitments

The following are five commitments I make to be a good Threefold Path virtual team leader and fulfill my value commitments. I navigate my Fourth Path by nurturing a network that is resilient, powerful, supportive, and valuable to me.

1. I take responsibility for developing mutually beneficial relationships. My professional power and influence depend on it.
2. Adaptability is key. I learn and evolve to keep pace, without losing integrity, adjusting quickly to different teams' rhythms and flows and learning their protocols.

3. I focus forward. Much is emerging that has no precedent, demanding innovation.
4. I "suit up and show up." My teammates can count on me.
5. I determine what and whom to hold on to, and whom to let go. Not everyone moves from teammate to network, nor does everyone in my loose network make it into my inner circle.

Connect in Different Ways

Get out and about physically *and* digitally.

We are social. We gain energy when we spend time physically with others, especially when we're meeting around a common passion. Get out of the home office.

Nurture Your Network

You want relationships that

- come from your current work colleagues and associates inside and outside your organization and profession;
- are fulfilling and functional; and
- balance loose and tight relationships—people who know you well, some you admire but who don't know you at all, and people who know you professionally.

You're growing a professional ecosystem that spans boundaries virtually, locally, and across business communities.

What I Learned From Rock 'n' Roll Photographer Bob Gruen

Bob Gruen toured for decades with the Rolling Stones and other rock legends, living an enviable career. A talented live action photographer, he was more than a photojournalist. He was an artist among artists. Gruen knew how to establish swift trust with rock stars accustomed to no-trust, temporary relationships. These were people who assumed everyone had an agenda.

Bob Gruen had an agenda, too, yet famous artists trusted him. Why?

He wanted to make a career out of hanging out with rock stars and taking pictures while doing it. *He had to be trusted and liked to have what he wanted.* Gruen's advice to photography enthusiasts sums up why he believed he was able to have what he wanted. It's great advice for today's Fourth Path career professional who will "hang out" with a lot of people in circumstances where you are a supporting player on their stage:

- Follow the flow and make the best of every situation.
- Meet people, and with those you like, try to stay in touch.
- When you like someone, give that person something. Show him or her what you can do.
- Get out and have a life.

The Fourth Path to a successful career in a mobile work world is a winding one. It isn't unpredictable, though, or doesn't need to be. Once you know yourself, you can follow the flow and make the best of each virtual team you join. Enjoy working with your teammates. Stay in touch with those you enjoy. Show up as a go-giver and have a positive impact. Expand the emotional bandwidth on your team and in your life.

Notes

1. Intuit 2020 Report, "Twenty Trends That Will Shape the Next Decade," *Intuit*, October 2010; Lauren Weber, "One in Three U.S. Workers Is a Freelancer," Wall Street Journal, September 4, 2014, http://blogs.wsj.com/atwork/2014/09/04/one-inthree-u-s-workers-is-a-freelancer/

2. Aarti Shahani, "Service Jobs, Like Über Driver, Blur Lines Between Old Job Categories," NPR.org, June 26, 2015, www.npr.org/2015/06/26/417675866/service-jobs-like-uber-driver-blur-lines-between-old-job-categories; Annette Nellen, "Über, Lyft and Others—Worker Classification in the 21st Century," *Proformative*, June 20, 2015, www.proformative.com/blogs/annette-nellen/2015/06/20/uber-lyft-others-worker-classification-21st-century

3. Press announcement from Uber's representing law firm, Lichten & Liss-Riordan, P. C. http://uberlawsuit.com/Breaking%20news%20-%20Uber%20will%20pay%20$100%20million%20to%20settle%20independent%20contractor%20misclassification%20claims.pdf

4. Dr. Tomas Chamorro-Premuzic, "Why Millennials Want to Work for Themselves," *Fast Company*, August 13, 2014, www.fastcompany.com/3034268/the-future-of-work/why-millennials-want-to-work-for-themselves

5. Ibid.

6. Marshall McCluhan, *Understanding Media: The Extensions of Man*, 1957.

7. *Golden parachute* is a lay term for a financial offer given to an employee who is being invited to retire early.

8. Apologies for being U.S.-centric, but I can't speak knowledgeably about the global picture.

9. Debbie Fledderjohan, "Tips and Tools for Negotiating Contractor Pay Rates," Top Echelon, updated September 16, 2014, www.topechelon.com/blog/contract-staffing-training/tips-and-tools-for-negotiating-contractor-pay-rates/

10. I'm also a fan of journaling and compassion-building activities, such as empathy walks and stakeholder interviews. The Presencing Institute has a helpful website to learn how to apply these tools: www.presencing.com

11."Online Discussion Forums Good for Well-Being, Study Shows," U. of Exeter, April 21, 2015; Dr. Louise Pendry and Dr. Jessica Salvatore, "Individual and Social Benefits of Online Discussion Forums," *Computers in Human Behavior*, April 20, 2015, www.exeter.ac.uk/news/featurednews/title_447204_en.html

12. Vanessa K. Bohns, "You're Already More Persuasive Than You Think," *Harvard Business Review*, August 3, 2015, https://hbr.org/2015/08/research-were-much-more-powerful-and-persuasive-than-we-know

13. Fareed Zakaria, *In Defense of a Liberal Education*, p. 69, Norton Publishing Company, 2016.

14. Bob Burg and John David Mann, *The Go-Giver: A Little Story About a Powerful Business Idea* (New York: Penguin Group, 2007); *It's Not About You: A Little Story About What Matters Most in Business* (New York: Penguin Group, 2011).

19

WHAT'S NEXT?

"A path is little more than a habit that comes with knowledge of a place. It is a sort of ritual familiarity. It is a form of contact with a known landscape. It is not destructive. It is the perfect adaptation, through experience and familiarity, of movement to place; it obeys the natural contours; such obstacles as it meets it goes around. A road, on the other hand, even the most primitive road, embodies a resistance against the landscape. Its reason? It's not simply the necessity for movement, but haste."

—Wendell Berry, *The Art of the Commonplace*

"I've always found that anything worth achieving will always have obstacles in the way, and you've got to have that drive and determination to overcome those obstacles on route to whatever it is that you want to accomplish."

—Chuck Norris

The Threefold Path

This book has shared the Threefold Path to organize and activate virtual teams. See Figure 19.1 to review the Threefold Path virtual team management model. There are many ways to navigate the Threefold Path, as long as all three tenets are there. A metaphor borrowed from Buddhism, the Threefold Path is a progressive path of action. Virtual workers are path followers who work with what is before them. They know that my success is our success. No worker is entirely separate from his team, and the team is not separate from the organization.

In my experience, when a team agrees to follow the Threefold Path, it finds its natural contours together while navigating the organizational landscape. *There is no one way.* Following the tenets of the Threefold Path, the virtual leader helps the team find *its own way.* The process strengthens team member ties. The team's deliverables connect them to the organization. The Threefold Path leads them from being a work group to a collaborative team whose members communicate, give honest feedback, hold passionate debate, and continuously hit their marks, fueled with lively interaction.[1]

245

Figure 19.1. The Threefold Path for high-performance teams.

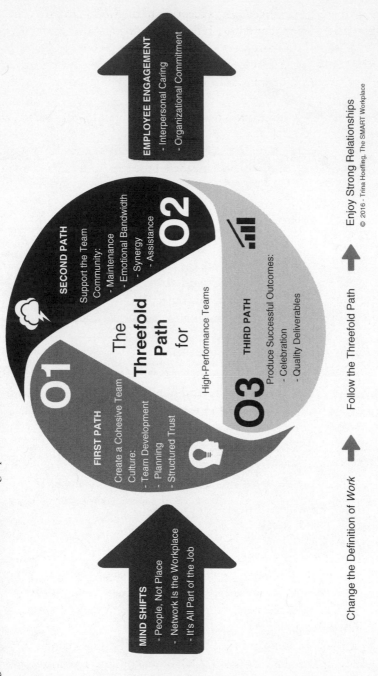

Working Virtually

Working virtually has changed our perception of the workplace. It's changed the way companies recruit and hire. HR, IT, learning and development, performance appraisal, and corporate cultures—all continue to evolve to meet the requirements of an interdependent, global, mobile, fast-paced work world. At a minimum, organizations have to do the following:

- Align strategy with people's hearts and minds, reinforcing it every day, to engage them.
- Engage virtual workers in the planning and design conversations while redesigning work spaces and business processes to fit all stakeholder needs.

What About the Next 20 Years?

It's been almost 20 years since I wrote the first edition of *Working Virtually*. I've seen dramatic technical progress and acceleration of change. The next 20 years will undoubtedly continue this trajectory. I've looked at workplace trends that will grow in importance. I highly recommend 12 responses.

12 Workplace Mandates

1. Organizations must get realistic and nimble at understanding and navigating complexity (*it's more than matrix management or better IT*).
2. Organizations must see themselves as participants in a larger world, forming creative boundary-crossing alliances and partnerships. They should continue to invest in global network architecture.
3. Competitive cultures and reward systems must transform, especially in virtual organizations, to be more team focused, empowered, and collaborative. (*I think most organizations and many leaders will stumble for a while, try to operate out of old cultures, and eventually learn from their progress. It may be a bumpy ride.*)
4. Organizations must facilitate learning and provide access to always available, on-demand learning and online curriculum as a worker benefit. (*Much can be outsourced, and learning and development budgets should increase somewhat.*)
5. Training departments embrace blended learning, using a combination of massive open online courses (MOOCs) and online, on-demand modular learning flipped classrooms, integrated with coaching and facilitated

employee/worker learning communities. (*There is still a need for classroom training as well.*)

6. Retiring boomers force increased attention to emerging leaders' training and development for succession planning (*usually an integration of courses and job aids/tutorials, heuristic knowledge management, coaching, and formal mentoring programs*).

7. Collaborative platforms and tools must continue to improve across organizational systems and processes, and be mobile app friendly.

8. Task and performance management technology (with Big Brother metrics) will be deployed first in organizations whose cultures don't shift to being more collaborative. (*It will meet with mixed reviews.*)

9. More robust artificial intelligence will be embedded in collaboration tools and equipment, embedding, even more, the indivisible relationship between technology and people. Some jobs will automate.

10. HR will employ more nontraditional worker-employer contracts and flexible work arrangements. Maybe government and tax regulations will catch up to how work is really being done.

11. Real estate footprints will continue to shrink with shared workspace designed around teams and drop-in work spaces.

12. Serious consideration should be given to redefining work and the value Western society places on it. Until definitions of *productivity* and *work* can be adjusted, most of us will stay in struggle to some degree. (*The U.S. tax code still reflects full-time work with one employer as normal. This prediction is somewhat my hope more than a prediction. It is, regardless, a looming conversation.*)

Attracting Talent

HR departments need to attract and retain the youngest generation of professionals. An organization is more attractive to millennials when it's designed around collaborative and mobile solutions, and supports a flexible work environment. Eighty percent of surveyed global HR executives have altered or are considering changes to their talent-sourcing strategy to accommodate millennials' expectations.[2] As a talent development strategy, LinkedIn and Alphabet Inc. (the parent company of Google) have three to five-year "tour of duty" contracts for high performers, for example. The mutual expectation is employees leave the company within five years unless that "tour of duty" suggests a deeper relationship be formed. If so, a new contract is negotiated. eBay keeps an active database of previous and current employees as a robust internal network. It welcomes "boomerang employees" who leave but often come back, or return for a temporary project.[3]

Trends indicate that by 2020 half of us will work on-demand or with a flexible work option. Seventy percent of millennials expect to spend part of their career working independently.[4] They approach their careers entrepreneurially, fitting today's business environment, intentionally navigating the Fourth Path of today's mobile work world—the self-led career path.

What's Past, Current, and Always—People Are Key to Team Performance

In a mobile world, virtual leaders are the connectors of team members to the corporate community. Virtual team members say their first loyalty is to their team leader, especially when working from a contract. I've written this book as a framework and manual for all virtual leaders.[5] Technology enables, the hiring organization provides the work environment, but *people are still the key*. Organizations have been underinvesting in their key asset, their virtual team leaders. *Underinvesting in leadership development is an expensive mistake.*

Executive teams are aggressively looking at how to integrate technically. They should be equally as committed to train people in how to collaborate, as well as how to use the tools. The team leader's primary role is *connecting people to get work done through networks of interdependent systems*—across silos and tribes, choices and distractions, boundaries and walls, and beyond traditional organizational structures and management habits. Leading from this priority helps a team come to collaborative team results.

In my professional and seasoned opinion, leaders need to prioritize their strategic attention and financial investment in two ways:

1. Support team leader training and development, especially virtual team leadership, facilitation, and social/relationship intelligence. Supporting management development demonstrates an organization's commitment to providing a desirable employee benefit. After all, the manager is the single largest determinant of employee satisfaction.
2. Support systemic organization program management and training for telecommuters, flex employees, and change managers. Flexwork experts report dismal progress over the last 20 years in how well organizations support their virtual workforce, despite how fast it's grown.[6]

Employee disengagement is a huge challenge in corporate America. With all the technical collaboration tools, people need to learn *how* to connect, link, and communicate *as a way of life.* My recommendation? *Hire to it. Then train to it.*

Networked organizations need virtual managers who actively engage and communicate with their teams. It takes many conversations and communication vehicles to embed a collaborative culture across a virtual workforce. Hanging cool posters in the hallways and break rooms doesn't reach virtual workers. Conversational leadership opens dialogue at all levels of the organization and isn't limited by place. People align when team leader conversations provide a virtual common ground upon which all stand together, connected by shared purpose and technology—across the distance.

Organizations can do better than they have to support virtual work. Managers can do better, too. It's not always an easy path, but it is a proven one. As one member of an online community stated, *"Get the commitment to the goal right, and you can put a team together with Dixie cups and string for communication devices, and they'll probably soar!"*

We Like Being on Teams

People enjoy working together, even if they are home-based telecommuters who seldom see teammates across an actual conference table. We are more satisfied at work when we

- feel safe and respected;
- know we're contributing because we get feedback; and
- believe others complement our talent for better results.

Interdependency makes a work group a team, as discussed earlier in the book and summarized in the first column of Table 19.1. The second column lists qualities that differentiate normal work groups from performing teams. *Notice how decades of data have verified the simple correlation between collaboration and effective teamwork.* You can see that managing an effective virtual team is simply a matter of bringing a group together and focusing on four components.

Leading virtual teams is a commitment to a facilitative, collaborative leadership style, leading by influence more than power or control and giving people a reason to work together and reinforce cooperation. Find the right mix of individual contribution and team interdependence, and the virtual team begins to see itself as a unit that gets the job done, bound together and committed.

TABLE 19.1

Collaboration and High-Performance Virtual Teams

Four criteria for collaboration—what makes a team a team?	Qualities of high-performance virtual teams—how will you know?
Give them a reason to work together.	Showing pride in delivering on its team promise
Make them interdependent.	Showing initiative, adjusting to each other, helping each other, coordinating work flow
Show commitment.	Committing to personal and team success
Hold them accountable to each other.	Delivering to the organization/customers

It Really Is Nothing New

I closed *Working Virtually*'s first edition with a story still poignant today. A colleague and I were discussing the question of virtual trust and the sustainability of global work relationships. This gentleman shared about his Scottish family's multigeneration lumber business. Three generations back, lumber was brought to Scotland from the United States and transported by suppliers through multiple countries. All contractual work was struck based on people's word—not even a handshake was involved over the ocean and miles when the business began. The technology did not exist for virtual signatures.

Relationships were built on trust, time, and results. Before there ever was a Threefold Path, there was this family-owned business. Along with several others across nations, it formed long-lasting, cohesive relationships (the development path) that supported all partners' longevity and profitability (the support path). Relationships were sustained by producing satisfied customers (the outcomes path). In this story is proof that while virtual work requires a shift in the *way* we work together *it really is nothing new*. Business has a tradition of virtual relationships that precedes the terminology and the technology.

If a three-generation family-owned business could function virtually 60 years ago without the tools, the technology, or the handshake, how much more is possible today?

A Final Author's Note and Confession

I may not have used the word *virtual* as much as some readers may expect. What has changed in the last 20 years is that work *is* virtual, wherever people's work space is. In some ways, virtuality is the water the fish lives in, inescapable and pervasive. I can find only two distinct differences between a telecommuter and a worker who goes to a location to work:

1. Telecommuters don't take transportation to get to and from work.
2. Colocated teams meet face-to-face all the time. (Even then, team members are often conferencing in, so these meetings are often virtual, too.)

You may be a reader who wanted to find more that is unique to virtual work. When I factor out what is true in both remote and colocated teams, the differences are few. Managers are key links between teams and organizations, and virtual managers even more so. If you want more focus on virtuality, consider two actions:

1. Follow a few wise blogs and join some communities of practice.[7]
2. Trick yourself. At the end of a meal with friends in an Asian restaurant, you are served fortune cookies. To spice it up, read aloud your fortune, adding the words *in bed* at the end. It's fun. Read this book again, and at the end of sentences, add *virtually*. I think you'll find it satisfying.

Notes

1. "Threefold Way," The Buddhist Centre, https://thebuddhistcentre.com/text/threefold-way

2. Deloitte University Press, "Global Human Capital Trends 2014/2015/2016: Engaging the 21st-Century Workforce," White Paper, Author, 2014, 2015, 2016.

3. Reid Hoffman, interview by Emily Chang, notes from discussion on Bloomberg TV Studio 1.0, June 30, 2014; Eric Schmidt, *Ask a Billionaire* interview on Bloomberg TV, December 30, 2014, Bloomberg.com

4. Hoffman, interview by Emily Chang.

5. Remember to download additional resources at www.WorkingVirtually .org

6. Go to http://clalliance.com/CLASEL/en/resources.asp to read more about success metrics when organizations support systemic flex work, including providing management training. While there, download a free report on a global workplace flexibility pilot.

7. Steve Willis, the author of *Power Through Collaboration*, has a robust community on LinkedIn by the same name. I'm a member and hope to see you in the conversation! I also invite you to my blog, accessed at www.TheSmartWorkplace .com or www.TrinaHoefling.com

The New Talent Acquisition Frontier
Integrating HR and Diversity Strategy in the Private and
Public Sectors and Higher Education
Edna Chun and Alvin Evans
Forewords by Andy Brantley and Benjamin D. Reese Jr.

"A must-read for both HR and diversity practitioners looking
to harness the power of diversity and inclusion to transform
their organization and enhance business performance, *The
New Talent Acquisition Frontier* offers dynamic principles,
state-of-the-art practices and insightful case studies that
outline how synergizing HR and diversity programs can
provide a competitive advantage."—***Rohini Anand***, *Senior
Vice President & Global Chief Diversity Officer, Sodexo*

For HR professionals and leaders, chief diversity officers,
line managers, and executives in the private and public sectors, this book presents a systematic
approach to integrating HR practices and strategic diversity initiatives to create the inclusive,
high performance workforce that every enterprise and institution needs to succeed in an
increasingly multicultural society and global marketplace.

Sty//us

22883 Quicksilver Drive
Sterling, VA 20166-2102   Subscribe to our e-mail alerts: www.Styluspub.com

Also available from Stylus

Training to Imagine
Practical Improvisational Theatre Techniques for Trainers and Managers to Enhance Creativity, Teamwork, Leadership, and Learning
SECOND EDITION
Kat Koppett
Foreword by Joel Goodman

"*Training to Imagine* is useful and wise, entertaining and generous. Based on rich experience and a great deal of thought, it's a splendid second edition."—***Paul Jackson***, *President, Applied Improv Network*

"In this revised edition Kat no longer has to call from the fringes. Clearly we are all performing, all the time, and business requires 'surfing' the waves of change. Why not get good at it? By outlining how the six core principles of improv apply to twenty-first-century leadership challenges, Koppett shows how we can trust ourselves to create together, not just in the safety of a team activity but out on the frontiers of business performance. I have used over half the activities in this book with excellent results! The 'yes/and' principle alone has the potential to reverse negative patterns and spark upward spirals of trust, collaboration, and excellence on any team."—***Elizabeth Doty***, *author of The Compromise Trap*

Creating innovative products and game-changing processes, and adapting to new cultures and communication styles, have all become imperative for business survival. Today's business leaders, from Fortune 500 companies on down, have discovered the value of improvisational theatre techniques to develop creativity and collaboration skills they need.

Building Cultural Competence
Innovative Activities and Models
Edited by Kate Berardo and Darla K. Deardorff
Foreword by Fons Trompenaars

"A new book of training activities is always welcome, but this volume offers something more: a thoughtful, careful analysis of how to design and execute relevant cultural training. You get the toolkit, in short, as well as guidance from some of the master builders."—***Craig Sorti***, *author, trainer, and consultant in intercultural communications*

"For HR directors, corporate trainers, college administrators, and diversity trainers, this book provides a cutting-edge framework and an innovative collection of ready-to-use tools and activities to help build cultural competence—from the basics of understanding core concepts of culture to the complex work of negotiating identity and resolving cultural differences.

(Continues on previous page)